DISCARD

ITALIAN HUMANISM

EUGENIO GARIN

ITALIAN HUMANISM

Philosophy and Civic Life
in the Renaissance

TRANSLATED BY PETER MUNZ

HARPER AND ROW, PUBLISHERS

NEW YORK

LIBRARY OF CONGRESS CATALOG CARD NUMBER: 66–10236

PRINTED IN GREAT BRITAIN FOR HARPER AND ROW, PUBLISHERS,
INCORPORATED, 49 EAST 33RD STREET, NEW YORK, N.Y. 10016.

CONTENTS

AD MEMORIAM

IUVENILIS AETATIS MEAE FLORENTINAE

HIC LIBER ANGLICE REDDITUS:

"*Per molti, Donna, anzi per mille amanti*
Creata fusti e d'angelica forma. . ."

INTRODUCTION TO THE TRANSLATION

DISCUSSION of the nature of the age of the renaissance or of the age of humanism has been bedevilled by a failure to distinguish the concept 'renaissance' as it was used by the humanists from the concept 'renaissance' which came to be used by historians from Burckhardt onwards, to describe a historical period. There is no doubt that the humanists of the late 14th and 15th century thought they were living in a 'new' age. But there is considerable doubt and a large measure of disagreement among modern historians as to when that age began, as to whether it was as new as the humanists thought and as to what the exact nature of the 'newness' was.[1] But these doubts and disagreements have all arisen from the fact that historians have ceased to take the word 'renaissance' in its original meaning and have used it to characterise a historical period.

There is a clear line of historical thinking that runs from the *Monumentum Ancyranum* to the early 14th century. It is concerned entirely with the fortunes of the Roman Empire and the view that the proper order in the world is the Roman order. The tone of the *Monumentum Ancyranum*, as can only be expected, was an optimistic one, for the Roman order seemed indeed established upon sound and permanent foundations. The belief in the soundness of that order was, at first, ineradicable, and was by no means confined to pagan writers. It was shared by Christians like Tertullian who proclaimed that the Roman Empire had indeed become the 'garden of the world'.

When the fortunes of that Empire began to decline and the economic prosperity of even the upper classes showed a marked deterioration, a note of genuine pessimism crept in which was to remain there for almost 1,000 years. Ironically enough, but not so strangely, the first note of pessimism was struck by pagan, not by Christian writers, i.e. in the all-pervasive view that the world

---

[1] For easily accessible bibliographies in English consult the indispensable work by Wallace K. Ferguson, *The Renaissance in Historical Thought*, Cambridge, Mass., 1948; F. Chabod, *Machiavelli and the Renaissance*, London, 1958; D. Hay, *The Italian Renaissance*, Cambridge, 1961; Karl H. Dannenfeldt, *The Renaissance, Medieval or Modern*, Boston, 1959; P. O. Kristeller and J. H. Randall, Jr., 'The Study of the Philosophies of the Renaissance', *Journal of the History of Ideas*, II, 1941; as well as the latest Italian edition of the present book, Bari, 1958.

was beginning to age; and, after 410 A.D. in the more precise conviction that the fall of Rome was to be attributed to the victory of Christianity and to the fact that the worship of the ancient gods had been abandoned. The pagans were answered by Augustine whose tenor, if anything, was much more hopeful. For he pointed out that though the Roman Empire might be declining, there was no real cause for commiseration since the City of God would remain valiant in its struggle for the ultimate salvation of man. Whatever transcendental hopefulness there was in this argument, it was used by later writers as a constant reminder that the fortunes of the earthly city were going from bad to worse and thus St. Augustine's argument served, perhaps in spite of itself, to reinforce the increasing pessimism as to civilisation, culture and political order.

The spread and development of this pessimism was punctuated several times by the naive efforts of the barbarian nations strenuously trying to acclimatise themselves on the soil of the Roman Empire. Fresh in their enthusiasm for the new religion they had adopted and conscious of their military prowess, they proclaimed, for instance in the Prologue to the *Lex Salica*, that a new nation, free of heresy and brave in battle, had been appointed by God to take on itself the task of re-establishing an order. Thence many others took their cue, and during the reign of Charlemagne a concerted attempt was made to mount a full philosophy of history in this optimistic tone. It was argued that the military victories and the fact that the whole of the West had been re-united under a Christian ruler could be taken to mean that the City of God, co-extensive with the Christian Empire of Charlemagne, was really on the march now. This forward-looking and enterprising argument, provoked mainly by the desire to reject Byzantine claims to leadership and predominance, had slender foundations. The concrete realities that had inspired it were precarious and did not long survive Charlemagne's death. In the wake of the new invasions from Scandinavia and Hungary, of the advancing might of Islam and of the rapid growth of feudalism, people very quickly lost sight of the Carolingian attempt to salvage or re-establish a Roman order. Some post-Carolingian emperors protested their intention of bringing about a *renovatio*, but the vociferousness of such protestations usually stood in inverse proportion to their chances of success. Thus the wave of pessimistic historical thinking continued until it reached its climax in the doctrine of the approach of the reign of the Antichrist and the apocalyptic speculations of Joachim of Flora. All these lines of historical analysis took it for granted that history was continuous from the biblical accounts onwards. The paramount power had eventually been transferred to the Romans, in the hands of whom it had turned Christian. Some argued that it had then been further transferred to the Franks, but even if such transfer was admitted, it did not really occur to anybody that in the hands of the Franks the imperial power could take a turn for the better or do anything but prepare the coming of the Antichrist.

One of the most interesting figures in this propagation of universal pessimism and gloom is bishop Otto of Freising. An uncle of Frederick Barbarossa and a Cistercian monk, he wrote his great chronicle of world history towards the end of the first half of the 12th century and gave free voice to his conviction that the misfortunes of King Conrad III and of the second crusade were sure signs of the approach of the final cataclysm. But even historians are human, and even when they are trying to encompass world-history they are often unduly moved and influenced by contemporary events. Less than ten years after Otto had completed his big, gloomy book he came to be drawn into the political circles surrounding his nephew Frederick Barbarossa. Frederick was then preparing his great show-down with Milan and the other Lombard cities and managed to enlist Otto's historical skill for this grand plan of re-establishing imperial power in the economically rapidly growing lands of Lombardy.

With this plan afoot, Otto was wrenched from his pessimistic historical outlook. He changed his mind—and this change was all the more remarkable as it took place during the very last years of his life—and began the composition of the *Gesta Friderici*, in which he allowed full rein to a spirit of liberation and the conviction that from now on the fortunes of the empire were about to be revived. The book is a most extraordinary document in more ways than one, and it is very regrettable that Otto did not live to complete it. As it was, Frederick battled for a good 15 years only to find that his plan could not be put into practice. The Italian communes were too tough for him. One must wonder what Otto of Freising would have concluded from Frederick's ultimate defeat in Lombardy, and whether he would have regretted that he had allowed himself to be temporarily swayed by his nephew's optimism.

But viewing the episode from the vantage point of later centuries one can discern that Otto of Freising, despite himself, was not nearly as wrong-headed as he must have appeared to himself, or would have, had he lived long enough to witness Frederick's failure. For the concrete changes that gave cause for a more optimistic outlook were indeed connected with the communes of Lombardy and the economic growth of northern and central Italy. In this sense, Otto was by no means as mistaken as a first glance seemed to show. The only trouble was that he had backed the wrong horse. He had imagined that the new era was to derive from Frederick's plan; whereas in reality it was to be connected with the Italian communes' resistance to that plan.

Having defeated Frederick Barbarossa and preserved their independence, the Italian communes did indeed rapidly progress from strength to strength. And it cannot come as a surprise that the first optimistic notes in historical writing were struck by historians mindful of their rapid growth. Even so it took almost another two hundred years before Leonardo Bruni, the Chancellor of the Florentine Republic, produced his *Historiarum Florentini Populi Libri XII*. This work was written no longer from the universal standpoint, but its attention was centred upon the city of Florence, one of the communes inside which the rebirth of life was taking place: 'Such cities throughout Italy as had survived the various barbarian floods began to grow and flourish.'[2] With this view the spell of the time-honoured tradition of focussing one's attention upon the inexorable decline of the Roman Empire was finally broken. The focus of attention was shifted from universal or Roman history to the history of the Italian communes. And it was their economic and cultural progress which furnished the evidence for a hopeful, forward-looking and optimistic outlook on history. Giovanni Villani had stated that Florence was rising while Rome was declining,[3] and before

[2] Muratori ed., XIX, 3, p. 23.

[3] *Chron.*, Dragomanni ed., 1844, II, p. 39. Dante's stubborn refusal to distinguish Florentine history from Roman history and its implied blindness to the vigorous growth of the Communes, is a telling measure of his 'medievalism'.

Bruni, towards the end of the 14th century, the Florentine historian Filippo Villani, concentrating on the history of culture, had struck an identical note, if anything even more explicit, concerning the revival of letters.

In this way the long period in which people had thought of the ageing of the world and of history as an inevitable decline leading to cultural decay on one hand and to the most fearful apocalyptic events on the other, was brought to a close. The conception of a renaissance, if not the word itself, gained rapid ground because historians began to interest themselves in the growth of the Italian communes. There is no need to trace the development of the concept, and finally, of the word, in detail. All that is necessary is to note that it was first fashioned in reaction to an age-old habit of pessimism in regard to a historiography that had remained concentrated upon the decline of the Roman Empire; and the pessimism of which had actually been independent of the apocalyptic fears introduced by Christianity.

But it was one thing to think that a new and more hopeful era of history was to be inaugurated by the growth of the Italian commune, and another to imagine that the word that came to be used to describe this awareness of hopefulness could be employed in order to describe the general culture of the age in question or, indeed, could be employed to describe a historical period with a beginning and an end. Villani's and Bruni's hopefulness could not envisage the possibility of an 'end'. If they had envisaged an end and if they had thought of the 'renaissance' merely as an age among many, they would have defeated their own purpose.

One could describe the long period of historical thought which was thus inaugurated as the period of innocence of the problem of the renaissance. This age of innocence lasted well into the 19th century: and Sismondi's *Histoire de la liberté en Italie* is perhaps its last and its greatest monument. Sismondi wrote of the growth of liberty and of the vicissitudes of that growth in the same spirit in which Villani and Bruni might have written about it. But in the generation after Sismondi the notion of the renaissance received its subtle transformation. When Burckhardt took it up and produced his epoch-making work on *The Civilisation of the Renaissance*, the notion had been narrowed and had received a new meaning. The renaissance was now a definite age, with a beginning and an end, and with certain well defined characteristics. Burckhardt had taken his cue from the humanists; but had ended up by seeing the renaissance as a new age in which the spirit of unbridled individualism had asserted itself in politics and art—a spirit which had produced the greatness as well as the guilt of the age. For Burckhardt was nothing if not a moralist and his general pessimism is a clear measure of the gulf that separated him from Petrarch and the humanists in general and from his immediate predecessors like Sismondi, in particular.

With this transformation of the concept of the renaissance, the flood-gates of debate were opened. For it soon became evident that the age of the renaissance did not necessarily have the characteristics which Burckhardt had said it had. It was argued that the preceding age had been much less barbarous and the age of humanism much more superstitious and that the only clearly recognisable dividing line between the middle ages and the renaissance was the fact that the humanists had claimed that there was a dividing line.

Some historians, concentrating upon the importance of Neo-platonic, Hermetic and Cabbalistic elements in the thinking of the humanists, have shown the enormous gulf that exists between genuine modernity and the renaissance, and have maintained that the modern age, far from beginning with the renaissance, was actually delayed by it. Others have singled out the contributions made by craftsmen and technicians and artisans to show the essentially technological and scientific orientation of the period (Olschki). Some have urged that the so-called revival of letters goes back to the 12th century and was therefore not characteristic of the renaissance proper (Haskins), and others have insisted that what was characteristic of the renaissance was not the revival of antiquity but a belief in a spiritual and religious renewal which goes back to St. Francis (Burdach). And Huizinga, by concentrating on Burgundy where Burckhardt had concentrated on Italy, described the 15th century as the waning of the middle ages. As in the case of Huizinga, there are other works where the confusion is more apparent than real because it depends so clearly on the chronological or geographical vantage point of the historian. Gilson, working backwards from Descartes, was able to show the persistent continuity of the well-organised medieval centres of learning; and Cassirer, working forward from Cusanus, treated the Italians of the 16th century as the forerunners of modern scientific thought.

Similarly, there is endless disagreement as to how the civilisation of the age of the renaissance was connected with the prevailing economic and social and political conditions of the time and a large number of different theories have been advanced as to the precise nature of what was being re-born as a result of these conditions. According to Baron, the new spirit was formed as a reaction of Milan's threat to the republican freedom of Florence. Others stress that it was related to certain social changes (v. Martin) or that it was an attempt to defend classical and Roman orthodoxy against the tide of medieval heresy and individualism (Toffanin). Some have insisted that this conception was really only a matter of the all pervasive influence of classical humanism, of a *renaissance des lettres* (Kristeller), and some have insisted that it had something to do with the economic recession that began in the 14th century (Lopez).[4] But the theory more persistent than any other is the one that maintains that the age of the renaissance was an age dominated by rebellious individualism, of which the concept in question was only one manifestation among many. This time-honoured notion goes back to Michelet and Burckhardt and has come up in one form or another in Gentile, to whom the anti-religious quality of this individualism was a cause for pride; and in Chabod, by whom it received a formulation that is so wide as to be identical with the way in which other observers have described the breakdown of traditional standards in other societies at other times. Chabod started with the notion that the renaissance was an age of unbridled and self-assertive individualism and worked his way through to the conclusion that what was so characteristic of the age was that art began to be done for art's sake, politics for politics' sake and so forth. In other words, men lost external and trancendental standards. This much seems already to have been surmised by Sir Walter Raleigh in writing about Hoby's translation of the *Cortigiano*: 'The purpose of the humanist was open and unashamed: man was to train himself like

[4] There is a judicious summary of the many doubts that may well cross one's mind by E. F. Jacob and A. S. Turbeville, 'Changing Views of the Renaissance', *History*, XVI, 1931–2. One ought also to consult the more specialized discussion by E. Panofsky, *Renaissance and Renascences in Western Art*, Stockholm, s. d.

B

a race-horse, to cultivate himself like a flower, that he might arrive to such perfection as mortality might covet'. Reflecting on this view, one cannot but be reminded of the trenchant description of the break-down of traditional German society after the first world war in the third volume of H. Broch's *The Somnambulists*, in which the hero—or better, the villain—appears as a man who is interested in business for business' sake. And with this reminder, Chabod's theory begins to lose its precision, for its outlines become blurred. If it is the characteristic of other periods of decaying traditions to do things entirely for their own sake without transcendental or external reference, ought we not to see the renaissance described in this way by Chabod also as a period of decline, as the end of an epoch, rather than as a positive formulation of a new way of life or a new civilisation? To Broch, who uses the same idea for the description of the decay of traditional German society, the protagonist of business for business' sake was certainly a villain, and not a hero. But once the outlines of Chabod's theory are blurred, and once we see that his attempt to describe the age of the renaissance has, instead, resulted in a description that reminds us more of a decline and the emergence of chaos than of a positive development, we have come full circle. For now once more, we wonder whether there is any point in speaking of the renaissance as an age. For Chabod's theory is such that, if it is true, it has proved not that there was a civilisation of the renaissance, but that what goes under this name is the period in which medieval civilisation broke up. But Chabod is by no means alone in formulating a theory that increases rather than diminishes the prevailing confusion. Burckhardt's idea that the distinguishing feature of the renaissance was individualism, is clearly incompatible with Toffanin's theory that humanism emerged as a reaction against individualism. And Burckhardt's view that the inspiration of the renaissance comes from medieval spiritualism is quite incompatible with Kristeller's notion that the renaissance was a *renaissance des lettres* as well as with Olgiati's view that humanism was only a new form of the traditional medieval faith—and the latter view is itself quite incompatible with that of Gentile who argued that the real mark of the renaissance was the rejection of religion.

These debates of historians are perfectly legitimate and are the necessary outcome of historical interpretation. The only thing that is *not* legitimate—and this, in fact, is the only thing that has made these disagreements appear so intractable—is to equate any one of these theories *about* the nature of a certain historical age or period with the concept of a renaissance as orignally fashioned by the Italian humanists and historians and claim that the latter concept affords hard and irrefutable evidence for any one of the many competing theories.

In the 20th century an entirely new factor has been introduced into the discussion—and it was introduced in a manner designed to increase the prevailing confusion. Burckhardt had seen the renaissance as the beginning of the modern age. To the 20th century historian, modernity without natural science is inconceivable; and hence he began to ask whether modern science stems from the renaissance. And it is now frequently taken for granted that the claim of the renaissance to have been a renaissance must stand or fall with its contribution, if not to science itself, then to the modern scientific outlook. The massive researches of Thorndike and Duhem have gone to show that in regard to the development of science, there was nothing very spectacular about the renaissance, which was lacking in originality. The sources of modern science are to be found in the middle ages. Both Duhem and Thorndike therefore, though perhaps prepared to accept the humanists' claim to have restored *litterae humaniores*, did not set much store on such an achievement and decisively rejected Burckhardt's claim that the renaissance was the beginning of the modern age. But one ought to note that this rejection was not really based upon a rejection of Burckhardt's theory as it stood; but upon a shift of emphasis due to the belief that 'modernity' means 'scientific attitude'—an emphasis which had been quite foreign to the 19th century Burckhardt. But it was not only that Duhem and Thorndike shifted the emphasis in the meaning of 'modern'. They also failed to see that what is important in the growth of science is not that this or that scientific doctrine actually went back to the middle ages; but the development of a mental and social climate favourable to scientific discovery and invention. If one can look upon the matter in this realistic way, one will find in spite of the shift of emphasis in the meaning of 'modernity', that the renaissance *was* important for the growth of science. Pico, for instance, was a humanist. His attack on astrology was based not on any scientific insight but upon the humanistic principle that astrology is incompatible with the dignity and freedom of man. Nevertheless it was a decisive influence on Kepler. Or consider the case of Galilei, whose mathematical skills were not derived from a teacher of mathematics but from a technical institute of *disegno* which he had attended. And even so staunch an advocate of the importance of Paduan Aristotelianism for the development of science and its debt to medieval Aristotelianism and the Latin Averroists of Paris as J. H. Randall, Jr., is obliged to admit that not the least contribution of humanism to the growth of natural science was to send men to the study of the original ancient sources in mathematics.[5] These and similar examples help us to understand how natural science no less than humanistic education and the study of history and politics, depended on the rise of a new society. They show us that the older view of the renaissance based on a study of 15th century humanism, has been confirmed by the discovery of the importance of the artist-engineer and of the practical humanist engaged in an active, civic life, for the development of science:

'Wherever creative individuals belonged to social groups which had direct contacts with the new life of work and action—whether we think of the official-secretary or the merchant-statesman or the artist-engineer—there the transformed relationship of life and thought rapidly gave to experience, interest and accepted values the shape that differentiates the modern from the medieval mind. . . . In the last analysis these varied views are not alternative but complementary to each other. They represent the different avenues along which recent scholarship has been developing the Burckhardtian thesis that at the basis of the 15th century renaissance there was a fundamental change in man's outlook on life and the world, the 'coming of the first born among the sons of modern Europe'.[6]

Probably in order to avoid the tantalising intricacies of these arguments, Eugenio Garin in the title of the work which is here

[5] 'Scientific Method in the School of Padua', *Journal of the History of Ideas*, I, 1940.
[6] H. Baron. 'Evaluation of the 15th Century Renaissance', *Journal of the History of Ideas*, IV, 1943, pp. 47–8.

translated, has imposed certain limitations upon his theme; it is no accident that in this title he avoided the words 'renaissance' and 'age'.[7] Garin's purpose is much more modest than that of most historians of this period. He leaves out politics, arts and science, and does not aim at giving a history of the period and of its characteristic tones. Instead he is concerned with a certain movement of thought. 'Movement' in this context must not be understood in the sense of a group of scholars and thinkers sharing a common purpose and therefore belonging to the same movement. The 'movement' he describes is more like a movement in music—a treatment of certain themes with variations, with counterpoint and fugue; it is a movement of thought in which one idea is linked to another dialectically rather than through pure logic. This movement stretched from the middle of the 14th century to the end of the 16th. It began with Petrarch and ended with Bruno and Campanella, and Garin sees it as one of the many movements in the history of philosophical thought, something comparable to the classical age of Greek philosophy or to German Idealism, although he would be the last to claim that in originality or depth the movement of Italian Humanism was comparable to either of these.

The humanists themselves, as a rule, did not look upon themselves as philosophers, and Burckhardt had completely omitted the consideration of philosophical ideas. The notion, however, that there is something like a philosophy of the renaissance goes back to Dilthey, who characterised it as a form of *immanentism*. People ceased to be occupied, he said, with an external principle sustaining the universe and looked upon reality as something *in* the universe, rather than above it. Hence the interest in neo-Platonism, in pantheism and in panpsychism. Dilthey's views on this matter were intuitive rather than scholarly and, for that matter, he was more interested in the renaissance as a kind of mid-wife to the reformation than in the philosophy of the renaissance itself. However, a sensitive thinker's intuition is valuable and Garin stands in a direct line of descent from Dilthey.

[7] The present book first appeared in German in 1947 and was published in Italian in 1952. The present text is a translation of the revised Italian edition of 1958. It is unabridged; but a number of quotations have been omitted. The sub-title was not used in the earliest edition.

But he has added to the notion that there *was* a body of philosophical ideas a great deal of erudition, and has thus been able to exhibit this body as a movement in the above sense. He begins with Petrarch's opposition to the reigning philosophy of Aristotelianism with its rationalistic and naturalistic interests, its collective and impersonalistic conception of human nature. And once the humanistic standpoint with its personal values is chosen as a starting point, the ensuing debate is of necessity represented from a humanistic and Florence-centred angle, and the Aristotelian developments in Padua, for instance, are depicted as so many reactions to the humanistic attack. Under this attack, Paduan naturalism tended to introduce personal elements of its own. Aristotle was not abandoned; but there began a tendency to replace Averroistic Aristotelianism and its fatalism by the Greek Aristotle and a consequent emphasis on scientific thought and a more humane individualism.[8] While all this comes out in Garin's presentation, one cannot help feeling that with his Florence-centred starting-point, he is perhaps a little bit less than just to Padua. Or perhaps one *must* see the humanisation of Aristotle as resulting from the growth of humanism in general. The only real weakness implicit in seeing the philosophical movement in this way is that its scientific interests as such tend to be neglected. Hence there is comparatively little attention paid to the great 16th century debate whether quality or quantity are 'the first accident of substance', and as a result Garin pays more attention to Fracastoro and Telesio who had opted for quality and thus were obviously linked with the general trend of humanistic thought than to the champions of quantity. And Galilei, who appreciated the fundamental importance of mathematics and of quantity, is seen as the beginning of a new movement; whereas a less humanistic centred treatment of the period's philosophy would have been more sympathetic to Galilei's position inside the philosophical movement that is the subject of this book.

All in all, and this much was stressed by Garin himself in the preface to the first Italian edition of this work, the treatment of the age under discussion singles out three strands of thought. And in selecting them, Garin, though ostensibly writing the

---

[8] For all this cp. O. P. Kristeller and John H. Randall, Jr., 'The Study of Renaissance Philosophies', *Journal of the History of Ideas*, II, 1941, pp. 492–493.

history of Italian humanism, has joined the ranks of those historians who have offered a theory as to the quality and significance of the age and its dominant philosophical movement.

There are three strands of thought running through this movement. The first is represented by the incessant, one might almost say obsessive, preoccupation with civic virtue and the rejection of the solitary, contemplative or monastic life. It begins with Petrarch and Salutati, though it is clear that in the 14th century both men still found it difficult to reach an unequivocal position in favour of the active life and social virtue. Petrarch was inclined to attribute enormous importance to the individual's awareness of death—so much so that at times he almost anticipates some of our modern existentialists. And Salutati too, continued to have a sneaking respect for contemplation. But from then onwards, the doubts disappear and the insistence upon the primacy of the active life tends to become both monotonous and aggressive. Except at times, when to the modern reader the argument used becomes almost humorous. For to us, Socrates' family life has become synonymous with marital strife and unhappy domesticity; but the humanists stubbornly determined to praise the active life and extol the civic virtues, kept reiterating, perversely so, that the life of Socrates is proof that man can successfully combine the pursuit of philosophy with a wholesome family life.

All this is clearly linked with the springtime republicanism of the Italian communes. When that republicanism gives way to the patriciate or even to tyranny, one can trace a corresponding flight from the preoccupation with the active life and civic virtue into the higher realms of metaphysics. Later, in the 16th century, when the political chaos has led to foreign domination, one finds a stubborn reiteration of the value of civic virtue and the active life as a sort of determined protest or a forlorn hope. And finally, at the very end of the period, these motives still play their part in the thought of both Bruno and Campanella, where they are now coloured by their religious vision of an entirely new society, reconstructed according to the insights of their metaphysical theories.

The second theme is represented by the fact that these humanists had freed themselves entirely from the scholastic style of

writing and thinking. Instead of dialectical reasoning and syllogistic deduction we are treated to the flow of rhetoric, both in
Latin and in Italian. The humanists considered the substitution
of rhetoric for the stern dialectics of the school-men an advantage.
The modern reader, though Garin very tolerantly does not say so,
cannot be so sure that they were right. It is undeniable that the
dialectical rigour of the school-men had a certain artificiality
about it; and often, at the very height of an argument, one sees
that they sacrifice genuine insight to the exigencies of a syllogism.
But at any rate, there was strenous intellectual labour there,
whereas there is really little joy in reading the pages of the humanists, full of repetition and intellectual imprecision as they are.
Instead of proof or demonstration, they pile assertion upon
assertion. Instead of attempting to produce arguments for the
truth of a proposition they recommend, they sing its praises; and
instead of giving a logical analysis of an opinion, they recommend
it by adding a metaphor. The humanists themselves called the
Latin of the middle ages 'barbarous'. But one cannot help thinking that this barbarous language, when placed under the yoke of
dialectical reasoning, proved a tougher discipline than the
discursive effusiveness of the humanists.

The third theme is possibly the most important one. It is
represented by the humanists' preoccupation with philology and
the study of the two ancient languages. They awoke to the
importance of such study because, unlike their predecessors, they
were alive to the fact that classical culture no longer existed and
that they were separated from it by 1,000 years. As we have seen
above, the whole of the historical thinking of the middle ages
had been oblivious to the disappearance of the ancient world.
They had known much of Plato and some of Aristotle. They had
had Latin and sometimes a little Greek. The influence of Cicero
and Boethius, of Virgil and Homer was very noticeable. And
much more was 'alive' of classical civilisation during the middle
ages than the humanists allowed. But all turns on the precise
meaning of the word 'alive'. Just because some of these ancient
authors had remained 'alive', they were really quite dead. For as
they continued to be read century after century—Gregory the
Great's injunction against classical studies had not been able to
survive the age of Charlemagne—nobody noticed that the world

in which they had been conceived, the people for whom they were written, and the social, economic and political conditions that had given rise to them, had disappeared. Hence, nobody noticed that the meaning of the words could not simply be assessed in terms of the new environment and that for instance what Aristotle had said about the government of a city-state could not easily be applied to the medieval empire or the management of a feudal manor. In short, nobody was aware that an understanding of Aristotle might require not only a new study of his language, but also an effort at imaginative reconstruction of the world in which Aristotle had lived. And for this reason the very 'aliveness' of the ancient authors was, in a sense, proof of their deadness. There is, therefore, no point in arguing whether and how many ancient authors were known in the middle ages; but only in how they were *interpreted*.

The formation of the idea that the people of the 14th century were separated from ancient civilisation by 1,000 years, which, as we have seen, was the origin of the conception of the renaissance, implied a complete reorientation towards the classical authors. It could no longer be taken for granted that they were 'alive'; and a determined effort had to be made to study their language and the conditions under which they had worked and lived in order to gauge their correct meaning. In this way, philology tended to become the queen of all sciences, the study that held the key to all wisdom and all culture. And paradoxically, now that it was realised that the ancient authors belonged to a dead civilisation, they were artificially brought back to life through philology and became 'alive' in a sense in which they had not been alive in the middle ages.

Garin is most insistent upon this point, and for a fuller elucidation one ought to consult his *Medioevo e Rinascimento* (Bari, 1954), pp. 105, 158 and 168. He argues that the real distinction between the middle ages and the renaissance must not be sought in whether or not the former showed an extensive acquaintance with classical writers; but in whether people were aware of the historical distance that separated them from ancient civilisation. His insistence on this criterion of distinction is clearly based upon the view taken of history by the humanists. But it is no mere mechanical application of it. For the humanists themselves merely derived pride from their knowledge that they had finally finished with the barbarism of the preceding centuries and used this position of pride in order to pour endless scorn upon scholasticism. And they considered that with the elaboration of philology they had fashioned the tool that would make contact with the lost land of antiquity possible. But in the last analysis they themselves only saw a simple dichotomy: ignorance on one side; philology on the other. Garin develops this view in a very subtle way into what must ultimately be considered a theory about the age of the renaissance. For he shows how the reliance upon philology became the dominant intellectual passion of the age and controlled all the discussions on beauty, rhetoric, love and metaphysics—discussions which were based almost entirely on commentaries upon the ancient authors on the subject. In this way he argues that the difference between the middle ages and the renaissance was not simply the difference between ignorance and philology; but consisted in the fact that medieval thinkers had no sense of history while the humanists had. In thus widening the simple upsurge of hope of the humanists into a general theory about the intellectual culture of the age, Garin has made his own contribution to the discussion as to what the salient characteristics of the age of the renaissance were.

Initially his theory is based upon a deep respect for the views of the humanists themselves. Only very cautiously does he proceed to extend its scope and turn it into a modern historian's theory about the age of the renaissance. But in the end, and I am sure he would not seek to deny this, the cloven hoof comes into view: time and again Garin reminds the reader that in such and such a respect the humanists anticipated Vico and the development of subsequent historicist thought in Italy. This is no simple piety in regard to the continuity of philosophical thinking in Italy. Garin himself, as a historian, is a member of this tradition, and his study of renaissance philosophy is therefore necessarily under the influence of the idea that all human thought, if it is to add up to a total truth, must be comprehended in its historical evolution. His interest in the philosophy of humanism is strongly determined by this view, and it is therefore not surprising that he should have come to see the history of that thought as essentially dominated by this view.

This insight is both a source of strength and a weakness. It is a source of strength, in the sense that Garin himself can write about the philosophy of the age of humanism as an insider. It is very noticeable how in the present book, which is a more or less formal history of the thought of the period, his own style of writing is, probably quite consciously, coloured by the rhetorical habits of the people he is writing about. In many cases the difference between the style of his quotations from the original authors and that of his own explanations is negligible. And, moreover, good historian that he is, he does not allow his hind-sight to intrude upon what the humanists themselves said. As a result he also keeps his explanations as to why certain changes in thought and shifts in accent occurred, to a minimum. In an English translation, however, the rhetorical flourish of the original text had to be toned down lest, in English, it sound too exaggerated. But some of it has been retained on purpose in order to preserve for the English reader the intention of the original.

There is no denying, however, that Garin's insight is also a source of weakness. For it is bound to make one slightly suspicious. He offers what one is forced to consider another interpretation of the thought of the age of humanism. One's confidence in the theory offered would have been increased if he had written a little more as an outsider. As it is, he himself seems so much part of the movement that is his subject; and the resolution of the arguments of the people he is writing about, so much part of the historicist tradition of Italian philosophy from Vico to Croce, that one cannot help wondering, at times, whether the humanists could *really* have been quite so much concerned with the same problems. Garin's employment of the word 'freedom' and the frequent play upon the alleged synonymity of words like 'spirit', 'mind' and 'soul' are certain to make English readers raise their eyebrows. But all this is not necessarily meant as a criticism of Garin. In one sense, of course, he confronts the dilemma which every historian must confront: if one writes as an insider, one may fail to mediate between one's subject and the modern reader. If one writes as an outsider, one can be sure of missing most of the essential points. And when all is said and done there remains the ultimately ineluctable fact that the Latin and the Italian the humanists wrote, contain the very same equivocality of the words mentioned. It is only in modern English usage that we have allowed secular, scientific, technological and non-religious considerations to teach us more precise and quite rigid distinctions between mind, soul and spirit. And even then it is not certain that these precise distinctions in a field that is by its very nature by no means very precise, are to our advantage. At any rate, a translator's task is not an easy one. The equivocations upon which much of Italian thinking thrives are impermissible in English. But if an attempt had been made to eliminate them, the book would not only have lost too much of its original character, but also appeared as a distortion of the ideas it contains. And if an attempt had been made to observe them meticulously, the English text would have been, in many places, quite incomprehensible. The translation therefore had to be built on compromise and discretion. And in these I have probably not been as skilful as I ought to have been.   P.M.

Wellington, New Zealand, October 1963.

INTRODUCTION

1. HUMANISM AND PHILOSOPHY

IT is almost a century now since Renan, in his book on Averroes, transformed Padua and Florence into symbols of an antinomy, capable of characterizing—so it seemed to him—the whole orientation of the so very complex culture of the Renaissance. On one side there was Padua, the stronghold of the Aristotelian-Averroist tradition, rigorously scientific and logical, in contrast to humanism and all it implied in the way of literature, the arts and *studia humanitatis*. On the other side there was Florence, the city of Ficino and Poliziano and of many others, thinkers as well as poets, who thought the Paduan masters to be 'strange and fantastic', according to a curious expression which is to be found in a letter of the year 1491 to Lorenzo.[1] This contrast was softened by the author's knowledge, always present if not always clear, of the profound significance of humanism and of the incontrovertible value of the unprejudiced critical position of humanism. Renan knew perfectly well that the Paduan philosophy of the 15th century was tired; that the tools it had perfected and which it had used were worn out and that its sources had dried up; that its subtle rationalizations moved in a void and belonged to the past. Galileo was to know well every single development of Aristotelian physics; but he was to draw the perspective that was necessary for a new synthesis from a very different cultural environment.

Unfortunately too many historians of the Civilisation of the Renaissance have been seduced by the possibility of transforming a mere contrast into an explanation, thus mistaking a negation for a positive factor. As a result the struggle between Florence and Padua has become one of the commonplaces of history, apt to characterize an attitude as a rebellion of literature against science, of poetry against philosophy, of law against medicine, of mystical rhetoric against heretical dialectics, of humanist-

[1] A. Poliziano, *Prose volgari inedite e poesie latine e greche edite e inedite*. ed. by I. Del Lungo, Firenze, 1867, p. 80.

Platonic *pietas* against Averroist impiety.[2] And finally all the
themes of the controversy about the Renaissance from Burckhardt
onwards have converged upon this famous contrast. And thus
'science' and 'philosophy' have from time to time become the
signs of medieval superiority and modernity, or of a radical
deficiency and a hopeless decline, as the case may be. And
alternatively, 'rhetoric' and 'grammar' have been looked upon
now as a pause in the progress of the spirit and now as an expression of a clearly modern culture. And finally, a large part
of modern historical writing has miraculously agreed to deny
the profound significance of the speculations of the Renaissance
and has declared them to be lacking in all originality. It is
alleged that there was nothing new or rejuvenating in their
literary aspects, and that philosophically they did not present
anything original when compared with the Middle Ages. Such
agreement was reached not only in obedience to a justifiable
desire for continuity with the Middle Ages but also on account of
a declared or hidden hostility to the values of modern philosophy.

Sarton, the historian of science, conducted a polemic against
the humanists whom he considered presumptuous dilettanti.
Without hesitation he came to the conclusion that they represented
an indubitable regression, both from the philosophical and from
the scientific point of view. Compared with the Scholasticism of
the Middle Ages, which, though dense, was honest, the philosophy
of the Renaissance, or better, the Neoplatonism of Florence,
was a heap of ideas too vague to be of any genuine value. Nardi,
a historian of philosophy, showed himself even more radical.
'If we wish to go back to the beginning of modern philosophy',
he wrote, 'we must jump back beyond the age of humanism.'
And Billanovich, a historian of literature, called the age of humanism an age of 'silence interrupted only by the silent declensions
of the grammarians', while the 'study of philosophy was degraded
to feats of philosophical and rhetorical astuteness' in the midst
'of a general intellectual disorder'.[3] One would like to reply

[2] Cp. E. Troilo, *Averroismo e Aristotelismo padovano*, Padova, 1939 (and G.
Toffanin, *Per l'Averroismo padovano*, Lettera a E. Troilo, 'La Rinascita', 1939, 5; B.
Kieszkowski, *Averroismo e Platonismo in Italia negli ultimi decenni del sec. XV*, 'Giornale
Critico della Filosofia Italiana', 1933, 4).

[3] G. Sarton, *Science in the Renaissance*, in J. W. Thompson, G. Rowley, F. Schevill
and G. Sarton, *The Civilization of Renaissance*, Chicago, 1929, p. 79 (cp. W. F. Ferguson,
The Renaissance in Historical Thought, Five Centuries of Interpretation, Cambridge Mass.,

that these grammarians and rhetoricians were none other than Lorenzo Valla and Leon Battista Alberti; that both Nicholas Cusanus and Paolo Toscanelli emerged from that sterile and empty atmosphere; and that the science of both Leonardo and Galilei originated precisely in that age which one is recommended to skip; that Machiavelli wrote during that very age and that the whole critical ferment that led to Bacon and Telesio took place at that time. And finally one would like to mention that neither Erasmus nor Montaigne could ever have been thought of without the specific mental climate of the 15th century. Thus one could indeed show very simply that the whole conception of an antithesis between Florence and Padua was totally wrong. The facts are at hand. If indeed 15th century humanism differed from place to place, it had nevertheless certain characteristics with which it penetrated everywhere. And thus it exercised every-where a profoundly and radically rejuvenating influence. It was the expression of an entirely changed human attitude.

If the truth were told, the real reason for this condemnation of the philosophical significance of humanism is a very different one. One can gauge the real reason from the constant hankering for that metaphysico-theological synthesis of 'obtuse but honest scholasticism'. It is in fact nothing less than the love for a kind of philosophy which the 15th century abhorred. The people who condemn humanistic philosophy lament precisely the thing which the humanists wanted to destroy, that is the grand 'cathedrals of ideas', the great logico-theological systematisations. The human-ists disliked that idea of a philosophy which deals with every problem under the sun and with all theological researches and which organizes and delimits every possibility within the pattern of a pre-established order.[4] The age of humanism considered that philosophy vain and useless and substituted for it a programme of concrete researches, precise and defined in two senses; one in the direction of the moral sciences (ethics, politics, economics,

1948, p. 384; L. Thorndike, *Renaissance* or *Prenaissance?*, 'Journal of the History of Ideas', IV (1943), pp. 65–74); B. Nardi, *Il problema della verità; Soggetto e oggetto del conoscere nella filosofia antica e medievale*, Roma, 1951, pp. 58–59 (and second ed. of 1952, p. 61, n. 105); G. Billanovich, *Petrarca letterato; I, Lo scrittoio del Petrarca*, Roma, 1947, pp. 415 sqq.

---

[4] Cp. B. Croce, *Lo storicismo e l'idea tradizionale della filosofia*, 'Quaderni della Critica', 1949, pp. 84–85.

aesthetics, logic and rhetoric) and one in the direction of the natural sciences which were to be cultivated *iuxta propria principia*, free of all chains and all *auctoritas*, and which have on every level that bloom of which an honest but obtuse scholastic knew nothing.

This was the accomplishment of humanism. It permitted such inquiries and saw that the logic of man's search is not necessarily that of Aristotle; that the logic of Aristotle is not the word of God, but a product of history. It produced concrete investigations and accustomed new generations to see and to think, and educated them humanistically. All this may appear to the purveyors of well balanced theologies of small importance. But to those that think of philosophy as a conscious search for human attitudes and as a discussion of concepts, all this was an invaluable conquest. And this conquest, one might add, was by no means impious and heretical, but was very often most respectful towards religious faith as an undeniable experience, even though the various single researchers were not occupied with it. They were modest and moved in other directions. The 'philological' and historical researchers were modest indeed and willingly abandoned those grave discourses about God and the intellect. They tried to determine instead the shapes of the human city, the nature of human customs and rituals; or, as far as the natural sciences were concerned, they endeavoured to define the nature of illnesses or the structure of living bodies with a 'grammatical' precision which, as the great Antonio Beniviene insisted, they had picked up in the schools of the grammarians as a method for the understanding of reality. This is in fact the very 'philology' which, as a historiography which is today only too easily despised had well understood, was of the essence of the new 'philosophy'. This philology is an altogether new method of looking at problems, and is therefore not, as some have believed, to be considered side by side with traditional philosophy, as a secondary aspect of the Civilisation of the Renaissance. It was essentially an effective philosophical method.[5]

[5] Cp. P. O. Kristeller, *Movimenti filosofici del Rinascimento*, 'Giornale critico della Filosofia italiana', 1950, pp. 275–88; and also, *Humanism and Scholasticism in the Italian Renaissance*, 'Byzantion', XVII, 1944–45, pp. 346–74. Cp. also the valuable contributions in which Kristeller confirms his point of view: *Studies in Renaissance Thought and Letters*, Rome, 1956.

2. New Philological Requirements

In this connection it is useful to take a look at the eulogy composed by Niccoletto Vernia for Ermolao Barbaro for his translation of Themistius. Or better still, to read Vernia's prefatory letter to the edition of Aristotle with Averroes' commentary. In that letter the least humanistic of all the writers of the 15th century insists at great length upon the trouble he has taken with the editing of the text and explains how he went about questioning the Greeks he knew in order to clarify the meaning of technical expressions and to understand the rendering correctly—for without being sure of the meaning of the text there would have been no point in empty discussions of non-existing problems. When one reads that prefatory letter—so important from the point of view of method—how can one stop oneself from comparing favourably the Paduan professor's edition of Aristotle with a codex that used to be kept in the library of the Monastery of St. Mark of Florence, and which contains the Latin version of Eustrach's commentary on the Nicomachean Ethics? The manuscript belonged to Coluccio Salutati. In the margin we find, by the great Chancellor's own hand, notes about the exact meaning of words and confrontations with the original Greek. Salutati was planning to obtain precise information on these matters from various Byzantine people who, for commercial as well as for political reasons, had come to live in Florence.[6] Later he even succeeded in obtaining the services of Manuel Chrysoloras. For Salutati, good pupil of Petrarch that he was, always insisted that one should, when confronted with a philosophical text, refrain from empty discussions and occupy oneself instead with the attempt to understand it in its exact original sense. On one page of the *De Fato*, concerned with the moral interpretation of Seneca, he mentions that when confronted with difficulties due to the corrupt state of the manuscripts, he collected *multos codices . . . non modernis solum, sed antiquis scriptos litteris*. Thus he managed to take account of the things obscured by the copyists, of the marginal glosses and of those between the lines which had

---

[6] An edition of Vernia appeared in Venice in 1483 (Cp. 'Rinascimento', II, 1951, pp. 57–66). The codex of Eustrazio is in the National Library of Florence, Conventi; I, V, 21.

C

eventually ended up as part of the text. Thus he also coped with
the presumptuous ignorance of those readers who were ready to
correct the text when they could not understand it. Moreover, he
added, one has to take care of the things that happen when
particular interests are at stake, such as when one is dealing with
sacred texts or the works of the Fathers in which all sorts of
motives have been the cause of various kinds of wilful alterations.
Thus various barbarians *nullum omnino textum philosophorum
moralium, historicorum, vel etiam poetarum non corruptissimum relique-
runt*. Hence the necessity for a collection of all copies of every
work so that those that were the most expert in the language
concerned and in history, would be able to restore to each its
original appearance.[7]

Vernia was to try to do for Aristotle, and Nifo for the *Destructio
Destructionis* of Averroes, what Salutati had tried to do for Seneca.
This meeting in spirit between Salutati and Vernia has a very
special significance. For one of the few writings by Vernia that
have come down to us is a posthumous attack on Salutati and on
his theory of the supremacy of the laws. This attack is written
in a singularly antihumanistic spirit. And nevertheless, even this
opponent of the supremacy of *studia humanitatis* had, without
himself being aware of the fact, availed himself of the major
humanistic achievement; that is, of the critical and historical habit
of sizing up authors in their proper dimensions. The prejudice in
favour of Aristotle was no longer confined to insinuating that a
more or less repugnant text is capable of a more or less heretical
interpretation. It began, on the contrary, to assume the shape of
an attempt to find out what the historical Aristotle really was like.
And such an attempt is an effective beginning for overcoming
Aristotle altogether and with him all those positions based on
Aristotelianism as a permanent truth. For this reason Ermolao
Barbaro agreed with certain points made by Vernia[8]; and for
that very same reason at a certain moment the lesson of the
'philologists' became decisive for the 'philosophers' who became
more and more alive to the need for original sources, for correct
texts, for historical accuracy. And at the same time, Aristotle

[7] Salutati, *De Fato, Fortuna et Casu*, II, 6, Laur. 53, 18, fol. II V–12 r.
[8] Cp. the edition of the *Destructio* of Averroes published by Nifo in Venice in
1497; and E. Barbaro *Epistole* ed. by V. Branca, Firenze, 1943, I, p. 45 sqq.

himself ceased to be an *auctoritas* and became a thinker like all the others, part of a certain historical age. When we find the open confession that Aristotle, because he was not aware of certain problems, no longer suffices, we are face to face with the distance between the old and the new way of thought. There is no more question of a text, given once and for all; and even less question of a certain Truth to be illustrated. There is instead a risky adventure where everything is still obscure, but where everything is possible. The real hero of the pillars of Hercules is not the man who defies the order not to sail beyond them—although he may well think himself a hero. At any rate, his heroism depends on their existence. But the real hero is the man who explains how they came into being and thus understands them and then leaves them where they are, an obsolete and elegant 'curio', to use an expression by Vespasiano da Bisticci. He leaves them alone without laughing at them and without crying over them, without contempt, but with full understanding. Compared with the true philologists, all the so-called heretics, the empty Averroists as well as the most ardent Aristotelians, are all poor fish. The philologists, though respectful of traditional forms, courageously faced every document, every piece of paper and every book, determined to treat it as it lay before them; a human fact, a vestige of human reasoning and as such to be subjected to critical examination and discussion.

3. HUMANISM AND HISTORY

On the first of February 1392 Colluccio Salutati wrote a letter to Don Juan Fernandez de Heredia. This letter is a distinguished monument of his thought. The Chancellor praised the advantages of history—the educator of mankind, the source of a knowledge far more concrete than all the subtleties of theology and philosophy. He called her the true creator of man, for humanity consists, above all, in the recollection of man's actions in this world and for this reason history is a kind of 'philanthropy', an encounter and a dialogue with all men. Civilisation takes shape and politics are defined through the dimensions of history: 'tolle de Sacris Litteris quod hystoricum est: erunt profecto reliquie res sanctissimae, res mirande; sed . . . taliter insuaves, quod non longe poterunt te iuvare.' It cannot be a surprise, therefore, that the first historian in the modern sense of the word, was the great pupil and friend of Salutati, Leonardo Bruni. It was the wide political experience which he had acquired in the chancellery that taught him to look into the causes of the facts which, to him, were always the free decisions of good men or bad men, of men capable of being understood.[9]

In this way the age of humanism, at the end of a long crisis, both focussed upon and overcame for good in its historical pictures the ancient vision of a static reality, rigid and unchanging. Such a static reality had been presupposed by Platonic as well as by Aristotelian logic. In this presupposition all movement had been an eternal return to identical positions and had thus resolved itself into the very denial of movement, while man's life and activities had been lost in total insignificance. And this is precisely what certain critics cannot understand: without the so-called 'rhetoric' of people like Guarino, Valla, Poliziano and other such 'pedants', it would never have been possible to dethrone the 'authorities', and nobody would ever have been able to see Aristotelian logic for what it really is—an admirable tool of human thought valid for, and to be used in, certain cultural regions only. That is, as the logic of Aristotle of Stagira and perhaps also of Euclid and several other equally subtle thinkers; but not as logic in an absolute sense. All this was taught by Lorenzo Valla on the day on which he ceased to pretend that he was discussing Aristotle from within and proceeded instead to attack him. In the preamble to his *Dialettica*, Valla defined his position: he pointed out that the logic of Aristotle was not the only logic. As a result he ceased to accept the obligation of the schools to swear that Aristotle, as far as fundamentals are concerned, could never be wrong. He wanted instead to supplant Aristotle and Aristotelianism root and branch.

Then, and only then, the efforts of these same pedantic historians made it possible to gain some detachment from Aristo-

[9] B. L. Ullman, *Leonardo Bruni and the humanistic historiography*, 'Medievalia et Humanistica', 1946, pp. 45–61 (Cp. H. Baron, *Das Erwachen des historischen Denkens im Humanismus des Quattrocento*, 'Hist. Zeitschrift', 1933). On *humanitas, studia humanitatis e* φιλανθρωπια cp. Guarino (Nat. Library, Firenze, II, I, 67, fol. 113v.). Cp. also H. Baron, *Aulus Gellius in the Renaissance and a Manuscript from the School of Guarino*, 'Studies in Philology', 48, 1951, pp. 107–25.

telian physics and from the cosmology of Ptolemy. At one stroke people became freed from their oppressive strictures. Even though it is true enough that both physicists and logicians both in Oxford and in Paris had for some time made breaches into the systems which had trembled ever since the blow aimed at them by Occam,[10] still it was only when people began to understand ancient civilisation in a historical sense—and this understanding was the essence of humanistic philology—that it began to be possible to regard those theories in a true light, that is, as human thoughts, as products of a certain culture, as results of certain partial and particular experiences. Humanistic philology ceased to look upon them as oracles either of nature or of God, revealed by either Aristotle or Averroes, and took them instead as human thoughts. In this connection it is worth while taking another look at the twelfth book of Pico's astrological discussions. In that book he gave a very precise account of the psychological and historical emergence and diffusion of astrology. As he succeeded in historicising the errors of astrology he succeeded simultaneously and with no less acumen, in historicising all human knowledge. His own nephew, Gian Francesco, pitilessly demolished all philosophical theories belonging to ancient civilisations by demonstrating their limitations. He did not want to do this, and was barely aware of doing it; but he managed, by different methods and with intentions diametrically opposed to those of his uncle, to prove precisely the same thing.[11] In every respect, people acquired a sense of human history. This was so when they underlined man's eternal unsatisfied search; and it was so when they fixed their gaze upon all the diverse positive achievements of man.

4. HUMANISM AND PLATONISM

In this connection it is worth remarking that the humanists' preference for Plato, which was a fairly constant factor in their thinking, was a sign of rebellion and, in a certain measure, a party

[10] Cp. A. Maier, *An der Grenze von Scholastik und Naturwissenschaft*, Roma 1952[2]; *Die Vorläufer Galileis im 14. Jahrhundert. Studien zur Naturphilosophie der Spätscholastik*, Roma, 1949; *Zwei Grundprobleme der scholastischen Naturphilosophie*, Roma 1951[2]; *Metaphysische Hintergründe der spätscholastischen Naturphilosophie*, Roma 1955.
[11] *Examen Vanitatis Doctrinae Gentium*.

badge. But in the very last analysis, this preference meant a preference for the conception of an open world, discontinuous and full of contradictions, incessantly changing and hostile to any kind of systematization. To such a world one could do justice only through incessant research which would never shrink from apparent inconsistencies, but which was sufficiently mobile and subtle and variegated to be able to respect the infinite variety of existing things. Such research, moreover, would reject all rigid articulations of a static logic incapable of catching the plastic mobility of all Being. At times it might use them in order to underline the inappropriateness of all static conceptions.

There were so many possible interpretations of Plato that he appeared as some kind of a peace-maker. The reconciliation which Plato seemed to recommend was not taken as a sign of speculative weakness, but as a frank admission of the fact that two alternative terms are likely to become contradictory no sooner than they have been coined. The seeming contradictions in the Dialogues revealed clearly how much the acute eye of the 'divine' Plato had appreciated the contradictions that are present in all Reality.

Platonic philosophy was sensitive to all problems and nuances. It was a moral meditation on a life shot through with hope, and it impinged upon the borders of mythology. Thus it was a human dialogue, rather than a systematic treatise; and the exasperation with all the many problems led to corroded systematizations. For all these reasons the philosophy of Plato served as the centre of a civilisation that had rejected all old certainties, and the idea of a closed, ordered and static world; and which had found itself in a historical crisis, in the course of which all venerable unity had gone by the board and all human relationships had been changed. These dialogues were full of the enigmatic figure of Socrates and his subtle searching, a witness both to the solid certainty of his convictions and to his sense of urgency. These dialogues are so humane—full of social and mundane problems—and yet intimately concerned with the divine. Their tenor alternates between hopefulness and the realization that the things that ought to be may never come to pass. Reading them, one never quite knows whether 'those distant lands' are lost in the memory of a tradition or whether they are perhaps so near because of the expectation of redemption. Throughout their pages one recognises that philosophy is a form of passionate love and a vision of well-nigh miraculous forms that stand over and above all sense-data; and at the same time one sees that it is also a matter of subtle logic and a discussion of different possible forms of logic. These, clearly, were the reasons why such different temperaments as those of Valla and Ficino, of Poliziano and Pico, of Bruno and Patrizi, worshipped the 'divine' Plato and contrasted him to that 'beast' Aristotle. They knew perfectly well, and lost no opportunity for saying so, that often enough Aristotle had done no more than sum up or tidy up Platonic themes with coherent rigour. But they opposed all such summations and crystallizations. It was this kind of crystallization (to mention only one example), which, in astronomy, had transformed a really elegant geometrical construction into the physical theory of the celestial spheres. And for this reason when they chose Plato, they chose, in opposition to all systematizations, the new spirit of research, unprejudiced and truly free. It was like a declaration of war on the oppressively closed, hierarchical and finite world of Aristotle. Thus the slogan *ubi spiritus, ibi libertas* joined forces with the new programme of *iuvat vivere*.

5. THE ORIGINS OF HUMANISM

'The return to Plato' brings to mind an old but ever recurring misunderstanding. That is, the opinion that humanism was conditioned and characterised by the discovery of new classical texts. It is believed that the revival of civilization was due to the study of Cicero, Lucrece, Seneca, Plato and Plotinus; and it is thought that an increase in the quantity of classical reading finally led to a change in quality. This is in fact the view of all those learned historians who comb the medieval texts and translations, compilations, anthologies and quotations, and thus gradually persuade themselves that the first century of humanism was not the 14th and still less the 15th, and that the first age of humanism was not to be found in Italy. They insist instead that humanism began in the 13th century—or, better still, in the 12th century and even earlier, in the age of Alcuin and at the court of Charle-

magne.[12] One must admit willingly that it was very important—
not the least reason being the desire to understand the peculiarities
of the Renaissance—to dispel the myth of the Dark Ages and to
show that the conception of the barbarousness of the middle ages
was purely polemical. But it does not follow that one should deny
that this whole question concerned the outward appearance of
culture and not its content.

There can be no doubt that one ought to remember that people
in the middle ages read and translated the classics; that at least in
some places, at certain times, they knew Greek; that they were
interested in nature, and so forth. It is equally important to recall
that the middle ages, far from being dark and barbarous, showed
both the light of civilization and greatness of thought and thus
fed upon classical culture and appropriated it. The point, however, is that the real problem is more intricate and consists in
something else. It consists precisely in the task of determining
the differences between the various modes and forms of culture.

The better one knows the middle ages, the more clearly one
recognises in their civilization the extension of antiquity. Methods
of teaching as well as views and doctrines survived in various
ways. Even though the ancient ways may have exhausted their
vital impulses, there still remained their echoes, caught in manuals
and in compilations, fixed by the scholastic method. Christianity
by no means substituted—as Tertullian hoped—the temples of
Jerusalem for the halls of Athens. Both Athens and Rome

[12] There is no need to repeat the expositions by Ferguson *op. cit.*, Cp. also F.
Simone, *La coscienza della Rinascita negli umanisti francesi*, Roma, 1949 and La *'Reductio
Artium ad Sacram Scripturam' quale espressione dell'umanesimo medievale fino al secolo XII*,
'Convivium', 1949, pp. 887–927. On the XIIth cent. cp. W. A. Nitze, *The so called
Twelfth Century Renaissance*, 'Speculum', XXIII, 1948, pp. 464–71; Hans Liebeschütz,
Mediaeval Humanism in the Life and Writings of John of Salisbury, London, 1950, p. 94:
'his thought . . . was determined on the whole by traditional forms of ecclesiastical
literature. . . His humanistic outlook, for which antiquity was a kind of picture book
illustrating the types of twelfth-century life, seems . . . to have been intimately
connected with the archaic stage of European systematic thought.'
  The conclusions of the learned studies by R. Weiss, *The Dawn of Humanism in
Italy*, London, 1947, and *Il primo secolo dell 'umanesimo*, Roma, 1949, are equally
negative. They show with very certain evidence that 'primitive humanism did not
result from a reaction to a certain kind of philosophical speculation or from a
conscious desire to bring about a *renovatio studiorum* or from the hope for a golden
age'. It was in no sense the parent of the humanism of the Renaissance but a 'spontaneous and natural development of the classical studies as cultivated during the
later middle ages'. Weiss' honest conclusion emphasises correctly the distinctive
character of the new form of culture—a form which amounted indeed to a new vision
of life.

continued to live in the medieval schools, even though the original doctrines of Plato or Aristotle or Lucrece seemed so distant, so elevated and so solemn. They lived instead in the expressions of a tired wisdom contained in very modest handbooks. What really mattered was neither the Platonic dialogues, nor Aristotelian metaphysics, but Porphyry and compilations from Porphyry. In this way the crystallized summaries of ancient culture were transmitted by school text-books to the middle ages. And the worshipful attachment of the middle ages to these books forced the masters to confine their work to obsessively tortuous commentaries designed to unveil the truth enshrined in the page by the sacred character of the written word. Some, perhaps, added a gloss to the text; others might arbitrarily correct the text. None of them were interested in knowing the historical truth about the origin and meaning of the text. They were only interested in the one perennial Truth that somehow existed at the root of everything that had ever been written down. They took the text itself, written by someone with authority, as the object of knowledge, and therefore dispensed with all direct research. All efforts towards a more profound understanding were directed towards discovering the truth in what has been written down. And things written were no longer taken to be human documents, but were considered oracles from which one had to wrest the secret meaning. A tenth century author explained well how one could overcome all difficulties of research. One went to Chartres to read the aphorisms of Hypocrates. If that was not enough, one consulted the commentaries by Galen and then the commentaries by Sorano, and finally the commentaries on the commentaries, and so forth.[13]

It was this kind of mentality that led, in part, to the famous theory of 'the double truth'. The books of Aristotle were taken to be the revelation of natural truth: philosophy disregards every direct reference to reality, and confines itself instead to an understanding of what an author has written. In this way, the truth is completely divorced from the historical personality of a philosopher; and the material vehicle in which it became manifest is considered to be of no importance at all. The man is unimportant.

[13] Richer, *Histoire de France* (888–995), R. Latouche ed., Paris, 1930–37, II, pp. 224–31.

The only importance attaches to the thought, and any change in the name of the person who happens to hold it is a mere accident. Hence those strange attributions and hence all those anonymous writers who make the individual disappear in the work or consider it the fruit of a collective effort. There is grandeur in all this; but also limitation. But one has to bear all this in mind in order to understand the emotion with which Valla, confronted by a word, by *verbum*, insists on the fact that we are confronted by a mere instrument of communication. This instrument, he admits, is something sublime; but all the same, something quite human. Through this new attitude both logic and dialectics were led back from the theological heavens to the plains of rhetoric and grammar, the most humble spheres of all mundane preoccupations. Guarino, at the beginning of his course on rhetoric, concurred and reminded his readers that both rhetoric and dialectics were human sciences. And, similarly, Ermolao Barbaro, at the opening of the course on Aristotle which he held in Padua at sunrise, felt it necessary to say that it was his purpose to make Aristotle come to life and to make him take part in a human conversation: *ut cum ipso vivo et praesente loqui videamur*. Aristotle was to be a man living and present, loved in all his limitations.

6. HUMANISM AND CLASSICAL ANTIQUITY

The essence of humanism is most clearly defined by its attitude to the civilization of the past. And that attitude is not confined to an admiration or a love for antiquity, nor to a greater knowledge of antiquity, but consists rather in a well marked historical consciousness. The 'barbarians' were not barbarous because they had remained ignorant of the classics, but because they had failed to understand them as a historical phenomenon. The humanists, on the other hand, discovered the classics because they managed to detach themselves from them and comprehend their Latin without confusing it with their own Latin. It is for this reason that it is true to say that antiquity was discovered by the humanists, even though both Aristotle and Virgil were equally well known to the middle ages. It was humanism which placed Virgil back into his historical context; and which tried to explain Aristotle in terms of the problems and the sciences of the Athens of the fourth century before Christ. For this reason one should never seek to distinguish between the humanistic discovery of antiquity and the humanistic discovery of man—for they amount to exactly the same thing. For the discovery of antiquity implied that one had learnt to make a comparison between antiquity and oneself, to take a detached view of antiquity and to determine one's relation to it. And all this implied, further, the concept of time and memory and a sense of human creation, of human work in this world and of human responsibility. It was indeed no accident that the majority of the great humanists were statesmen and men of action, accustomed to participate freely in the public life of their age.

This point of view assumed concrete shape in the critical discussion which was started about the documents of the past. Such a discussion, whether or not it was to have any specific results, made it possible to establish a proper sense of distance between the humanists and the past. And in between, the humanists discovered those seven centuries of darkness—for no less were counted by Leonardo Bruni. During those centuries the spirit of criticism had been in abeyance, and all knowledge of history as a story of human activity had been absent. The 'philology' of the humanists gave concrete shape to that crisis which was occasioned by the new awareness of the past as past, by the new vision of reality as something earthly and by the new attempt to explain history as the story of men.

As soon as one opens the *Miscellanies* of Poliziano one comes across, in the very first chapter, the 'Endelechia', the soul. But the soul of which he treats has nothing to do with the Goddess of which Bernardo Silvestre had sung in the 12th century, or with the sort of soul which, according to so many Platonic commentators, was an entity of some kind or other. Nor does he discuss the unity of the possible intellect and of its relations with individual human beings. The question *he* discusses is a question of vocabulary: should it be *entelechia* or *endelecheia*? i.e., is it a matter of eternal movement or of a perfect act? With extreme lucidity and with classical witnesses at hand, Poliziano illustrates the origin of two conceptions of the soul by referring the whole matter to the relationship between the thought of Plato and the thought of Aristotle. He points out the meaning of the different premisses, and thus explains the thought that resulted from these two premisses. He shows the genesis of two theories and of their historical relationship, and we are made to understand the significance of an episode in the history of philosophy.

Or let us take a look at Valla, at his famous 38th chapter of the sixth book of the *Eleganze*. He deals there with the term *persona* and in a purely grammatical discussion, having reduced *persona* to a *quality*, he solves a grave theological problem with the help of Occam's Razor. It is no accident that Valla refers to his 'dialectics' for his dialectics is a rigorous reduction of philosophy from theology to an analysis of the structure of thought such as it is revealed in speech.

Or let us open the *Notes to the New Testament*. There we will read that 'none of the words of Christ have come to us, for Christ spoke in Hebrew and never wrote down anything'. And with reference of St. Jerome's observation that all biblical codices were corrupt, we read: 'if after only four hundred years the river had become too murky, need we be surprised that after a thousand years—for we are separated from St. Jerome by that many years— that river, never having been purged, carries both mud and refuse?'

While the most venerable texts were being re-examined in the light of their historical reality, and while the charters of ancient privileges were subjected to devastating criticism, people were also tracing back the origin of equally well enshrined ideas about the cosmic order to old superstitions and ancient errors. Poliziano smiled at the sight of the Codex of the Pandects that was exhibited in the Palazzo Vecchio by the light of candles. For these parchments were to him nothing but a historical problem, and he considered them sacred only because he considered any valid human creation sacred—that is, any human creation which was meant to open paths for mankind rather than to obstruct them for good.

This, then, is the true meaning of humanistic 'philology'. And it is not hard to understand that these same humanists were indeed extreme pedants, for they were sensitive to the fertility of their own method. For this reason they showed a very touching love in their exasperating desire to recover as many records of human labour as possible. Poliziano, confronted by a verse of Theocritos or Statius, wanted to rediscover every flavour, every allusion.[14] For the truth that is manifest to all men is entirely contained in those works which bear witness to man's indefatigable *poiein*. To understand its meaning is to understand our own meaning, our own limitations as well as our own potentialities. Before he wrote his *Miscellanies*, Poliziano wrote some pages that contain not only a grand lesson for mankind, but also define a method valid for any kind of research. In reading those pages one understands why the Renaissance was not only an age of artists, but also an age of scientists like Toscanelli and Galilei. And one understands why the sterile, though often very subtle, debates of medieval physicists and logicians could become fertile only after the new lesson had been learnt—even though that lesson seemed still so far distant.[15] One will also understand that eventually even a new kind of physician emerged from those schools of philology. And in view of this rigorous (one is tempted to say pitiless) critique, one can understand, finally, the doubt of Descartes. And similarly, one will understand why, for roughly two centuries, Italian culture should have dominated the whole of Europe, and why Italy during this period should have become a country so productive of so much philosophical talent.[16]

[14] Cp. Laur. XXXII, 46 (Theocritus), Magliab. VII, 973 (Statius).

[15] Cp. E. Callot, *La Renaissance des sciences de la vie au XVIme siécle*, Paris, 1951, pp. 14 sq. Callot notes this positive function of humanism without being able to explain it. But the explanation is not difficult to find and must be sought, precisely, in 'education' and the acquisition of a logical method.

[16] Cp. the curious and important text by Naudé published by Croce, 'Quaderni della Critica', 10 March 1948, pp. 116–17. On the general questions discussed above see: B. L. Ullman, *Studies in the Italian Renaissancce*, Roma 1955; G. Sarton, *The Appreciation of Ancient and Medieval Science during the Renaissance*, 1450–1600, Philadelphia 1955; C. Dionisotti, *Discorso sull'umanesimo italiano*, Verona 1956. On the problem of periodisation see D. Cantimori, *La periodizzazione dell'età del Rinascimento nella storia d'Italia e in quella d'Europa*, X Congresso Int. di Scienze Storiche, 1955, Relazioni, vol. IV, Firenze 1955, pp. 307–334. For other aspects cp. W. K. Ferguson, *Italian Humanism: Hans Baron's Contribution*, and H. Baron, *Moot Problems: Answer to Ferguson*, 'Journal of the History of Ideas', 19, 1958, pp. 14–34.

CHAPTER I

THE ORIGINS OF HUMANISM:

FROM FRANCESCO PETRARCHA TO
COLUCCIO SALUTATI

1. HUMANAE LITTERAE AND CIVIC LIFE

'PETRARCH was the first man to have had a sufficiently fine
mind to recognise the gracefulness of the lost ancient style
and to bring it back to life'. Thus wrote Leonardo Bruni in 1436
in his Life of Petrarch. He merely confirmed a view that was
widely held by humanists. According to that view Petrarch's
work had been the light of a new day which had dawned after the
barbarities and the darkness of the middle ages.[1] In the same
connection, Coluccio Salutati often also mentioned Albertino
Mussato, who used to love ancient thought and who had written
widely on the subject of *Fortuna*.[2] But there was general agree-

[1] Leonardo Bruni, *Vita di Messer Francesco Petrarca*, Philippi Villani *Liber de
Civitatis Florentinae Famosis Civibus* . . . ed. by G. C. Galletti, Florentiae, 1847, p. 53;
Julii Caesaris Scaligeri Poetices libri VII, vi. i (Apud Petrum Santandreanum,1594,
p. 765): 'de integro rediviva novam sub Petrarcha pueritiam inchoasse . . . visa est';
G. J. *Vossii De Historicis Latinis*, Lugd. Batav. 1651, p. 524. This did not exclude the
possibility that the 'darkness' lasted only for three centuries, i.e. until the advent of
Charlemagne. Domenico Silvestri, friend of Salutati, author of *De Insulis et Earum
Proprietatibus* (ed. C. Pecoraro, Palermo 1955, 'Atti d. Acc. Scienze, Lettere e Arti', s.
IV, vol. 14, 1953–4: On S. cp. P. G. Ricci, *Per una monografia su D.S.*, 'Annali Scuola
Normale Sup. Pisa', 1950, pp. 13–24; R. Weiss, *Note per una monografia* su *D. S.*,
ibid., pp. 198–201) in a letter to Giuliano Zonarini (ms. Nat. Library, Firenze, II, IV,
109, f. 79 v) says: 'cum Florentia tribus seculis latuisset'. Similarly Donato Acciaiuoli in his Life of Charlemagne (ms. Nat. Library, Firenze, II, II, 10). Filippo
Villani claims that Dante rescued learning *ex abysso tenebrarum*. In fact, people soon
learnt to distinguish the political renaissance and the renaissance of theology from
the awakening of *studia humanitatis*. Cp. Raffaele da Volterra, *Commentarii Urbani*,
dedicated to Julius II. In the 15th century the consciousness of a renaissance
became a rhetorical commonplace in Italy and thence was taken up in France. Cp.
F. Simone, *La Coscienza della rinascita negli umanisti francesi*, Roma, 1949 and the
observation in 'Rinascimento', 1950, pp. 91–7.

[2] On *De Lite Naturae et Fortunae* (ms. in Bibl. Colombina of Seville, 5, 1, 5; ms·
B.P. 2531, Bibl. Civica di Padova) cp. *Giunte e correzioni* by Zippel on the Italian
edition of Voigt, *Il risorgimento dell'antichità classica*, Firenze, 1888–1897; A. Moschetti,
Il 'De Lite inter Naturam et Fortunam' e il 'Contra Casus Fortuitos' di A. M., 'Miscellanea di studi critici . . . in onore di V. Crescini', Cividale del Friuli 1927, pp.
567–90; G. Billanovich—G. Travaglia, *Per l'edizione del 'De Lite inter Naturam et
Fortunam', 'Contra Casus Fortuitos', di A. M.*, 'Boll, Museo Civico di Padova',

ment that the true father of the new devotion to *humanitas* had been Petrarch. It had been he who had approached literature and the *studia humanitatis* in the full knowledge of their significance and of the value which an education of the mind through conversation with the great masters of antiquity was bound to have for the whole of mankind. These masters alone had understood the full importance of the soul which was to result from the study of the highest products of the human mind.

In one of his letters, Petrarch tried to show the way in which eloquence or literary discipline and philosophy or care of souls were related. Speech—*sermo*—is a form of expression which exhibits its own measure as well as that of the soul of which it is an expression. 'Speech is no mean index of the soul'. It is brought to light and submits to the control of other men. It accepts a discipline and reveals a certain attitude. 'Speech can have no dignity unless the soul has dignity'. At the same time, as we communicate with other people by speech, our own inwardness gains measure and concrete sense. 'Indeed, if our passions are not in harmony with each other, there can necessarily be no concord between our inner habits and our speech. But a well-formed soul remains always calm and collected, on the heights of serenity, as it were. . . . And though it may not be well versed in all the artifices of eloquence, it is likely to enunciate clear words, appropriate to its nature'. There is an insoluble connection between the interior and the exterior, between mind and speech. There is no point in praising the solitary form of speech, or monologue, which man conducts with himself. If we wish to be human, we must communicate with other men. 'We must endeavour to help those men with whom we live and no one can doubt that we are of great use to their souls through our words'. This does not mean that we should attribute great importance to the moral content of a sermon. The value of speech lies rather in the fact that human conversation has the power to elevate. For conversation is able to make us communicate across deserts and across centuries and thus soothes and shapes our minds.[3]

XXXI–XLIII, 1942–54. Salutati added Geri d'Arezzo to Mussato; on these 'prehumanists' cp. R. Weiss, *The Dawn of Humanism in Italy*, London, 1947, and *Il primo secolo dell'umanesimo*, Roma, 1949.

[3] Petrarca, *Familiar. Rer.*, I, 9, Rossi-Bosco ed., Vol. I, Firenze, 1933, p. 45 sqq.

We must not allow ourselves to be disturbed by the thought that our works will be forgotten. Nor must we be discouraged by the fact that our efforts are useless and will be subject to the vicissitudes of fortune and to the transitoriness of all things. 'Let millenium follow millenium . . . neither virtue nor the love of God will ever be sufficiently praised; and vice will never be finally overcome. Man's mind will always be astute enough to find ever new ways open for research. Let us therefore be cheerful: our efforts will not be in vain. Not even the efforts of those who, after many, many centuries, will begin their lives at the dawn of the last age will be in vain'. *Ceterorum hominum charitas*—the love for one's neighbour: this, to Petrarch, is both the reason for and the end of *studia humanitatis*. And, ideally speaking, 'our neighbour' is always with us, even in the very retreat of our solitude where the most solemn words of the ancient sages sound familiar and friendly—not only to the heart but also on the lips—and arouse the sleeping soul.

Two of the most characteristic motives of humanism are in evidence here. First, the value of *litterae humanae*; and secondly, the social character of humaneness. In a letter to a friend who had expressed the intention to devote himself to a monastic life, Petrarch developed at great length the value of the active life.[4] He cited a letter by Cicero which was to become one of the favourite texts of the moralistic literature of the 15th century: 'there is nothing more pleasing to God Who governs the world than men united by social bonds . . . there is a place reserved in heaven where all those who have laboured to preserve, augment and assist the fatherland, can enjoy eternal blessedness'. This is by no means, as it may seem, incompatible with Petrarch's praise of solitude. For he insisted above all that it is necessary to find first one's own self and to discover in oneself one's true humanity. Only then can one rediscover oneself as a man among men. The love of the fatherland and the love of one's neighbour are not only not incompatible with, but are closely connected with, that inward education which is the condition of all fruitful earthly activity. For this reason the vague journey towards the discovery of his own soul which, for Petrarch, lasted all his life, was at the same time a journey towards a more solid link with other people.

[4] Petrarca, *Familiar. Rer.*, III, 12 (vol. I, pp. 128–131).

In the name of this link Petrarch vibrated with patriotic enthusiasm when Cola di Rienzi launched his appeal in Rome for a *renovatio* of 'sacred Italy'. In spite of all this, all Joachimite dreams and mystical hopes about the coming of the Third Age with which Cola di Rienzi intoxicated himself remained completely foreign to Petrarch. This is a very important difference which we must bear in mind when we come to compare the work of Cola di Rienzi with the position of Petrarch. For the latter cherished no dreams of an Eternal Gospel, but longed for the complete *humanitas* of a Scipio and a Caesar.[5]

2. THE ANALYSIS OF THE INNER LIFE

The withdrawal into solitude signified for Petrarch the rediscovery of the whole richness of the inner life, of the contact with God. It also opened the road towards effective contact with one's neighbours. Such solitude was not a monastic retirement into a barbarous isolation, but an initiation into a truer society, into a more effective form of love. The appeal in favour of inwardness, renewed by Petrarch in terms reminiscent of St. Augustine, has nothing to do with isolation as usually understood, but is an exaltation of the world of man, of the world of values and of actions, of language and of the sociability that links men through time and space and defies all limits. The famous letter to brother Dionigi da Borgo San Sepolcro, in which he described the ascent of Mont Ventoux, is a very vivid example of that conversion from nature to spirit. This conversion was a necessary condition for a re-valuation of the realm of the spirit. 'Antonius, when he had heard these words, ceased to search; Augustine, having read them did not go further. Thus I also, reflecting silently on those words, understood the stupidity of man. For man neglects all that is noblest in him and loses himself in so many external things and swoons at the appearances of the external world and seeks outside what he already possesses in himself.' The mountain which seemed to rise so high at first, appears now a

[5] The texts in K. Burdach, *Rienzo und die geistige Wandlung seiner Zeit*, Berlin, 1913–28. On the *Vita Caesaris* and the ideal of the perfect man see R. de Mattei, *Il sentimento politico del Petrarca*, Firenze, 1944, p. 103 sqq. Cp. also G. Martellotti, *Petrarca e Cesare*, 'Annali Scuola Normale Sup. di Pisa', 1947, pp. 149–158.

D

contemptible thing. 'I looked at the peak,' exclaimed the poet, 'and by comparison with the profound depth of human contemplation it seemed to be no higher than three feet.'[6]

The whole richness of Petrarch is to be found in his insistence on those fundamental experiences with which man, once he has torn away the veil which hid him from himself, finds himself in his own misery and in his own nobility. He dwells particularly on the thought of death and admonishes his fellow-men to recognise their own nature through serious meditation upon their deaths. 'Nobody,' he exclaims, in a letter, 'believes in his own death'. And in another place he describes how he imagines his own death agony, the decomposition of his own body, the pain and the extinction of all strength. 'Return to your self; . . . tear the veil to pieces and gaze into the darkness that opens in front of you. Make sure that not a single day or a single night goes by in which you are not reminded of your death.' All this was not so much a question of ascetic renunciation as a restituton of one's self to oneself. Indeed, earlier, Petrarch had sung the praises of glory. But he is concerned that man, to live in a truly human fashion, should see himself as he truly is and be always mindful of his condition.[7]

This and nothing else was Petrarch's problem. His whole philosophy, so profoundly antagonistic to the empty disputes conducted in the schools, is research into the life of man. His friend Bonsembiante Badoer, though he himself had remained confined entirely within the patterns of late scholasticism, had clearly foreseen the bankruptcy towards which the intellectual efforts of the last thousand years had been moving. We do not know whether he communicated to his friends in those 'long conversations' to which Petrarch refers, the outcome of his own search.[8] But it is certain that Petrarch was always proudly opposed to the official philosophy of Padua, of Bologna and of Paris. For that philosophy was completely entangled in the logical and physical problems of a decadent nominalism. His cruel condemnation of

---

[6] Petrarca, *Familiar. Rer.*, IV, I (vol. I, p. 153 sqq.). On the famous letter of 26 April 1336 see U. Mariani, *Il Petrarca e gli agostiniani*, Roma, 1946, p. 31 sqq., p. 41. (Dionigi had also written a commentary on Valerio Massimo).

[7] Petrarca, *Famil. Rer.*, VIII, 4 (vol. II, p. 164): 'nemo est qui se moriturus credat'. *L'Autobiografia, Il Secreto, Dell' ignoranza sua e d'altrui*, ed. by Angelo Solerti, Firenze, 1904, p. 170.

[8] Petrarca, *Seniles*, XI, 14.

all naturalistic research, of medical science and of Averroistic knowledge amounted to an appeal in favour of the mental sciences; an appeal in favour of the investigation of human life and of the human soul. 'There are people who know a great deal about wild beasts, about birds and fish; and they know very precisely how many hairs a lion has on his head and how many feathers there are in the tail of a hawk and with how many arms the octopus clings to ship-wrecked sailors; ... they know how the phoenix consumed by aromatic fire, rises from the ashes, how the sea-egg can stop a ship no matter how fast it is travelling even though once outside the water it has no strength at all .... Most of these things are not even true; but even if they were true they would be of no consequence as far as beatitude is concerned. I may well ask myself what the use of knowing the nature of animals, birds, fish and serpents really could be, if one has no interest in discovering the nature of man, whence man comes, where he goes and why he is born.'[9]

Petrarch decidedly opposed the investigation of the nature of man to the vain search for knowledge about the nature of mere things. He was looking for a humble philosophy that would concern itself with man and with the terrestrial city built by man. The world of God, he insisted, is closed, as far as the finite mind is concerned, with seven seals. It would be senseless and impertinent to attempt to penetrate it. 'There are fools who seek to understand the secrets of nature and the far more difficult secrets of God, with supercilious pride, instead of accepting them in humble faith. They cannot approach them, let alone reach them. Those fools imagine they can grasp the heavens with their hands. Moreover, they are content with their erroneous opinion and actually imagine to have grasped truth. They are quite happy in their illusion. Not even the telling words addressed by the Apostle to the Romans are able to deflect them from their lunacy: 'Who knows the secrets of God? Who is a party to His counsels?'.[10]

[9] Petrarca, Dell'ignoranza sua e d'altrui, pp. 272–73. Cp. P. O. Kristeller, Petrarca's 'Averroists'; A note on the History of Aristotelians in Venice, Padua and Bononia, 'Mélanges Augustin Renaudet', 'Bibl. Humanisme et Renaissance'. IV, 1952, pp. 59–65; and, Il Petrarca, l'Umanesimo e la Scolastica a Venezia, in: La civiltà veneziana del Trecento, Firenze, 1956, pp. 147–8; B. Nardi, Letteratura e cultura veneziana del Quattrocento, in: La civiltà veneziana del Quattrocento, Firenze, 1957, pp. 101–45.
[10] Petrarca, loc. cit., p. 289.

3. THE POLEMICS AGAINST THE SCIENCES OF NATURE

Petrarch's persistently hostile attitude to the natural sciences was conditioned by his demand for humane and moral research. His polemics were directed with implacable precision against physicians, for medicine presupposed knowledge and care of bodies. In his *Invectiva Contra Medicum Quendam*, which was to play no mean part in the 15th century debate about the relationship between the sciences of nature and the sciences of man, Petrarch exclaimed: 'Carry out your trade, mechanic, if you can. Heal bodies, if you can. If you can't, murder; and take the salary for your crimes. . . . But how can you dare, with unprecedented impertinence, to relegate rhetoric to a place inferior to medicine? How can you make the mistress inferior to the servant, a liberal art to a mechanical one?'[11] The following proposition contained in the *Senilia* reads like a commentary on this invective: 'It is your business to look after bodies. Leave the care and the education of the mind to genuine philosophers and orators.'[12]

Even though Petrarch knew Cicero and Plato only by their reputation, especially through the rôle they played in Patristic tradition and in St. Augustine, rather than directly, it was through these authors that he sought a new orientation of thought; an orientation that was to differ from the rigid logic and physics of Occamism, of Averroism and of Parisian and Paduan Scholasticism. It is true enough that the experienced eye of the historian can discover certain subtle analogies between the extremes of Nominalism and the new philological and rhetorical interests. And it is equally true that there exist certain close connections between Parisian physics and the new natural sciences of the Renaissance.[13] But as far as Petrarch was concerned, the appeal to

[11] Petrarca, *Invectiva in Medicum Quendam*; *Opera*, Basilea, 1581, p. 1087 sqq. There is a good critical edition of the *Invective* by Pier Giorgio Ricci (Roma, 1950) together with the translation by Domenico Silvestri.

[12] Petrarca, *Senil.*, III, 7; *Opera*, p. 778.

[13] Some fruitful themes in connection with the dissolution of scholasticism, capable of further development, are to be found in the studies by Michalski, published 1924 and 1938. See the list in *Giornale critico di filosofia italiana*, 1948, pp. 386–7. For this reason it is difficult to overlook the friendship between Geri d'Arezzo and the ardent Occamist, Brother Bernard. The latter was acquainted with Nicholas of Autrecourt and was in fact the Bernard mentioned by Weiss, *Il primo secolo*, p. 190. It is equally difficult not to notice what Salutati wrote to the

Plato and the development of Ciceronian themes amounted to an insistence on a philosophy which aimed at moral reform; at a spiritual renaissance of man and of the body politic; and at a new conception of the whole tenor of life. Petrarch knew exactly the same Platonic dialogues which had been known and ransacked during the middle ages: the *Timaios*, the *Phaidon*, the *Menon*.[14] Of the other dialogues he possessed the codices; but as he was ignorant of Greek, they meant nothing to him. It is therefore wrong-headed to insist on tracing his thought back to Platonic influences. All he did was to use Plato as a polemical weapon in his battle against the predominance, based on Aristotle, of purely theoretical interests. All he wanted from Platonism (for that matter, from rhetoric) was a return to the problems of human communication; that is, of human society. In brief, the intention was to rediscover the concrete meaning of the earthly city and to place once more value upon those political virtues which find favour in heaven. This is how Petrarch, following Macrobius and, by implication, Plotinus, explains it. Even though he did not actually defend the primacy of virtue active in this world, he insisted nevertheless upon the necessity of recognising its value side by side with that of contemplative virtue. As if this were not enough, he also pointed to a motif that was to be developed more fully later. He insisted that all the liberal studies are related to the active life and to the civic life. By contrast, the natural sciences are deserving of the utmost contempt. Pure contemplation was relegated to the life to come, but all earthly existence is a fertile field for human activity and human morality. The new philosophy was born on the plane of morality and owes its existence to the sharp contrast between nature and humanity—or between fate and *fortuna* and virtue.

Petrarch himself planned and even began writing a treatise 'against that ranting dog, Averroes, who, excited by hellish wrath, abused and blasphemed the holy name of Christ and the Catholic faith by his sacrilegious insults and cursing.' In this sense he had

nominalistic logician Pietro Alboino da Mantova who was converted to poetry. Cp. my remarks in *Giornale critico*, 1948, pp. 203-4, 389-90: 'enuda sophismatum apparentiam; redde nobis rerum noticiam . . . tum velim de poetica cogites'.

[14] Cp. L. Minio-Paluello, *Il 'Fedone' latino con note autografe del Petrarca*, 'Rendic. Acc. Lincei', Cl. sc. mor., IV, 4 (1949), pp. 107–113; *Plato Latinus*, II, *Phaedo*, Londini, 1950, p. XII.

written to Luigi Marsili, an Augustinian, and recommended him to follow the examples of Lactantius and Augustine and combine *studia humanitatis* with *studia divinitatis*. He also enjoined him to persevere in his work and to construct a *pia philosophia*.[15] The mention of Marsili reminds us of the conversations that took place in the *Paradiso degli Alberti*, that lively centre of humanistic culture in the monastery of Santo Spirito in Florence. It also draws our attention to that circle of scholars among whom Coluccio Salutati was one of the most eminent ones, and which Leonardo Bruni described in his *Dialogi ad Petrum Histrum*.[16] Leonardo Bruni sang the praises of that same Marsili; for Marsili was a noble figure and a pious priest who relentlessly attacked the papal corruption at the court of Avignon: 'He keeps in his mind not only those things that are important for the faith, but also those that are commonly described as pagan. He talks constantly of Cicero, Virgil, Seneca, and mentions other names famous in antiquity. He not only quotes their opinions and sayings, but their very words, and made them completely his own'.[17] Salutati called him the 'incomparable teacher of all Florentines'. For he was indeed the greatest heir and the most faithful upholder of the tradition of Petrarch. Salutati stressed especially the moral worth and the human interest of his thoughts. On the occasion of Marsili's death, Salutati wrote a letter to Count Roberto Guido di Battifolle, which has become famous. He compared the subtle search for the motions of the soul, the school of life, the elevation towards God—all central topics of Petrarch's philosophy—to the empty dialectics of the schools. 'Not to mention the liberal arts . . . he was eminent in that philosophy which is a divine gift, a guide for all virtues, a purification from all vices . . . mistress and instructress in all sciences. But I am not thinking of the philosophy which modern sophists frivolously praise in their schools. I am thinking rather of that wisdom that shapes the soul and the

[15] Petrarca, *Senil.* XV, 6–7.
[16] Alessandro Wesselofsky, *Il Paradiso degli Alberti; Ritrovi e Ragionamenti de 1389: romanzo di Giovanni da Prato*, Bologna 1867. On Marsili cp. U. Mariani, *op. cit.*, pp. 66 sqq. Among the documents edited by Wesselofsky, the short poem in praise of Occam by the Cieco degli Organi is of special interest. Cp. now C. Vassoli, *Polemiche occamiste*, 'Rinascimento', III, 1952, pp. 119–41. For the rhetorico-dialectical polemics see, besides Bruni's dialogues the texts published by A. Manetti, *Roberto de' Rossi*, 'Rinascimento', II (1951), pp. 33–35.
[17] Leonardo Bruni, *Dialogi ad Petrum Histrum;* Mehus, *Historia Litteraria Florentina* (Ambrosii Traversarii, *Latinae Epistolae*, I), Florentiae, 1759, p. CCLXXXIII.

virtues, exterminates vice and illuminates the truth, far removed from all subtle dialectics.'[18]

4. COLUCCIO SALUTATI

Coluccio Salutati's eminence was precisely in this new field, the investigation of man's life. In his moral treatises and even more in the admirable pages of his voluminous correspondence he offers his sensitive reflections about his rich inner experiences. He was well trained in logic and grammar, and learned in questions of law, and played an outstanding part in the political life of Italy as Chancellor of the government of Florence. He was an uncompromising fighter for *Florentina libertas*, which he considered to be the only worthy heiress to *Romana libertas;* and as a result, according to a famous pronouncement by Visconti, his letters were more dangerous than a whole army. It is no accident that Pius II praised the wisdom of the Florentine authorities because they appointed the greatest humanists as Chancellors of their Republic.[19] It is certainly true that in Coluccio Salutati, as, later, in Leonardo Bruni, political life and intellectual activity were most happily brought together. As far as these men were concerned, the sage and the scholar were not hermits remote from all accidents of life. Sages and scholars appeared as men who followed their vocations by serving the Lord of Heaven in the midst of earthly life. Salutati's words in his *De Saeculo et Religione*, addressed to Nicolò di Lapo da Uzzano and encouraging him to lead a fighter's life, are at the same time a motto and worthy summary of Salutati's own life. Or, for that matter, one could choose for this purpose a similar admonition, directed towards the end of his life to Fra Raffaello Bonciani: *standum est in acie, conserendae manus, luctandum pro iusticia, pro veritate, pro honestate*.[20]

Man's vocation lies on this earth. He must endeavour to lay the foundations of society and to establish a state. 'The fairest things on earth are the fatherland and one's friends'. In a

[18] Coluccio Salutati, *Epistolario*, Francesco Novati ed., vol. I, Roma, 1891, pp. 178–79.

[19] G. Manetti, *De Illustribus Longaevis*, Cod. Urb. lat. 387 (in F. Novati, *op. cit.*, IV, 2). *Invectiva Lini Colucii Salutati . . . In Antonium Luschum Vicentinum. . . .* Florentiae, 1825, pp. 21–22, 54. Cp. *Aeneae Sylvii In Europam sui Temporis*, LIV (*Opera*, Basilea, 1571, p. 454).

[20] C. Salutati, *De Saeculo et Religione* I, i, Cod. Riccard. 872, fol. 30–42.

letter addressed to Pellegrino Zambeccari, who intended to dedicate his life to monasticism, we find an outspoken praise of the active life. 'Do not imagine, Pellegrino, that one can seek perfection by fleeing from the crowd, shunning the sight of everything beautiful and locking oneself up in a monastery or a hermitage. Do you really believe that God prefers a solitary, inactive Paul to a creative Abraham? Do you not think that God looked with greater pleasure upon Jacob and his twelve sons, two wives and large herds than upon the two Macarii, upon Theophilus and upon Hilarion? In an attempt to run away from the earth, you may well tumble down from heaven to earth. But I, while I am busily engaged on earthly things, can always raise my heart from earth to heaven. As long as you are serving, as long as you are striving for your family, children, relatives, friends, and for the fatherland which comprises them all, you cannot help lifting your heart heavenwards and thus please God'.[21] In the life to come we will be able to rise to pure contemplation. But we will be able to do this only if we have fought the battle of this life and have completed our daily tasks. In his *De Saeculo et Religione*, which is the most severely ascetic of all his works, Salutati depicts the religious life as one of activity, struggle and work. 'Religion is the hard way of virtue . . .; it is the strenuous path which leads, through the cliffs of this world, to the sweet peace of heaven'. Religion, thus, is never a refuge, but constant trial, labour and effort: *summus hic profecto labor*. And this effort makes for concord. For when Salutati, during an epidemic, was advised to flee, he replied with indignation that no man had the right to evade the bonds of communal life which link him to his brothers.

According to this conception, philosophy was a reflection on earthly activity, a quickening of the consciousness of community tasks, of the human condition and of human fate. It was also a reflection on the behaviour of man and the forms of his life. In short, it was a deepened appreciation of the highly dramatic problems of experience. For this reason Socrates was taken to represent the highest type of philosopher; the saint of philosophy, so to speak. Had he died in the true faith, he would have been regarded as the greatest of martyrs: *princeps nostrorum martyrum*.[22]

[21] C. Salutati, *Epistolario*, II, p. 303–307.
[22] *De Fato*, II, 8, Cod. Vat. lat. 2928, fol. 16 r.

On every single page written by Salutati we find this demand for
a philosophy that is a school of life, a serious and deep meditation
upon the problems of life. He held that only a clearer consciousness of one's self could give rise to a philosophy superior to
scholastic disputations and abstract constructions. The latter
kind of philosophy is more likely to lead away from reality than
toward it. Even the dramatic thought of death, to which Petrarch
had appealed, is to be found again in Salutati. He considered it a
fundamental experience, bound to undermine all the ancient and
consoling theories as well as the many fictitious ideas which men
in the past had used in their attempts to escape the seriousness of
their problems. On the other side, it was bound to lead back to
the original sources of all thinking and to the humblest of all
philosophical topics: 'Why was my Peter, still a child in the full
blossom of his youth, why was he taken away from me. . . .? Even
though the soul may be immortal and survive the body; even
though the body made of earth may become earth once more:
man unfortunately ceases to exist once the harmony of the human
unit is destroyed'. There is not a single consoling doctrine
capable of explaining away the sorrow caused by the loss of a
loved one or by the fear of one's own end: 'consolations are but
sophistical verbiage. Once the words are spoken, they leave no
echo in the mind, for they are lacking in rationality and are without solid ground'.[23]

5. THE PRIMACY OF THE WILL ACCORDING TO
SALUTATI

Given these preconceptions, Salutati's philosophy was bound to
stand in sharp contrast to the whole ballast of traditional syllogism
and reasoning. His whole philosophy was a reorientation of
thought based upon Socrates, Christ and St. Francis. All these
teachers had established their own lives as the message of truth.
In the narrower sense, however, the reorientation rested on the
defence of the primacy of the will and thus on the doctrines of the
Franciscan schools which had held that the innovations of
Thomistic Aristotelianism had endangered and even eliminated

[23] *Epist.* III, pp. 416–20.

the essence of Christianity. The controversy between Salutati and Dominici turns precisely upon the question of the primacy of the will, of the active life and the connection between *studia humani-tatis* and civic life. Dominici was a man of unusual stature, very alive to the problems of his age. In all his writings he fully recognises the earthly vocation of man. But his Thomistic premisses obliged him to adopt a hostile attitude to all criticisms of the view that behaviour is rationally determined. Moreover, the efforts of humanism, often degenerating into pure rhetoric, had made him highly suspicious of all easy going enthusiasms for antiquity. Salutati himself was prepared to recognise the danger of exaggerations. But nevertheless he insisted on the value of the new education. The training in grammar, after all, was only apparent. In reality the new education taught *sub cortice* the intended meaning of words which custom (*consuetudo*) had been apt to obscure. This was to be done through an elucidation of the expressions in question by their intimate intellectual meaning. Words and things, Salutati emphasised, must not be separated. The word is born together with the thing. There can therefore be no serious grammatical instruction unless it is at the same time an approach to real things. For this very reason grammar was taken to be the preparation for all genuine under-standing. Without the ability to understand language and its expressions in their profoundest meanings, there can be no knowledge of the Scriptures, the word of God. All serious knowledge is communication. In this sense, the *studia humanitatis* are closely connected with the *studia divinitatis*, for they are the means by which the spirit can be discovered in the letter; and the soul in the body to which it is inseparably linked. The study of the divine message amounts to an acquisition of a spiritual directive. This acquisition is dependent upon an adequate under-standing of these literary monuments which are the expression of the fact that there is a spiritual community between their authors and the people who wish to understand them.[24]

This, approximately, was the answer given by Salutati in 1406 to one part of Dominici's criticisms. As far as the other parts were concerned, the whole of his thinking was an answer to Dominici. 'I do not know how and why,' Dominici wrote with

[24] *Epist.* IV, pp. 205–40.

irritation in his *Lucula Noctis*, 'some people have dared to give primacy to the will and its expressions rather than to reason and the authority of the saints. But perhaps those people discuss for discussion's sake. Or else they base their views on certain observed facts, such as that there are houses in which the woman commands and the man obeys, or poultry farms where the hen cackles and the rooster remains silent.' As a matter of fact Salutati had solved the difficulties and contradictions which the problem of fate poses to man's reason. He had done this in his work *De Fato, Fortuna et Casu* by pointing to a practical certainty. He insisted that man is made free through a free act of the will, whereas a reliance on reason would prove to him that freedom is an impossibility.[25]

But the full justification of his position is to be found in his *De Nobilitate Legum et Medicinae*. This is a small work which looks as if it amounted to no more than a narrow-minded attack on physicians. It continued the assault first started by Petrarch, an assault which was to be repeated from time to time right until the end of the 15th century. But owing to its speculative depth, Salutati's work reaches far beyond the scope of mere polemics.

In discussing the value of jurisprudence and of laws as compared with that of medicine, Salutati wishes to demonstrate the value of the knowledge of things human as against the investigation of mere nature. In his argument, law is represented as the rules governing the activities of human families in their harmonious endeavour to promote the common weal. He stressed that 'the goal of naturalistic speculation is the knowledge of truth. The goal of law is the regulation of *human* activity. Its object is the well-being of man. But this well-being is not any arbitrary kind of well-being; but the truly divine well-being of a human community.' How could one possibly refuse to recognise that well-being or the good is superior to mere truth? One is compelled to arrive at this conclusion especially when one considers that the good in question is by no means a mere natural good which one obtains as one might obtain a gift; but that it is a good which has to be *willed* and which is therefore something precious, something that has to be worked for with great effort.

[25] *De Fato*, II, 10–11, fol. 23 v-31 v. Johannis Dominici, Card. Sancti Sixti, *Lucula Noctis*, E. Hunt ed., Notre Dame, Indiana, 1940.

For, in short, it is a good which, in a sense, makes us fellow-workers with God. 'The common good aimed at by law is not the sort of good that happens to make us naturally good: but it is the sort of good that persuades us to *become* good. The former is a value given by nature; and if we pursue it, we are not entitled to praise . . . But we do deserve praise for the kind of good that is created by us . . . provided God enables us to act and to perform meritorious actions in conjunction with Him.'[26]

In another place he explained that laws were a kind of divine seal, through which, after the commission of original sin, God had re-opened to human societies a path for the re-acquisition of goodness. They are given by God and engraved in the human soul. As such they possess yet another superiority over the laws of nature. For it is possible to know them in their full extent with a *certainty* which it is impossible to achieve in the natural sciences. 'They have their origin not in external things, but *in us*. They inhere in our minds as of nature. Thus we know them with such a certainty that they cannot escape us and that it is not necessary to seek them among external facts. For, as you see, they inhabit our most intimate selves'.

'The laws,' Salutati continued, 'are infallible because they are promulgated by human beings. They contain man's natural reason which every sound intelligence can understand and discover by reflection and discussion. By contrast, the principles of medicine, once experience fails, are misleading and uncertain and are lacking the universality of reason.' The value of jurisprudence, as against that of the natural sciences, is very different and corresponds to the higher dignity of morality. The critique of knowledge advanced by the Occamist schools had left its traces on Salutati. In fact, Salutati simply took this critique for granted when he composed the magnificent praise of the laws which he put into the mouth of medicine: 'When I contemplate the mystical body which consists of a crowd of human beings, united in families, countries, cities, nations, kingdoms and empires, and when I observe how all this is ordered, regulated and sustained by laws . . . I recognise that the true blessings of human societies do not depend on medicine but on spiritual concord. . . . Woe to me! Why do you glorify my certainty? . . . Laws

[26] *De Nobilitate Legum et Medicinae*, 5.

exist unshakeably in the relations of human minds of each other. And they are not only certain, but also fully known. But however will you get to know *me*, if you can only grasp with effort and labour a minute portion of all the things that are to be known? . . . For the whole of experience changes . . . according to the place and time of the observer . . . I am of the earth; but the laws are born of God's wisdom. God has proclaimed the laws through his words. But I am relegated by him to the realm where accidents in experience cause constant variations. I am exposed to accidents and I myself belong to the realm of the accidental. But the law is based upon eternal and universal justice.'[27]

Ego de terra, lex vero de mente divina. This was Salutati's final summary of his ideas, and as it stood it implied a conception which was to be developed later by Vico. It was both the slogan and the programme of humanism; for humanism turned its back upon nature and moved the existence of man into the centre of its interests. It dealt with men who had tamed the earth in order to discover their own identity. In his *De Hercule eiusque Laboribus*, Salutati praised these men as 'powerful beings who had accomplished the most horrible labours of the earth'. He considered them worthy of the stars. The same treatise also contains an examination of the art of poetry. He considered the latter too, generically, a human creation. There is, further, a treatment of rhetoric which it is argued possesses the same creative and inspiring power as love. 'It is no accident that we attribute rhetoric to Venus, the goddess of love whose task it is to inspire souls and set hearts afire.'[28]

6. LAW AND MEDICINE

Salutati's vigorous discussion of the primacy of the mental sciences did not remain without repercussions, and we can detect

[27] *Ep. Regi Navarrae* (1376), ms. Marucell. (Firenze), C. 89, fol. 48 r.

[28] Cod. Magliabech., cl. VIII, 1445, fol. 166 v. On mythology and poetry in Boccaccio cp. V. Branca, *Motivi preumanistici nell'opera del Boccaccio*, in *Pensée humaniste et trahition chétienne au XV me et XVI me siécles*, Paris, 1950, pp. 69—85 [*De Hercule* by S. has been published by Ullman, Zürich, 1951, 2 vols.; also *De Saeculo et Religione*, Firenze 1957. For the development Mussato-Petrarca-Boccaccio, cp. G. Billanovich, *Pietro Piccolo da Monteforte tra il Petrarca e il Boccaccio*, in *Medioevo e Rinascimento*, Studi in onore di B. Nardi, Firenze 1955, pp. 1–76].

its echoes throughout the 15th century. Even such a famous
physician as Andrea Benzi of Siena took his cue most probably
from Salutati, although he does not mention him by name. Benzi
was well known for his zeal in the classical disputes about Aristotelianism and owed his glorification of law and of civic life in his
inaugural lecture, delivered in Florence, probably in 1421, to
Salutati. 'If the laws were abolished, would not every community,
every house, every family decay? Would this not result in the
destruction of the whole of human nature?'[29]

Salutati's greatest pupil, however, Leonardo Bruni,[30] was of a
different opinion. He contrasted law, focusing his eye upon its
purely coercive character, with literature. For the former pays
attention to wrong-doers rather than to good men and changes
according to the time and the place. 'Things that are legitimate in
Florence are condemned in Ferrara'. Poggio Bracciolini went
even further. In his dialogues between Carlo Marsuppini,
Benedetto Accolti and Niccolò da Foligno, composed in 1450, he
not only despises law but dares to argue that the greatest deeds are
accomplished only when the will of an individual transgresses the
law which binds the majority. 'Only the mob and the common
people are bound by your laws. The ties of legality exist only for
them. Serious, intelligent and modest men need no laws. Their
lives have their own laws, for their education and the formation
of their character leads them automatically to the exercise of
virtue and to good manners. . . . Strong men transgress and reject
the laws that seem suitable enough for the weak, for cowards, for
pedlars and the miserable rabble, for the lazy and the poor. . . . It
is a fact that all great deeds worthy of being remembered have
their origin in injustice and violence, in short, in the breaking of
the law.'[31]

Nevertheless, both Bruni and Bracciolini, except for this
interesting glorification of violence, did not really concern themselves with the problem which had troubled Salutati. Salutati had
moved the problem to another plane in order to defend the very
humanitas which they too had wanted to praise. The laws which
were the object of Salutati's praise were the foundations of moral

[29] *Oratio Andreae Hugonis De Senis* (Laur. gadd. 89, sup. cod. 27, fol. 125 a; cp.
K. Müllner, *Reden und Briefe italienischer Humanisten*, Wien, 1899, p. 113).
[30] Leonardo Bruni, *Epist*. VI, Mehus ed., II, Florentiae, 1741, p. 50.
[31] Poggio Bracciolini, *Opera*, Argentorati, 1513, fol. 19 r v.

life, the soul of every human society. They were the basis of the whole richness of human communications. There is a significant dialogue by the physician Giovanni d'Arezzo. Shortly after the death of Pietro it was dedicated to Lorenzo de' Medici. In this dialogue Marsuppini, Niccoli and Bruni converse *De Medicinae et Legum Praestantia*, and the refutation of Bracciolini's thoughts is attributed to Bruni. 'In my opinion,' he is made to say, 'the laws can never be praised enough. For they not only guide the peasants or the ordinary citizens or the rich, but they also limit the activities of judges and keep them in check. They rule over lords and kings and exercise their power over emperors . . . They protect the weak against the strong and maintain harmony among equals . . .' One ought not to object that they are variable. 'Even though nations change their views with the passage of time, they do not succeed in touching the sacred and old laws. They merely manage to deceive themselves.' The norm of justice is truly eternal. It is a guide and mistress of all laws. The latter are the concrete foundations and the firm bonds of human societies. 'The name of the fatherland is both sacred and sweet . . . there is something great in belonging to the same city, especially when it is a free city. There is much that the citizens have in common: the law, *forum*, Senate and the Magistracies.'[32] Thus Lapo da Castiglionchio, even though he was anything but pliable as far as the claims of lawyers were concerned. But he too was very clear as to the social value of *humanitas* and represented it in an *Oratio de Laudibus Philosophiae* as the builder of cities and the conqueror of nature.[33]

On the other side, the philosophers of Padua entered the foray in order to defend medicine. Their spokesman was Niccoletto Vernia, a subtle and elusive thinker. He was very interested in these discussions and he kept, among his manuscripts, a *Quaestio* by the Augustinian theologian Giovanni da Imola. It bore the title *Utrum Scientia Civilis vel Canonica sit Nobilior Medicinali*. The monk began 'that it seemed that the question ought to be answered in the affirmative, provided one considers *that*

---

[32] *Johannis Aretini Physici de Medicinae et Legum Praestantia*, Laur. lat. plut. LXXII, 22: For this and other texts see my *La disputa delle arti nel Quattrocento*, Firenze, 1948.
[33] Lapus Casteliunculus, *Epist. Roberto Strozzae* (Cod. Ottobon. lat. 1677, fol. 218 v). Cp. Müllner, *Reden und Briefe*, p. 249 sgg.: *Oratio de Laudibus Philosophiae, ibid.*, pp. 139 sqq.

science the nobler one which makes man nobler.' But Vernia held the opposite view and defended it with a wealth of proofs. It is true, he granted, that politics enable man to live in peace. But medicine, he explained, keeps him alive. And without life no other activity is possible. Also, the natural sciences were more noble because they were based upon logical reasoning rather than on human authority. He considered moreover that the main concern of the *Quaestio* was the concept of happiness and he could not grant that happiness was to be found in social activity. Rather, it belonged to pure speculation. 'Legislation aims at a certain happiness with regard to social life and with regard to communication in civic assemblies. But this is not the true happiness. . . . We can approach God only through speculation, the blessedness of which consists in the contemplation of its own essence'.[34] Antonio de Ferrariis, 'il Galateo', did not move far from these thoughts in his treatise *Della dignità delle discipline*. Not without insult to Salutati, he did not hesitate to rate, as far as sociability is concerned, both bees and ants more highly than men. 'Who does not know of the great prudence that exists in the forms of society of bees and ants and similar insects? Both justice and compassion are much more developed among certain animals than among certain men.' The true nobility of man lies entirely in his knowledge, not in his actions.[35]

This was indeed a battle between two opposing conceptions of life and of philosophy. The one could be described as a human conception. It held that the essence of man consists in his becoming and in his doing. At bottom, it was a Christian conception. The other conception was linked to the Aristotelian ideal of knowledge and contemplation and considered action and works as something secondary and inferior.

[34] *Magistri Joannis De Imola Quaestio utrum Scientia Civilis vel Canonica sit Nobilior Medicinali*, Marcianus lat. cl. X, 218, fol. 79–82. N. Vernia, *Quaestio an Medicina Nobilior atque Praestantior sit Iure Civili* (In Vernia's edition of Burley's commentary on *Fisica*, cp. *Gualterii Burlaei de Physica Auscultatione*, Venetiis, 1589).

[35] *Vari opuscoli di Antonio De Ferrariis detto il Galateo*, Lecce, 1868 (Collana di scrittori di Terra d'Otranto, III) pp. 10, 13, 25–26.

CHAPTER II

CIVIC LIFE

1. THE SCHOOL OF SALUTATI AND BERNARDINO
OF SIENA

THE search for the origins of the ideas of Salutati about the
value of earthly activity and the primacy of the will is likely
to take us back to Francisan traditions and to certain themes of
Scotist philosophy. This much has already been indicated above
in connection with the discussion of the polemics with the
Thomist Dominici. A confirmation of this view could be found
in St. Bernardino of Siena. Bernardino was a pupil of one of
Salutati's pupils. He was a great admirer of both Petrarch and
Salutati whom he considered to have 'accomplished mighty
things, for which they deserve great praise'. He was very aware
of the enormous value of the soul, for the soul was superior to
all other created things; a point he was fond of stressing in his
attack on the astrologers. Bernardino emphasised especially that
in the soul the primacy of the will is undeniable. 'The will is
the emperor of all the three . . . powers (of the soul) and of all
our feelings; the will is the king of our mind. . . The firm will
is the emperor of the universe.' While in his true fatherland, in
heaven, man may be destined to lead a contemplative life, it is
his calling in this world to act and to love. Even the keys of
wisdom are in the hands of love: 'he who loves, knows more
than he who does not love'.[1]

The warm praise which Leonardo Bruni lavished upon the
gentle saint of Siena is no mere convention. It was a sincere

[1] On the attack on astrology and on the infinite value of the soul cp. S. Bernardino
da Siena, *Le prediche volgari* ed. by P. Bargellini Milano, 1936, predica II, p. 56 sqq.
On the critique of abstract philosophy cp. *Le prediche volgari* ed. by P. C. Cannarozzi,
vol. II, Pistoia, 1934 (Quaresimale of 1424), p. 97, and p. 213; Sermon XVII,
1425, Cannarozzi ed., vol. III, p. 297 sqq. (*L'educazione umanistica in Italia*, Bari,
1949, p. 39 sqq.). On the relations with Scotism, D. Scaramuzzi, *La dottrina del B.G.
Duns Scoto nella predicazione di San Bernardino da Siena*, Firenze, 1930. The letter by
Bruni referred to by Cannarozzi, I. p, XXXIX, is from Laur. plut. 90, 34, fol. 206.
B.s official letter of 1439 is more important (ms. Panciat. 148, 112r).

E

encounter of two minds which had taken place in the idealistic atmosphere of Salutati's school. There was on one hand the heir of Duns Scotus; and on the other, the zealous restorer of classical studies. These studies were to him, as they had been to his beloved teacher, no mere pedantic literary exercises. They were a genuine restoration of the life of the mind. The enthusiastic exclamations with which Bruni greeted the beginnings of Greek instruction by Chrysoloras are anything but rhetorical. They are his tribute to an age in which the human mind had rediscovered lost treasures and learnt to enjoy once more the fruits of its own wealth. 'Even though Greek is the source of every doctrine, it is seven hundred years since anyone in Italy has known any Greek'. The *litterae* are about to return with all their fertility, to form whole men, not just scholars. 'They call themselves *studia humanitatis* because they shape the perfected man'.[2]

The human mind can enter into an ideal community in which God's word is heard by means of the human voice through the knowledge of the thoughts of other people—provided, of course, that such knowledge is not a barbarous misrepresentation, but consists in a humble reconstruction of the whole of the thoughts in question. For this reason the conversation with the great minds of past ages, to which the *studia litterarum* lead us, is by no means a form of 'vulgar erudition'. It is, on the contrary, a discovery of the common human links and the development of the ideal basis for a commonwealth. When Angelo Decembrio introduced the school of Guarino in his *Politia Literaria* he took great pains to explain that he was using the expression *politia* not in the Greek sense of city or republic, but in the Latin sense of culture. This human culture in which human minds 'converse urbanely' is situated outside the limits of time and space. It is an ideal republic in the soil of which our spiritual life strikes roots and finds its nourishment. Civic and political discourse are prepared, illuminated and sustained through that culture.[3]

[2] Bruni's words on the return of culture, in L. *Aretini Rerum suo Tempore Gestarum Commentarius*, in Muratori, *Rer. ital. script.*, XIX, 3, ed. C. di Pierro, 1926, p. 403 sqq. On *studia humanitatis* cp. *Epist.*, Mehus ed., Florentiae, II, p. 49: (See *Caroli Sigonii de Laudibus Studiorum Humanitatis*, in M. A. *Mureti Orationes*, Lugduni, 1590, p. 97).

[3] *Angeli Decembrii Mediolanensis ad Summum Pontificem Pium II de Politia Literaria*, Basileae, 1562, p. 6. *Politia literaria* means here both the *honesta disciplina* of Crinito and the *elegantia* of Valla.

In his biography of Dante, Bruni wrote as follows. 'After that battle [of Campaldino] Dante returned to his home. He devoted himself to his studies more than ever. But he did not neglect for this reason the practice of urbane and polite conversation . . . On this occasion it seems to me appropriate to correct the erroneous opinion of many ignorant people that only those can be numbered among the scholars who hide themselves in solitude and leisure. I for my part have never known one of those remote people, hostile to all convivial conversation, who was able to read as much as three consecutive letters . . . Dante not only cultivated conversation with other men but even took a wife . . . who bore him several children. . . Boccaccio could not tolerate this thought and therefore said that studies and marriage are incompatible. He seems to have forgotten that Socrates, the greatest philosopher ever, had a wife and children as well as offices in his city; and that Aristotle who had never been surpassed in wisdom and knowledge by anybody, had two wives, one after the other, and children and very considerable wealth. Marcus Tullius, Cato, Seneca, Varro, all great Roman philosophers, were all married. They all had children and held offices in the Republic. . . It is the opinion of the philosophers that man is a political animal. The first community, the proliferation of which gave rise to the city, was the community which consisted of man and wife. And there can be nothing perfect when such a community is lacking'.[4]

The close connection which Bruni assumes to exist between culture and civic life corresponds entirely to the theories of Salutati. Salutati too praised industrious families, flourishing states, worldly activities, and insisted emphatically upon the positive value of matrimony. Salutati spoke very highly of the latter and thus touched upon a topic which was to be discussed frequently in the moralistic literature of the 15th century and the treatment of which can be taken as the yard-stick by which the various attitudes can be measured. We see, for instance, that Manetti agreed with Bruni in the praise of Socrates as a philosopher, citizen and head of a family. Further we have the treatises De Re Uxoria by Francesco Barbaro and De Dignitate Matrimonii

---

[4] Leonardo Bruni, *Vita di Dante* in Philippo Villani *Liber*, p. 46 (cp. also A. Solerti, *Le vite di Dante, Petrarca e Boccaccio scritte fino al sec. XVI*, Milano, 1904).

by Campano. And finally there is a very temperamental work by Guiniforte Barzizza.[5]

Both Salutati and Bruni had warned against the tendency to reduce *humanitas* to a purely cultural matter and *litterae* to mere rhetoric. The necessity for this warning was clearly revealed by another attitude to this fundamental way of participating in the life of human society. For some, culture was a form of communication and a human conversation and thus a full participation in civic life. In spite of his Platonic asceticism even Ficino exclaimed, praising matrimony: 'Man, almost like a god, maintains his species through having descendants. Gratefully he restores to nature what she has given him . . . Like a happy and true sculptor he sculpts his living image in his children . . . Moreover he is in possession of a domestic republic in miniature in which he exercises the force of his whole intelligence and virtue. . . . And finally there is this to be considered: either wife and family are a sweet solace and take many a burden from us, or they are a thorough schooling in moral philosophy.' In the eyes of Marsilio Ficino the priest, i.e., the man who despises marriage, is lacking in humanity. For humanity consists in the participation in the life of society. 'For this reason, if you wish to be men and genuine sons of the gods, you must legitimately multiply by generating, nourishing and educating children. Because in this way you are similar to God and imitate Him. And remember that you, in guiding your family with the utmost care, are educating yourselves to be experienced and honoured members of the earthly city, worthy of the heavenly city.'

Thus the tone and the opinions of the old Salutati turn up again in Ficino. Similarly Ficino has the same ideal of the complete man able to harmonise culture and morals. As against this, rhetoric triumphed in Ermolao Barbaro. In a letter to Arnold of Bost, of the year 1486, he sharply condemned marriage. 'There is nothing as harmful for culture as marriage and the care for children. I do not condemn marriage absolutely, for without it

[5] Fr. Barbari *De Re Uxoria Liber in Partes Duas*, ed. A. Gnesotto in 'Atti e Memorie d. R. Accad. di Padova', vol. XXXII, 1915, pp. 8–103; The *Dialogi* of Bruni, the *De Ingenuis Moribus* of Vergerio and *De Re Uxoria* of F. Barbaro represent, taken together, a characteristic picture of a typical Florentine attitude of the early 15th century. *De Dignitate Matrimonii* by Campano in *Opera*, Venezia, 1595. For a bibliography see R. Kelso, *Doctrine for the Lady of the Renaissance*, UrbanaI/ll. 1956.

not even *litterae* could exist. But I am of the opinion that the
scholar and the man who investigates God, the stars and nature,
ought to be free of this yoke.'[6] We can see the sharp contrast
between the *humanitas* of Bruni and the rhetoric of Barbaro. For
Bruni, culture is *humanitas* and therefore community. For
Barbaro, on the other hand, culture is isolation, contemplation,
literature.

2. LEONARDO BRUNI

Leonardo Bruni's ideal was to use *humanae litterae* and *studia
humanitatis* as means for the education of the complete man: *inest
auctoritas magna propter elegantiam, et ingenuitas quaedam liberis
hominibus digna.* As he sees the formation of a complete man as the
goal of humanism, he paid special attention to the civic virtues. In
his preface to his translation of Aristotle's *Politics* he maintained
that 'among the moral doctrines through which human life is
shaped, those which refer to states and their governments occupy
the highest position. For it is the purpose of those doctrines to
make possible a happy life for all men. And if it is praiseworthy to
assure the happiness of one being, how much more beautiful it is to
gain happiness for the whole state? The more universal the well-
being, the more divine it must be considered to be.' The civic
life is made by man and is at the same time the full realisation of
the individual who, without it, fails to reach his highest perfection.[7]

Bruni's interest is always directed to worldly affairs and to the
affairs of his city, for the latter is considered the frame in which
virtues are maintained and tried. The natural sciences, on the
other hand, do not attract him. 'They have an uncommon

[6] *M. Ficini Opera*, Basileae, 1565, I, pp. 778–79. Ermalao Barbaro, *Epistolae,
Orationes et Carmina*, V. Branda ed., Firenze, 1943, I, p. 96. Valla goes much further
in exalting the flesh: 'melius merentur scorta et postribula de genere humano quam
sanctimoniales virgines et continentes' (*Opera*, Basileae, 1543, p. 924).

[7] H. Baron, *Leonardo Bruni Aretino. Humanistisch-philosophische Schriften mit einer
Chronologie seiner Werke und Briefe*, Leipzig-Berlin, 1928, p. 73, contains the texts. On
the Aristotelian translations cp. my *Le traduzioni umanistiche di Aristotele nel secolo
XV*, Firenze, 1951 ('Accademia di scienze morali La Colombaria', VIII). The
fifteenth century Florentine commentaries on the *Ethics* and *Politics* deserve to be
treated on their own. Cp. my *Giovinezza di Donato Acciaiuoli*, 'Rinascimento', I,
1951, pp. 43–70.

theoretical value, but no value for life; the other part of philosophy is our concern.'[8] Like Socrates, he insists that nothing that
takes place outside the walls of his city is of any interest to him.
As a result he does not favour monastic withdrawal, but expresses
a Socratic devotion to his fellow-citizens, a form of Christian love
of one's neighbour. As we saw above, the well-being that is
enjoyed in solitude is a very sad affair, for we can really enjoy
only when we dedicate ourselves to others. There is no value in
the static, withdrawn life envisaged by Aristotle, the βίος
θεωρητικός; in Stoic asceticism or in a monastic existence. Men
are meant to live on a level on which they can love their neighbours. According to the letter, Bruni's problems appear to be
Aristotelian ones. They are especially reminiscent of Aristotle
the moral philosopher. But the spirit which is active in Bruni's
writings is completely Christian. It is a form of Christianity
which opposes quite consciously the active will for the well-being
of the community to the Greek ideal of pure contemplation.
Hence Bruni's admiration for Cicero and for Roman ethics which
endeavour to resolve thought into concrete concepts. Hence also
his admiration for Dante as the ideal of the complete man as
opposed to the solitary man of letters who is stoically cut off from
the world and leads a useless existence. 'Great and high-minded
intelligences do not need those tortures (of solitude). And it is
certain that things that are not apparent at once will not come out
later. Therefore, detachment and withdrawal are becoming to
those who have an inferior mind, incapable of starting any
enterprise.'

When he presented his translation of Plato's letters to Cosimo
de' Medici, he sang a hymn on the Platonic meaning of the
political life. In his beautiful introduction to his translation of
Aristotle's *Politics* we find an elegant presentation of the thesis
that our activity is fertile in proportion to the number of people
who derive benefit from it. In the centre of his thinking there was
the emphatic belief that man 'is a weak being, incapable of

---

[8] The same meaning is contained in the philosophical pronouncements of the
Dialogi ad Petrum Histrum of 1401. They ridicule the natural science and the logic of
the Occamists who had even in Florence an important representative in Francesco
Landini, the so called Cieco degli Organi (1325–1397). These dialogues are related
to Vergerio's *De Ingenuis Moribus* and amount to an exaltation of antiquity and of the
value of Cicero's golden eloquence. But there is no idolatry in them and modern
writers are warmly defended by the old Coluccio.

achieving anything. Perfection can only be reached in a civic community'. Therefore 'there is no more important branch of knowledge for man than to know what the state and the city are, and how they can be maintained and how they decay'. This classical insistence upon common well-being which, according to Bruni, was of the essence of Plato, Aristotle and Cicero, is, in his view, completely in harmony with Christian morality. He wrote to Eugene IV thus: 'The part of philosophy which treats of the customs, the governments and the best way of life, is common to pagan and Christian thinkers.' For this reason he took the study of the ancients to be the sole foundation of a clear consciousness of one's own humanity.[9]

3. POGGIO BRACCIOLINI AND THE VALUE OF EARTHLY GOODS

In his introduction to his translation of the pseudo-Aristotelian *Economics*, Leonardo Bruni had emphasised the value of wealth. According to a metaphor by Davanzati, money is to the city what blood is to an individual. Given the general revaluation of the whole world in its various manifestations, economic activity too was reconsidered and assessed more positively. Between 1428 and 1429 Poggio Bracciolini wrote his dialogue *De Avaritia*. In this work Antonio Loschi attacked monkish hypocrisy and argued that the love of money is something quite natural and even useful to society.[10] If one considers that all men, no matter what sex, age, status and race, desire money, one cannot deny that that desire is a natural one. 'One cannot tolerate the objections raised by hypocrites, parasites and coarse men who are running after food under the cover of religion. These people do not work and take no pains and preach that others ought to seek poverty and despise earthly treasures! We cannot build our cities with these pseudo-men who can afford to be lazy only because our labours keep them alive.' But these attacks on monks, though they were to become more bitter in the *Contra Hypocritas*, were immediately

[9] On the meaning of full participation in civic life cp. Bruni, *De Militia Liber Singularis*, appendix to *Osservazioni e dissertazioni varie . . . concernenti . . . Antonio da Pratovecchio*, Livorno, 1764, p. 81 and sqq.
[10] Poggio Bracciolini, *Historia Disceptativa de Avaricia*, *Opera*, fol. 7 r.

followed by a more constructive consideration. These pages were indeed informed by a peculiarly modern appreciation of the importance of money—one is almost tempted to say, of capital. These pages eluded Max Weber's attention as well as that of his critics who concentrated entirely upon the social preoccupations of St. Antonius and the reflections of Leon Battista Alberti. Poggio Bracciolini described, with considerable polemical emphasis, the social upheaval that would take place if every individual were to seclude himself in a completely autarchic economy. Everybody's efforts would be exhausted by the exigencies of a purely vegetative life. 'All splendour, all beauty, all charm would disappear from our cities. There would be no more temples, no more monuments and no more art. Our whole existence as well as that of the state would be disrupted if everyone endeavoured solely to provide for his own necessities. . . . For the commonwealth, money is the nerve of life and those who lust for money are its foundation.'[11]

Work, which was to provoke the enthusiasm also of Giordano Bruno, is here counted as a blessing and not as a punishment. It is a means for the full development of human faculties. With its help man tames the world and makes it human. Wealth becomes thus almost the tangible sign of divine approval. We have seen above that Salutati maintained that God looked down with pleasure upon the fat herds and the massive property of Jacob. Alberti's exclamation that poverty is hateful to men as well as to the gods was probably nothing but a rhetorical phrase; but the story told by the unfortunate lawyer of Pesaro, Pandolfo Collenuccio, is highly significant. Labour, an active deity, could not remain a bachelor. Therefore he married the industrious Agenoria, the daughter of Usus to whom Pallas gave eight noble virgins: Politia, Opis, Pales, Arachne, Larunda, Doris, Bellona and Panacea. These virgins provided harvests, hearths, clothing,

[11] In view of this the attitude attributed by Filelfo in the third dialogue of the still unpublished *Commentationes Florentinae de Exilio* (Cod. Nat. Firenze, II, II, 70) to Poggio, is of great interest. Poggio is made to praise Cosimo as well as the concreteness of *res* which somehow are the tangible expressions of human activity. Cp. fol. 93r and 92r. For a criticism of ascetic attitudes see fol. 98r. The third book (*De Paupertate*) is particularly significant. It attributes the triumph of the Medici to the power of money (foll. 83–4). For Filelfo and Landino cp. the texts published by me, *Testi inediti e rari*, Firenze, 1949. Characteristic texts are to be found almost anywhere. Cp. e.g., the letters exchanged between G. Manetti and D. Acciaiuoli, ms. Magliab. VIII, 1390; or the letters of Niccolò Luna to Palmieri, ms. Ricciardino, 1166.

houses, goods, protection and safety. 'They were obedient and their efforts were guided by Politia. Seven children issued from this happy marriage: Life, Industry, Virtue, Victory, Plenty, Truth and Joy'.[12]

But let us return to Bracciolini. There is not a single humanistic motif which cannot be found in his writings. He wrote to Niccoli that *litterae* were well and truly necessary *ad vitam et mores*. With him too, the first place was occupied by attacks on all forms of fruitless asceticism and monkish solitude.[13] 'Our virtue, without the slightest doubt, would freeze, become solitary and infertile, if we were deprived of health, wealth and fatherland. Without these things, virtue could never take up, among men, the life that is appropriate to her. Instead she would give rise to a coarse nobility which is alien to every genuine nobility.' Campanella's invitation to Pico della Mirandola to leave the libraries and to venture forth into the excitements of life, has often been taken as a manifesto of modernity. But already Bracciolini despised the scholar who remained buried in his codices and strove for nothing but a kind of rural virtue. 'I, on the other hand, approve of and aim at that virtue that is confirmed by life'. He was talking of the true *virtus* which is a glorification of the whole of man, which is measured in terms of the world and which is able to enjoy the world. Already Salutati had exclaimed *standum in acie*. And similarly, Bracciolini openly faced the two subjects, *gloria* and *fortuna*. *Gloria*, so to speak, is the tangible manifestation, the body, of virtue. It is the echo virtue evokes in human society and is therefore inseparable from true civic virtue. *Litterae* are connected with *gloria*; for they are responsible for making the memories of great deeds live for posterity. They are the concrete expression of the fact that in every great deed there is a collaboration of minds which transcends the boundaries of time and of space.

The contempt for *gloria* in the name of virtue is tantamount to an ideal of monkish, solitary and therefore sterile and senseless, virtue. Against this, a full-fledged virtue cannot live in the hearts of men without an echo. For the echo serves both as an example

[12] L. B. Alberti, *Opera Inedita et Pauca Separatim Impressa*, Firenze, 1890, p. 169. Pandolfo Collenuccio, *Agenoria*, in *Operette morali*, Bari, 1929, pp. 15–17.

[13] For the letters of Bracciolini see the edition by Tonelli, 3 vols., Firenze, 1832–61.

and a goal to other men. *Gloria* is the external sign of the radiation of virtue in society.

Nor must the problem of *fortuna* be neglected in the discussion of man's life and virtue. *Fortuna* is, so to speak, the web of earthly accidents in their uncontrollable succession—the result of fortuitous actions, the sum total of which makes up the course of reality. It is therefore impossible for man to remain indifferent to *fortuna* by seeking refuge in the illusory fortress of solitary virtue. For virtue, if it is to be taken seriously, must be social and must lead to growth and to the enrichment of the commonwealth. True virtue cannot remain indifferent to the social fruits and to the success of actions. In his *Liber de Nobilitate* Bracciolini insists that virtue ennobles and that nobility, in turn, is the expression of a fruitful virtue. Such virtue must be victorious over *fortuna* and change the world of men. Virtue can effect this transformation even when it is present only in the intellectual labours of philosophers 'who educate men in the arts and sciences through their studies and their vigils, though they themselves may, in fact, be living far away from human contacts'.[14]

On the other hand, in his *De Nobilitate* Bracciolini especially emphasised the two fundamental topics of the humanistic discussion of nobility. These two topics led to the writings of Buonaccorso da Montemagno[15] and, towards the end of the century, to the work of Landino. There was, first, asceticism and the stress on the significance of nobility as a sign of virtue. And secondly, there was the appreciation of the value of nobility, provided that nobility is the result of virtue and work and not a hereditary right. 'Virtue is at the disposal of all. Whoever embraces her, can possess her. Men who are lazy, wicked, evil and perverse and think they can simply inherit from their ancestors, are men who ought to be despised more than others the farther they have removed themselves from their ancestors.'

[14] Poggio Bracciolini, *Ad Insignem Omnique Laude Praestantissimum Virum Gerardum Cumanum de Nobilitate Liber, Opera*, fol. 3r. v-32 r. On the concept of *gloria* cp. *De Infelicitate Principum* and *De Varietate Fortunae*. The *Oratio in Laudem Matrimonii* can be found in ms. Magliab. II, IX, 14, c. 119r-127r.

[15] *De Nobilitate* by Buonaccorso da Montemagno (*Prose e rime*, Firenze 1718), translated by Giovanni Aurispa, is nothing but a rhetorical exercise in which nobility of blood and nobility of action are compared with one another.

4. THE WORLD OF THE PASSIONS AND THE VALUE OF PLEASURE

The works of Bracciolini, often written in an admirable style, are pervaded by a very positive assessment of every healthy and vital manifestation of life. We owe his famous descriptions of nature and of the perfect gracefulness of the human body to his fresh sensitivity to all forms of human life. We always find in him a lively (for that matter, a very Christian) consciousness of the incarnation of the spirit. To his mind, man is not exclusively a soul, but a man—that is, a body which is animated by something spiritual. In a letter of the year 1450, Filelfo put it as follows: 'I cannot understand how one can forget the body, for man is by no means pure soul'.[16]

The great value of the researches of Francesco Filelfo, who was a fertile rather than a profound writer, lies in their attempt to discover a balance suitable for the various needs of man—a balance which would enable a man to lead a quiet as well as a moral life. In a letter to Bartolomeo Fracanzani he gave an obviously Aristotelian outline of his ideal of *alipia*. This outline is more precise than the one given in his far-flung treatise *De Morali Disciplina*. By *alipia* he meant a securely established equanimity of the soul capable of coping with any storm. It amounts to a sort of peace, albeit a peace that stems from the measured contentment of the body as well as of the soul or spirit.[17] For that matter, his whole work follows the tendency to reconcile opposing viewpoints, especially those of Plato and Aristotle. The devotion to Socrates and to the Aristotelianism of the earlier humanists had eventually come to be confronted very outspokenly by the belief in Plato. Filelfo defended the thesis which came to be the guiding principle of the whole school of Ficino that the two great philosophers of antiquity are fundamentally in agreement with one another. The only thing was that

---

[16] Filelfo, in ms. Magliab. VIII, 1445, c. 308–9. In *Commentationes*, fol. 81 *r*, he writes: 'si hominem scimus non animum, non corpus, sed tertium quiddam, quod et animo constet et corpore, immortali mortalique natura, nequaquam ambigere nos oportet. . . .'

[17] Cp. Filelfo, besides the *Epistulae*, Venetiis, 1502, the *De Morali Disciplina*, Venetiis, 1552. Further texts in C. De Rosmini, *Vita di Francesco Filelfo*, Milano, 1808, 3 vols.

Filelfo's attempt at reconciliation was completely lacking in depth. He was dominated by a very superficial form of rhetoric and thus emptied *studia humanitatis* of all true humanity. In his lectures he allowed, therefore, the philosophy of life to degenerate into a set of grammatical artifices. When he preferred Cicero, on account of his elegant oratory, to Socrates, Plato and Aristotle, he placed himself outside the great humanistic tradition—even though in this preference he was in agreement with certain views of Poliziano and Ermolao Barbaro. In the end, only the faintest traces of genuine humanism can be detected in Filelfo. As an example one might cite the praise of wealth put into the mouth of Bracciolini in the third book, entitled *De Paupertate* of the dialogues of the *Commentationes Florentinae de Exilio*.

As against this, the praise of Epicureanism that is to be found in the epistle by Cosimo Raimondi of Cremona, strikes a completely different note. Raimondi was a highly erudite Latinist who committed suicide in 1445. His polemics, like those of Valla, were directed against the Stoics, those 'hard and inhuman philosophers, whose senses have gone to sleep and become atrophied, proof against all calls of joy'. He argued that it was the fundamental error of all asceticism not to consider that every virtue is a virtue of the whole of man, who consists of body and soul in an ever newly achieved harmony. It was the great merit of Epicure who was more than merely human—in fact a divine being—to have understood this fact. 'People condemn Epicure because they think he had too easy a conception of the highest good, when he identified it as pleasure and maintained that all efforts ought to be related to pleasure. As against this, I, when I consider him more closely, approve his opinions every day more fully—as if they were not just the guiding line or the principle of a single man, but of a higher spirit. He placed the highest good in pleasure because he had looked more deeply into nature and had understood that we have emerged from nature and are formed by her so that nothing is more appropriate than to maintain all members of our body healthy and whole . . . and to keep all evil from our soul and our body.'[18]

[18] The letter by Raimondi, his only philosophical statement, was published by Santini, *Cosma Raimondi umanista ed epicureo*, 'Studi storici', 1899, pp. 153–66; cp. my translation in *Filosofi italiani del' 400*, Firenze, 1942, pp. 133–49. Later I was able

Raimondi stressed the beauty which we perceive through our senses and the joy of life which we experience as pleasure and appreciate as such, with very impressive words. Epicureanism was known through the works of Diogenes Laertius and from the poetry of Lucretius, discovered in 1418 by Bracciolini and immediately communicated to Niccoli. It offered a fine foundation for this new appreciation of nature in her whole integrity. At times, however, this new valuation took such an irreligious turn that it led to an anti-Christian attitude of the kind we can observe in Rome in the circle of Pomponius Laetus. 'These men held that there was no world other than this one and that the soul dies with the body, and that therefore nothing mattered except the full enjoyment of all pleasures and lusts. For these men were followers of Epicure and Aristip. . . .'[19] Even if one discounts the probably polemical exaggerations of Galeazzo Maria Sforza's ambassador, to whom we owe this description, it is nevertheless true that this report mirrors the attitudes of certain *literati* of the Roman group, especially the views of Filippo Buonaccorsi (Callimaco Esperiente) whom we know also from other sources as an opponent of the Platonic separation of the body from the soul. Platina, on the other hand, always insisted on his own orthodoxy, although he too attacked monks, ascetics and contemplatives of all kinds very sharply.[20] 'Many Egyptians and Greeks have shown a preference for contemplation and have written much about the beauty and the wonders of creation. But I praise and admire above all the Romans who neglected the excellences of individuals and the pleasures of the mind and, writing instead about laws and morals, were mindful of the needs of men.' Even science and culture in *De Falso et Vero Bono* are represented as instruments of human communication, as a language which

to identify a copy in the anonymous Laur. Ashb. 267 of the 15th century under the title *Defensio Epicuri contra Stoicos, Achademicos et Peripateticos* ('Rinascimento', 1950, pp. 100–101).
[19] The full text in Pastor, *Storia dei Papi*, tr. Mercati, Roma, 1925, vol. II, p. 742.
[20] On Callimaco Esperiente and his writings cp. B. Kieszkowski, *Filippo Buonaccorsi detto Callimaco e le correnti filosofiche del Rinascimento*, 'Giornale critico della filosofia italiana', 1934, pp. 281–94. Note the *Quaestio de Peccato* addressed in the form of a letter to Pico referred to by Zeissberg, in 'Arch. für österr. Gesch.' vol. 55, 1877 and partially published by me, 'Rivista critica di storia della filosofia', 12, 1957, pp. 16–21. The *Rhetorica* was published by Kumaniecki, Varsavia, 1950. The writings of Platina, Colonia, 1540. *De Optimo Cive*, translated by F. Battaglia, Bologna, 1944, together with Matteo Palmieri's *Della vita civile*.

overcomes time and space as well as other differences between
nations and races. 'Only the scholar is never an alien in a foreign
land. . . . Wherever we happen to be going culture accompanies
us and leads us into a port'. People who are shipwrecked and
thrown by the waves upon an unknown shore, are immediately
of good cheer when they discover in the sand geometrical figures.
And the philosopher among them will greet them with the
following words: 'Tell my fellow-citizens that parents cannot give
better provisions to their children than an education in the
liberal disciplines'.[21]

Litterae, conceived as *honesta disciplina* and *studia humanitatis*
are the firmest and widest human bond there is.

5. VALLA AND THE MORAL SCIENCES

Lorenzo Valla stood for a positive valuation of life in this
world, and was opposed to any form of ascetic denial. His
polemics against Stoicism and his satire on monks derived from his
demand for a full life to be lived in a purity that sought to recognise in nature as well as in the flesh the work of God. The whole
of man, body and soul, is fashioned by God. And there is no
part in him which comes from the devil. We said 'purity': he is
indeed dominated by a veritably chaste desire to free himself of
all overgrowth which only too often harbours perversions and
all manner of degeneration, sinister refuges of barbarism. We
ought, he insists, to rediscover under all accretions, the spon-
taneity of an erstwhile innocence that has been betrayed. Ideally,
it is impossible to separate this appeal to nature and to pleasure
that is to be found in his *De Voluptate* from the fideistic tone
which he strikes in his *De Libero Arbitrio*; from his search for a
logic that is in conformity with actual processes of thought; for a
law, free of all fossilisation; for a language that is language in the
original sense of the word.

Valla had a predilection for sharp and pitiless polemics. His
harsh tone lent a special and almost scandalous colouring to all the
attacks which he was so fond of mounting against the past. The
literary conceits with which he glorified *voluptas* have to be

---

[21] *De Falso et Vero Bono*, II (ed. Colonia).

numbered among them. But the most intimate indication of his personality is to be found in his appeal to the nature which is alive and ferments in us; to a nature which is of divine origin and which mediates between God and men. Whoever suppresses or prunes nature commits a sin against her. Therefore it is the vocation of man not to kill his own self but to display his own love of action and to enjoy the serene movement of the soul, the agreeable gaiety of the body which is called ἡδονή. Valla objected to Christian and Stoic asceticism: pleasure is to be enjoyed in this world and valued as the goal and prize of action. It is a sign of true wisdom if one seeks once more to enjoy pleasure in the next world as a divine reward for one's actions. Valla insisted that the traditional relationship between means and ends, honesty and pleasure, was not only immoral and false, but ought to be completely reversed; or, better still, eliminated. The honourable ought never to be taken for the pleasurable; and the pleasurable ought never to be taken for the honourable. *Voluptas* ought to be desired for its own sake: action has intrinsic value and is not valuable only in respect of something else. It is as if in these thoughts of Valla's there had taken place a suffusion of pleasure with morality, something akin to the human incarnation, so that there had ceased to be a clear distinction, or, more correctly, an opposition, between flesh and spirit. The defence of nature in her totality is the centre of the first book of *De Voluptate*. It does not aim, as some people have maintained, at a substitution of nature for God but at a sanctification of nature and at a proclamation of the perfection of nature. For nature is taken to be God's first minister and the minister of the whole, wise providential *ordo rerum* to which our attitude ought to conform. For the *bonum* is to be found in all activity that follows nature; that is, in the precision with which actions are fitted into reality. At least this is true of the *bonum* which is genuinely fertile and concrete rather than abstract and hollow like the *bonum* which the Stoics opposed so bluntly to the natural order of things. *Voluptas*, divine pleasure, is the sign of the fertility that descends upon human actions like God's blessing. In pleasure, nature expresses herself in her complete strength and reveals positively her potential development. In enjoyment and in joy we sense the influx of that same pleasure which is to be found in a heightened measure in

Paradise. Thus the close links between beauty and pleasure are strengthened. These were the links which Panormita had stressed in the first dialogue. They dominate men's minds and even the barristers in the courts of law exploit this fact in order to penetrate the hearts of men and to win them over. Not without a certain sensuous delight, physical love was praised; for physical love is closely related to beauty. And the fertility of *voluptas* was given a thoroughly physical meaning: the propagation of the human species. If asceticism should ever succeed in imposing radical abstention, *quantum naufragium de genere humano*! One must add that at this juncture the polemics against the monks and the praise of matrimony came up again—both commonplaces among 15th century publicists.[22]

The whole of *De Voluptate* is concerned both with this pointed criticism of Stoicism and other forms of asceticism and with the development of this extremely refined concept of *voluptas*. This refinement reaches its climax with the praise of divine gaiety and of the whole of Christian experience which occupies the whole of the last book of the work. Stoicism, so the argument runs, sinned through its extreme dualism: the opposition of reason to sensuousness, of soul to body, implied a tacit antithesis of the Manichean type. Valla considers it fair game to show up the contradiction between asceticism and the facts of life; and to oppose the absurdity of a doctrine which, at the very moment in which it insists that man's existence is confined to this earth, demands that man forego everything positive which life on earth might have to offer. By comparison, Christianity became a programme for the unity and the wholeness of man and a principal opponent of the Manichean postulate.

[22] For anti-monastic polemics cp. *De Professione Religiosorum*, Vahlen ed., 1869, *Opuscula Tria*, Sitzungsberichte der Wiener Akad. d. Wissenschaften, phil.-hist.Kl.61, pp. 7–67, 357–444; 62, pp. 93–149. This is not the place to take up the question of the various versions of *De Voluptate* and of the eventual modifications and qualifications due to Valla. All the same, it is possible that a first version of 1431 is preserved in the Paris edition of 1512; a second version of 1433, in the printed editions of Louvain and Cologne of 1483 and 1509 respectively; and a third, final version, in the Cod. Ottobon. Lat. 2075 of the Vaticana. The Bâle edition of the *Opera*, however, is supposed to contain a fusion of the first two versions. Cp. M. de Panizza, *Le tre redazioni del De Voluptate del Valla*, Giornale stor. d. letteratura ital., 1943, 121, p. 1–22. The same author has returned to this question in order to integrate and correct, in her *Le tre versioni del De Vero del Valla*, Rinascimento, VI, 1955, pp. 349–64. There is a good Italian translation of Valla's *Scritti filofici e religiosi* by G. Radetti, Firenze, 1953.

The canonisation of *voluptas* (conducted, by the way, entirely in the sense of Lucretius), is a defence of the divine element in nature, regarded as the marvellous revelation of the clearly ordered and providential goodness of God. The position of Valla, like any radical rejection of Manicheism, comes dangerously close to Pelagianism and to a deification of nature and, through nature, of pleasure, *hominumque divumque voluptas*.[23] All the same, this consideration does not affect its validity which depends instead on the appeal to that Christian experience which promises the salvation not only of the soul but of the whole of man—of body and soul—and which thus stands in contrast to pessimistic asceticism or any other open or disguised form of Manicheism.

The final speech in *De Voluptate*, in which Niccolò Niccoli confronts Panormita's praise of nature with the praise of God, is by no means a clever mask which Valla chose to wear in the end for purely opportunistic reasons. It reflects his genuine reasons. It reflects his sincere thought that nature is the work of God and that everything that is natural is divine and must therefore be regarded as a sacred language. He argues that we ought trustingly and naively to follow the divine law that orders all things: *totum ad voluntatem Dei esse referendum*. This is where true joy is to be found.

The treatise *De Libero Arbitrio* contains Pauline accents, a severe condemnation of Aristotelian theology and an enthusiastic proclamation of a faith which amounts to a total dedication of the soul to God. Although it shows complete agreement with the voluntaristic thoughts of Salutati's *De Fato*, the treatise is no alien in Valla's world. For its concern is to break through the syllogistic armour of scholastic dialectics and to remove the barrier which Aristotelians had erected between man and nature and between man and God. Only when we trust reality, Valla argued, and lay ourselves open to the divine, only when we find our way back to the primordial in *our* nature and thus to the innocence of the whole of nature, can we once more become worthy of God.[24]

[23] Valla, *Opera*, pp. 906, sqq., 909 sqq., 926 etc. 'Stoicos pre ceteris imitari studebimus, qui sunt evangelio propinquiores', wrote Enea Silvio in 1444; *Lettere*, Wolkan ed., I, I, p. 342.
[24] Valla, *De Voluptate*, I, 10. The reference to Lactantius' Hermetic text is significant. It was to be used by Giannozzo Manetti. Useful parallels between *De Voluptate* and Manetti's work on man could be found in many places.

F

Whether one is reading the *Dialettica* or the *Eleganƶe*, one always comes across the same theme. Valla wants to grasp the precise original meaning of words, a meaning that lies beyond any meaning that can be established by traditional logical discussions. In going back to the oldest meaning of a word he aimed at determining its connotations and denotations. And thus he hoped to advance to the sources of the thought that is enshrined in words. This explains his vehement criticism of Aristotle, of Boethius and of the whole of medieval *barbarism* as well as his grammatical and philological investigations. He endeavoured to return to the genuine meaning of words and to strip off those fantastic ones that had been forced upon them as a result of untenable theories. Words that have suffered thus have to be once again looked at in the light of their original function and be freed once and for all from the bonds of over-clever discussions. For this reason he spoke of the *sacrament* of classical Latin as if he were dealing with a sacred being or a divine seal which embodies the first thought of man in its purity.[25] For this reason, too, he established the rule that the word ought to be met with respect; that one ought not to do violence to language; that one ought to listen humbly and piously to the message of the living spirit that has become word.

Only if these rules are observed can the word regain its value as a method of communication and as a link between man and man. Only if these rules are applied can thought and word cease to be contradictory elements. Valla, as Poliziano was soon to do, assigned a very special role to philology. He regarded it as the road that leads to the understanding of thought. We can indeed follow in the history of a word, the history of an essential human relationship; of an institution and of a concept; a custom or a form of life. When reading the acute explanation of the connection between law and philology in the preface to the third book of the *Eleganƶe*, one can understand what the study of the *Digests* must have meant. And at the same time we can appreciate the philological substratum and the moral and political relevance of the treatise on the Donation of Constantine in which a mere question of language ended up by becoming a social and religious

[25] *Elegant. praef.*: 'magnum ergo Latini sermonis sacramentum est, magnum profecto numen. . .' Cp. anche *Dialectica, Opera*, p. 643 sqq.

commitment.[26] Language, as already indicated, became once again a tangible manifestation of the unity of the human mind, the texture of society and the incarnation of the Spirit. A contemporary of Valla wrote to Giovanni Tortelli, a humanist to whom the *Elegantiae* had been dedicated, that all forms of man's intellectual life were re-born and met in eloquence.

This is the very theme which, following Cicero, all the most important of the humanists sought to develop: the whole spiritual life of man has its roots in *studia humanitatis*. 'Who does not know, wrote Gasparino Barzizza, that all arts that are concerned with *humanitas* are connected with one another by a common bond? Who does not feel that all human evidence, without that bond, would not only be mutilated and barren but also inferior and more contemptible than that of many animals?'[27] One could well argue that Valla's generous conception of philology as the investigation, growing awareness and education of the whole of man in the orbit of *humanitas*, anticipated Vico's conception that philology had to be transformed into history. If Platina praised history as a teacher of eloquence, Valla conceived it as the synthesis of all branches of human knowledge. 'In my view, historians show a greater seriousness in their speeches, greater insight and greater civic wisdom than the philosophers with their general maxims. For truly, from history there flows a comprehensive knowledge of all things natural, which were reduced by others to a system; and a deep knowledge of customs and of other kinds of wisdom. And since we have demonstrated the superiority of historians to philosophers, we are entitled, where religion is concerned, to consider both Moses and the Evangelists . . . to have been historians'.[28] History is thus the *magistra vitae*. But in the first

[26] *Elegantiae*, Lugduni, 1543, p. 156: 'perlegi . . . digestorum libros . . . et relegi cum libenter, tum vero quadam cum admiratione. Primum quod nescias utrum scientia rerum an orationis dignitas praestet. . . .'

[27] *Tortellio Aretino Viro Sapientissimo Cassius*, in 'La R. *Accademia Petrarca di Arezzo a F. Petrarca*', Arezzo, 1904, p. 87 (dal Vat. Lat. 3908). *G. Barzizii in Principium quoddam Artium Oratio* (Müllner, op. cit., p. 57). Cp. Cicer. *Arch.* 2.

[28] L. Valla, *Historiarum Ferdinandi Regis Aragoniae Libri Tres*, Neapoli, 1509; cp. Poliziano, *Praefatio in Svetonium*, *Opera*, Lugduni, 1528, vol. II, pp. 392, 399; Platina, *Proemium in Vit. Pontif.*, *Opera*, Colonia, 1529, p. a r. (Cp. also the beautiful book by F. Gaeta, *L. Valla, Filologia e storia nell'umanesimo italiano*, Napoli 1955; G. Radetti, *La religione di L. Valla*; F. Adorno, *Di alcune orazioni e prefazioni di L. V.*, 'Rinascimento', V, 1954; G. Zippel, *L. V. e le origini della storiografia umanistica a Venezia*, ibid. VII, 1956, pp. 93–133; C. Vasoli, *Le 'Dialecticae Disputationes' del Valla e la critica umanistica della logica aristotelica*, 'Rivista critica di storia della filosofia', XII, 1957, pp. 412–33).

place, it is itself the concrete life of the mind and an unfolding
of the mind into all its ideal dimensions. And therefore all history
is contemporary and living history. It is the method by which
man takes survey of himself and which leads to the greatest
possible enlargement of the horizon. In the middle of the 16th
century Gianmichele Bruto, of Venice, was to exclaim in his *De
Laudibus Historiae*[29]: 'We are educated not by the inactive and
barren philosopher, but by Scipio in arms; not by the schools of
Athens, but in the Spanish camps. We are educated not by
speeches but by deeds and examples.' The morality taught by
history does not consist of one universal justification of what has
happened, but in casting merciless and disrespectful light and
shadow and in the irrevocable dismissal from the history of
mankind of all those who find it impossible to participate in it.
'The true judge of the world is he who makes history. He is the
sole, pious and incorruptible judge.'

6. GIANNOZZO MANETTI AND THE PROBLEM OF THE DIGNITY OF MAN

Giannozzo Manetti followed the same lines of thought as
Leonardo Bruni. He remembered his predecessor in a warm
obituary notice. Manetti was a pupil of Ambrogio Traversari,
the learned monk of Camaldoli, the translator of Diogenes
Laertius. He had been present at the sessions of Santo Spirito
during which he had absorbed the ideas of early humanism, the
teaching of Petrarch, Salutati and Marsili. He was thoroughly
conversant with Hebrew, Greek and Latin 'and used to say that
there were three books which through a long-standing acquaintance he knew by heart: the letters of St. Paul, St. Augustin's *De
Civitate Dei* and, of pagan works, Aristotle's *Ethics*'. He gave
public readings from these books and lectured on them. He was
a staunch Aristotelian in so far as Aristotelianism was compatible
with civic virtue—but added to it his firm Christian faith. 'He
used to say that our faith ought not to be called "faith" but
"certain knowledge".' His faith, however, was mainly concerned

[29] *Joh. Mich. Bruti De Historiae Laudibus*, Colon. Brandeb., 1698, pp. 703–4, 731,
743–4.

with *caritas*, the love of the neighbour. His high-minded and earnest conception of life was manifest in his refusal to make political compromises and he was therefore forced to taste the bitter fruit of exile. With Bruni, he shared the conviction that Dante was the very embodiment of dignity—even as Socrates had been its embodiment in classical times. For Socrates had been a conscientious citizen, had fought on the field of battle and exposed himself without fear to the dangers of political life and had been an exemplary husband and father. 'Though a sublime philosopher, he lived, in Athens, a citizen's life like any other citizen. He conversed with the Athenians, took a wife, served as a magistrate and neglected none of those things which he considered to belong to the life of society.'[30] When Manetti was confronted with the inhuman, monkish ideals of Stoicism, he reacted violently. In his *Dialogus Consolatorius de Morte Filii* he incessantly criticised those who plan to eradicate the passions. Virtue is a glorification of *humanitas* and is its valid expression. 'You have to appropriate virtue with all the forces of your soul and body, because, according to Cicero, the word "virtue" is derived from *virilitas*.' But if one followed the plan of the Stoics to change men into stones, one would destroy humanity instead of elevating it.[31] When Agnolo Acciaiuoli, a follower of the Stoa, reminded him of the maxim of Terence according to which men ought to bear the painful blows of destiny without emotion, he replied: 'Though I remember Terence's maxim well . . . I am also mindful of another memorable saying by the same poet: "when we are healthy we are all given to giving good advice to the sick". And I can also recall another marvellous saying by the same poet: "I am a man, and nothing human is alien to me." Therefore I am of the opinion that all the pain that fills me is due to my humanity rather than to frivolity.' Acciaiuoli was a radical Stoic and therefore, in Manetti's opinion, quite inhuman. Manetti, on the other hand, good Aristotelian that he was, defended the life of the emotions: 'The peripatetics, who are much more human, believe that all passions have their

---

[30] *Vita Socratis*, Cod. Laur. LXIII, 30.

[31] *Dialogus Consolatorius de Morte Filii*, Palat. 691 of the National Library, Florence, which contains also Manetti's Italian version. Cp. the noteworthy orations by G. Manetti on justice (e.g. in Palat. 51 e 598 of the National Library, Florence). One of the orations was printed in Turin by Fanfani (*Collezione di opere inedite o rare*, vol. II, 1862, pp. 195–201). The oration by Palmieri appeared in Prato, 1850.

origins in nature . . . and I follow this belief because it is more
consonant with human nature.' To be human, according to this
view, meant to feel with men, to suffer and to enjoy; to love
children and fatherland and to see in reason not an enemy but the
guide and the measure of the emotions. 'For this reason the
memorable and golden saying of the wise emperor Antoninus
Pius has always pleased me very much. Someone once reproached
Marcus Antoninus (who first was a philosopher and then an
emperor) because he, though both emperor and philosopher,
bemoaned the death of the man who had brought him up.
Antoninus Pius is alleged to have replied to that reproach as
follows: "let him be a human being, for neither philosophy nor
the possession of power can ever suppress the emotions of the
soul". In order to reinforce his views, Manetti repeated with
Cicero that if the emotions were eliminated, there would cease
to be a difference 'not only between a sheep and a man, but also
between the trunk of a tree and a man. Even the difference
between a stone or any other lifeless object and a man would
disappear'. Hence the anti-Stoic conclusion: 'One should not give
credence to those who maintain that virtue is a hard, a well-nigh
iron, thing. If we see that at times the death of a puppy or of
another graceful and charming little animal is so painful for those
who have bred them, that they shed tears because they can no
longer enjoy the pleasurable sensations caused by the animal . . .
what should the fathers do on the death of their children when
they realise that they are forever bereft of those much more
certain and more expressive children's charms which are by no
means mere vain and frivolous joys? And at the same time they
know that they were flesh of their flesh and that, when alive, they
had the same nature as their fathers.'

If it is becoming to man to submit with humble devotion to
all misfortunes sent by God, it is equally human to suffer and to
shed tears. 'In frivolous and uncontrolled men such sentiments
may well appear to be opposed to each other. But in the wise and
the prudent they often are reconciled'. Such deeply understanding
words reflect the wide spiritual horizon of the humanism which
also inspired Guarino's sharp condemnation of every Stoic,
monkish and solitary hardness: 'They tear all mutual benevolence
from the heart of man. They eliminate the love of mankind, all

friendship, all compassion and nothing can be more cruel and more bestial, nothing more inimical to human society.'[32]

Manetti's famous eulogy of human dignity is based upon this Socratic and Aristotelian and, at the same time deeply Christian, conception. This eulogy, although it goes back at times, via Lactantius, to the Hermetic glorification of the god Anthropos, takes its cue mainly from the positive evaluation of earthly activity. According to the report of Vespasiano da Bisticci, it was Alphons of Aragon who induced first Fazio and then Manetti to write a dissertation on man. It is well known and especially mentioned by Pandolfo Collenuccio, that Alphons had a predilection for literary discussions, for he was convinced that 'a king ignorant of literature was a crowned ass'. He had come to treasure especially a dialogue about felicity by Bartolomeo Fazio, a Ligurian pupil of Guarino's. This dialogue was an attack on Valla but was lacking in speculative power. Moving entirely outside the orbit of the humanistic tradition, Fazio had returned to the praise of pure contemplation, for he was convinced that it was destined to reveal to us the secrets of nature: 'thus will we get to know all the stars, and nothing more brilliant, decorative and diverting can be imagined.' But when Fazio presented his treatise *De Excellentia et Praestantia Hominis*, the king was said to have been disappointed. He had every reason to be, for the arguments were both banal and superficial and exhausted themselves in the praise of God's gifts to the soul, especially of 'philosophy, guide and mistress of the righteous life who teaches us the worship of God and all virtuous actions'.[33]

Dissatisfied with Fazio's treatise, the king approached Giannozzo Manetti and 'after long discussions . . . he asked him what, in his opinion, the essential definition of man was. Manetti replied: *agere et intelligere* '. But in the four books of his work, Manetti emphatically placed human activity into the foreground. Knowledge came second and eventually turned out to have been derived from active attempts to control nature. It was a promo-

[32] Guarino Veronese, *Epistolario*, R. Sabbadini ed., vol. I. Venezia, 1915 ('Miscellanea di Storia veneta edita per cura della R. Deput. Veneta di Storia Patria', Serie III, vol. VIII).

[33] B. Fazio, *De Vitae Felicitate*, Antverpiae 1556; published with *De Excellentia et Praestantia Hominis* together with the *Epitomae de Regibus Siciliae et Apuliae* by F. Sandeo (Hanoviae, 1611), p. 106 sqq., 149 sqq.

tion of the arts and the construction of a splendid, harmonious world of human monuments on the basis of nature.

Manetti opposed both Lactantius and Cicero to the rhetorically pessimistic prose of *De Contemptu Mundi* by Pope Innocent III. Following Lactantius, he produced that glorification of man which had been so characteristic of the Hermetic tradition. But he did not dwell upon the metaphysical significance of man's central position, as Ficino and Pico were to do later. This significance came later to be taken as consisting in such an inward deepening of human understanding as to make all human knowledge appear as the confluence of the whole of nature in the one centre of human thought. In this way, nature came to be conceived as raised to the level of the realm of the mind. True, Manetti mentioned the account of *Genesis* and points to the fact that man is similar to God. He even went so far as to borrow from Patristic tradition the idea that the plural used in Scripture ('We create man') in reference to the act of creation, signifies the co-operation of all three persons of the Trinity. But the dominant theme in Manetti's hymn to man is the theme of the over-riding value of human activity. Thus we can watch him conjure up for us Jason's sea voyage, the courage of sailors, the magnificent buildings not only of antiquity but also of *his* Filippo Brunelleschi, *architectorum omnium nostri temporis facile princeps*; the works of all the arts, of literature, of law; in short, of the whole world of the mind, i.e. of the 'realm of man'. In the centre there stood human freedom—the splendid gift which was gift and achievement at the same time. Through his work man incessantly shows himself deserving of freedom. And this freedom enables him to make all the things created by God ever more beautiful and more perfect.

Pico and Ficino were to emphasise even more the cosmic significance of man and of the way in which he stands at the cross-roads of the universe. On eloquent pages they were to transform man almost into a god. But in the simple prose of Manetti the value of man was derived from the dignity lent to him by his Creator. According to Manetti, man shines mainly through his earthly works, in his daily construction of the earthly city, in the serious dedication to civic life.

7. LEON BATTISTA ALBERTI

In spite of the variety of his interests and the width of his horizon, Leon Battista Alberti remained confined very much to the same circle of earthly experiences and predominantly worldly preoccupations. In one of his most important dialogues he insisted solemnly on the finitude of the human condition. In *De Fato et Fortuna* he tells of the strange dream of a philosopher to whom, in a marvellous vision on the banks of the river of life, are revealed the contrasts between souls. The shadows that meander aimlessly along the banks of the rushing stream are the divine sparks in expectation of incarnation. They warn all over-curious investigators of the pointlessness of all fool-hardy speculative daring. 'Desist, oh man, desist from the attempt to investigate God's secret more than is becoming! Remember that the gods allow you as well as every other soul incarcerated in a body to know only those things that happen to fall under your eyes.' Whoever tries to penetrate the divine secrets is like the child who wants to catch the rays of the sun.[34]

In another place, the *De Iciarchia*, the withdrawal from human society for the purpose of pure research is branded as treason. 'Whoever, driven by the desire to know what he does not know, leaves the father and other invalid relatives, is a criminal, is inhuman. *'Man is born in order to be useful to other men'*. The most useful man is he who co-operates with his neighbours and who directs all his efforts 'upon the fatherland, the common weal, and the advantage of all citizens'.[35] The typical motif of the Renaissance, *virtù vince fortuna*, (virtue triumphs over accidental luck) is connected by Alberti with the glorification of human work. The latter finds its justification in the well-being of families and cities. For the accumulation of wealth is both symbol and expression of God's favour. In this connection one ought to re-read the admirable and justly famous preface to his *Della famiglia*, in which all pessimism and all asceticism are banished and replaced by the assurance that human work is valuable. Poggio Bracciolini had reproached the malevolence of *fortuna* because she had enjoyed turning the solemn buildings of Roman magistrates into

[34] *Opera Inedita et Pauca Separatim Impressa*, G. Mancini, ed. Firenze, 1890, p. 137.
[35] *De Iciarchia*, in *Opere volgari*, Bonucci ed. (Firenze, 1843–49), vol. III, p. 92.

pig-sties. Alberti, thoughtfully, asked for the reasons for the sudden collapses of glory which the varying accidents of time force us to witness. 'Alas! How many families there are, fallen and overthrown? One could hardly count all those who used to work in our country for the common weal, like, for example, the Fabii, the Decii, the Drusii, the Gracchi, the Marcelli, and many others, respected by the ancients. They protected the authority and the dignity of the fatherland and showed themselves modest, prudent and strong in times of war . . . Of all those families there has disappeared not only the wealth and the splendour but the very men. And not only the men, but the very names. They are not remembered and all knowledge of them is almost completely obliterated. For this reason it seems to me very appropriate to inquire whether *fortuna* is so powerful in human affairs, and whether she is endowed with unlimited and arbitrary power to overthrow the most respected families in an inconsistent and pusillanimous manner.'

The answer to this serious and anxious question is clear. 'I can see many who have suffered misfortune as a result of their own frivolity. They complain about *fortuna* and allege that they are thrown hither and thither by her ceaselessly moving waves. Whereas in reality their stupidity alone is responsible for their having fallen prey to those waves.' Man himself is the cause both of his misfortunes and of his good fortune. Virtue always defeats *fortuna*. And by 'virtue' is meant a human virtue, an earthly efficiency 'the good and sacred discipline of life'. 'Good laws, virtuous rulers, prudent counsellors, energetic and determined deeds, the love of one's fatherland, faith, industry, the citizens' decorous and laudible obedience (to the laws) have always been able either to gain recognition without *fortuna* or to achieve even greater fame and enlarge their scope with the help of *fortuna*'. As far as *fortuna* is concerned, it is impossible to distinguish the effects of a favourable one from those of a hostile one. But a virtuous efficacy, in the full sense of a civic virtuous efficacy, will never fail to achieve a genuine triumph in history. 'As long as we observe the oldest and most sacred order, as long as we endeavour to behave according to the example of our ancestors and as long as we endeavour to surpass the ancients in glory—as long as our fellow-citizens believed that all our activities, all our industry and skill and everything is devoted to the fatherland and is useful to the other citizens—as long as people were willing to risk their property and their lives in order to maintain the authority, the majesty and the renown of the Latin name—as long as people were prepared to do these things, was there a single nation, no matter how wild and barbarous, which did not respect and fear our decrees and laws?'

Efficiency and virtue are here taken to mean *humanitas*—a humane, prudent, wise and virtuous form of behaviour, which, thoughtfully planned, can be adjusted by subtle intuition to fit into the play of all earthly forces. 'Should we ascribe those things which men do forcefully after mature reflection to the arbitrariness and fluctuations of *fortuna*? And how is it possible to maintain that *fortuna*, with her pusillanimity and her uncertainty, has the power to scatter and destroy those things which we prefer to be subject to our vigilance and our reason rather than to foreign wilfulness? Can anyone argue that those things that we decide to maintain and preserve with care and industry belong to *fortuna* rather than to *us*? It is not in the power of *fortuna*, nor is it an easy matter, to vanquish those who do not wish to be vanquished. She can only defeat those who submit willingly.'

It is hardly possible to exaggerate the significance of virtuous efficacy. For it signifies human deeds in the fullness of their moral and political value. *Fortuna* merely represents the limitations imposed by physical events, limitations which are by themselves powerless to prevent human action. For human action, provided it is virtuous, must always remain victorious. This is so, even when it fails to achieve success: for virtuous action finds its intrinsic fulfilment within an earthly community which sanctifies even those meritorious actions that turn out to be failures. And what is more, such actions are always educationally fertile. 'True (the Romans') enormous renown was often obscured by the envy of *fortuna*; but in the long run virtuous efficiency never fails to achieve renown and as long as (the Romans) were convinced that virtuous action and patriotic discipline adorn and strengthen the empire, *fortuna* always remained willing and inclined towards them. As long as those serious and mature counsels and that deep faith in the fatherland were effectively available; as long as the love for the common cause outweighed all private affairs and the determination to maintain the country was stronger than any personal interests, empire, glory and *fortuna* were preserved. But when the imprudence of tyrannical rule, private advantages and debauches . . . began to prevail over good laws and the sacred customary disciplines, the Roman empire began to become weak and powerless.'

With Machiavelli, the antithesis *virtù-fortuna* was to assume a completely different guise. For Machiavelli, *virtù* and lack of scruple were not contradictory. They can co-exist and collaborate, as they did in that Roman emperor who was at the same time a great virtuoso (i.e. very strong) and extremely criminal. Machiavelli was more concerned here with *virtù* as a force of nature which is to be deployed skilfully amidst other forces of nature. To Alberti, on the other hand, *virtù* is a moral good, a fertile and effective good, but nevertheless a good. It is a mind of justice that builds a world in which it cannot remain without echo and effect. 'In civic affairs and in the lives of men, industry, the good arts, consistent works and mature decisions, honest practice, manifest acts of the will, rational expectations alone are of value.' Human reason, a splendid quality of the human soul and the very light of the spirit 'which distinguishes us from animals, is for man the means by which he can experience and sense what honesty is'.

As a result, the dignity of man is to be sought in work—and only in work. 'Who could believe himself to have any dignity or value without the burning will to explore the perfection of the arts, without the most consistent application, without sweat in order to attain to laborious and manly goals?' According to Alberti such activity consists in the relationships between the citizens 'for men . . . are born for the sake of their fellow-men'. In a civic community, happiness and effective virtue coincide and become, as it were, a solemn prayer addressed to God. 'For this reason I am of the opinion that man is born not in order to rot away in laziness, but in order to be active . . . He ought to be convinced that he is not in this world in order sadly to prolong his existence through lack of action, but in order to aim at great and far-reaching goals. Through this he will please God and will worship God and for himself he will thus attain to the exercise of perfect virtue as well as to happiness, the fruit of perfect virtue.'

Alberti envisaged a community that was organised as harmoniously as one of his palaces; a community in which nature bent
herself to the intentions of art as the stones of the Florentine hills
were wont to bend themselves when they were being used for the
construction of palaces. The idea of open conflict, so apparent in
Machiavelli, was absent. Nor did Alberti share Guicciardini's
notion of perennial discord. And there is nothing here of the
Aristotelian conception of the 'good *fortuna*' so peculiar to
Pontano. To Pontano, 'good *fortuna*' had appeared as the
necessary element of good luck, but it had nevertheless remained
completely independent of human liberty. To Pontano, therefore,
there was, in the field of politics, an unbridgeable gulf between
the blindness of natural urges and civic prudence. To Alberti,
however, man alone was the creator of communal life. Nature,
and thus also *fortuna*, are merely so many tools and opportunities.
Even if there are limitations, they are never insuperable, provided
man is prudent and takes account of them in his calculations.
They are obstacles to efficiency, but obstacles which efficiency can
remove—for virtuous efficiency exercises an absolute sovereignty
in the realm of the spirit. And in that realm, not even when misfortunes happen, can virtue be deprived of its eternal, educative
value and of its fame.[36]

Landino said of Alberti that he was 'a master in geometry,
astrology and in music'. And, true enough, astrological doctrines
can be discovered time and again in *De Architectura*. Their purpose
is less to intrude into the world the shadow of dark forces, than
to underline the world's perfect regularity. The universe is
presented as part of a perfect network of relationships. In these
relationships there is no apparent rupture and it appears that
natural efficacy is the firm foundation of all human activity. For
Alberti, mathematics is, indeed, the secret code of the universe.
When he speaks of painting as the 'flower of all art', and when he
seeks the root of its 'divine power' which, 'even after centuries,
can recall the dead to life', he finds it nowhere but in mathematics. For mathematics 'gives birth to this graceful and noble
art from the roots that are in nature.'[37]

[36] *Tre libri della famiglia* by Alberti, Mancini ed., Firenze, 1908. *De Fortuna* by
Pontano in *Opera Omnia*, Venetiis, 1518, p. 275 sqq.
[37] Alberti, *Il trattato della pittura*, Papini ed., Lanciano, 1913, pp. 13, 43, 45, 49,
95.

8. Matteo Palmieri and the Transition to Platonism

In his dialogue, Cristoforo Landino repeatedly tried to make the character of Alberti appear in the light of Platonism and of a Platonic synthesis. In historical reality Alberti stood well outside this sphere, even though at times he was no stranger to certain lines of that Platonic-Pythagorean conception of nature which, made common property through the school of Ficino, was to become an influence upon the views of Leonardo.[38] But for the most part Alberti's mind was still completely absorbed in this world and was very far from desiring an ascetic flight towards a deity. 'I desire that in your troubles you invoke the help of God. But I do not want you to devote yourself entirely to Him and to cherish the belief that you cannot achieve on your own those things for which your own strength suffices. Stop molesting the gods always with a lot of prayers and vows! Make use of your own power. Our mind will be healthy if we want it to be healthy'. Earthly activity, with him, always assumed concrete forms, especially in practical, economic matters: there it was transformed into success, and this success was embodied in 'goods', in money and in 'domestic property'. 'One ought not to despise wealth. One ought, however, to control avarice. And thus we shall live freely and serenely in the midst of plenty. . . .' We will be free of those material wants which, since they affect the body, depress, in the end, also the soul. This re-valuation of economics and of earthly goods also found its full expression in the fourth part of the *Summa* by the saintly bishop of Florence, Antoninus, who, though going back to St. Thomas Aquinas, brought the old insights up to date.[39]

Close to Alberti we find Matteo Palmieri. There was a striking similarity with Alberti in certain of his demands and even in his literary attitudes—even though they were influenced by newer currents. He was praised by Alamanno Rinuccini as a

[38] Cp. *Disputationes Camaldulenses* and *De Vera Nobilitate* (ms. Corsin. 433). Cp. Ficini *Opera*, Basilea, 1561, vol. I, p. 936. In the *De Iciarchia* (*Opere*, Bonucci ed., vol. III, p. 118 sqq.), Alberti was to speak in Stoic and Ciceronian terms of the sparks placed by nature in the souls of men so that they can illuminate the mind with the rays of reason.

[39] Cp. A. Masseron, *S. Antonin*, Paris, 1926.

typical and miraculous example of a complete equilibrium between active and contemplative elements.[40] In order to outline the ideal of the *civic life*, Palmieri wrote a dialogue by the same name. This work is one single condemnation of all sterile research and of pure, abstract knowledge, cut off from life. 'He who puts all his industry and all his care into honest things which are worth knowing and the knowledge of which results in either a private or a common advantage, deserves to be praised. But those who waste their time in the pursuit of arts that are obscure and abstruse and contribute nothing to anybody's well-being, deserve to be reproached by the whole world, for they yield no fruits.' Hand in hand with the rejection of vain contemplation goes the contempt for a very solitary, monkish virtue. The good consists in *caritas* and is a bond of love, a life in society. 'There is no human love which is as powerful as the love of one's country and the love of one's children.' We are not only absorbed by the community, but through it alone, it seems, can we survive. Hence the deep desire to perpetuate ourselves in it for the future. 'It is not possible to say whence a man comes; but it is certain that there is in our hearts a longing for future centuries which compels us to seek eternal fame, a happy condition for our country and enduring health for those who are about to descend from us.' For this reason the truly human and real virtue is the virtue that aims at the common weal: 'for this reason it is asserted that there is no human achievement greater, more eminent and more worthy than to secure the safety and the growth of the fatherland —for the best possible condition of a well-ordered republic. . . . No work can be more meritorious among men than the care for the safety of one's country, to maintain cities and to guarantee the concord among harmoniously organised crowds of men.'

In Palmieri, Ciceronian ethics came to be fused with Plato and Aristotle; but tended, nevertheless, to assume the colouring of Plato. 'The greatest minds have maintained with certainty in the course of centuries that the just leaders of states come from heaven and return to heaven.' True, it was a very peculiar brand of Platonism, for the praise of Dante as an unsurpassed writer and a perfect citizen, the myth of Er and the *Somnium Scipionis* were

[40] *Alamanni Riunccini Oratio in Funere M. Palmerii,* in Fossi, *Monumenta ad A. Rinuccini Vitam,* Florentiae, 1791.

curiously mixed. And at the same time, its centre remained concerned with the glorification of human society, of human work, its successes and its fertility. Virtue separated from utility was considered empty and sterile. Palmieri's words to this effect are very significant and deserve to be emphasised. He considered that 'to value what is honourable as distinct from what is useful, amounted to straying from the correct road . . . People who despise what is useful and what can be achieved reasonably, deserve to be reproached and cannot be considered virtuous . . . The true merit of virtue lies in effective action and effective action is impossible without the faculties that are necessary for it. He who has nothing to give cannot be generous. And he who loves solitude can be neither just, nor strong, nor experienced in those things that are of importance in government and in the affairs of the majority. . . . It follows that it becomes those who are virtuous to seek what is useful, so that they can lead a righteous life . . . He who increases his property through honest skills without causing any damage to anyone, deserves to be praised.'[41]

At this point Salutati's old attack on solitary virtue and his passionate glorification of the common weal reached their zenith. Yet, even with Palmieri, whom Ficino was to eulogise as a theological poet, this mundane attitude came eventually to be fitted into a framework of Pythagorean and Platonic motifs and of themes culled from Origen. The great philosophical poem, *The City of Life*, which remained unpublished because it came under the suspicion of heresy, shows in heaven the prologue to the earthly battle. The human souls are nothing but those angels who, according to Dante's word, 'stood by themselves' and would not fight either for God or for Lucifer. They are offered an opportunity to stand a final trial. They are turned into flesh and are thus sent to fight their battle in human shape on the stage of the world. Thus the world becomes a kind of stage on which the last act of the divine drama is performed. In this way all human activity is, on one hand, fitted as a simple episode in the history of the mind into a classical plot. But on the other hand, it is filled with an enormous significance and value. With every

---

[41] Matteo Palmieri, *Il libro della vita civile*, Firenze, 1529, pp. 42–43, 62, 75–76, 120–125. Cp. *Una prosa inedita di M. Palmieri fiorentino*, Prato, 1850, or the *Protesto* of 1437. The collection of orations of this kind, Riccardiano 2204, is important.

human decision on earth, there goes a decision about the destiny of an immortal 'syllable of God'. This world is the arena which God offers to the souls so that they can decide freely about their own destiny. And thus on humanity's great world-stage, the fruits of action become for all eternity the seal of a victory over evil.

In spite of this, there was a tendency to cast a glance also towards other worlds. The notion that the earth might be regarded as a parenthesis—albeit as a very important parenthesis —crept into the *City of Life*. And for this reason, Palmieri associated his eulogy of action for the sake of the love of mankind with a eulogy of pure contemplation and of the mystical ascent of the soul to God.[42]

9. PHILOLOGY AND RHETORIC IN POLIZIANO AND BARBARO

If, on the one side, speculative interests were directed towards Platonic metaphysics, on the other side the appeal to antiquity and to the study of the ancients tempted people to lose themselves in grammatical discussions. Under the pressure of various forces the clear and solid culture of early humanism came to be obscured and fissured. Among those forces there was first of all that of official culture. Although it accepted, with a certain suspicion, certain themes of the new philosophical movement, it insisted upon pushing forward its own demands as well as the distinction between *res* and *litterae*, between form and content, which had already been opposed by Bruni with the utmost vehemence.[43] Those humanists who had been admitted teachers of grammar and rhetoric, established themselves with their translations and commentaries in the closed academic circles. They demanded the right to undo dialectics, medicine, law, metaphysics,

[42] M. Palmieri, *La città di vita*, ed. by M. Rooke (*Smith College Studies in Modern Language*, VIII, 1–2) Northampton, Mass. 1927–28.

[43] In the 16th century, Paolo Sacrato, nephew of Sadoleto, wrote thus to his father: (*Epistolarum Pauli Sacrati Libri Sex*, Lugduni, 1581, p. 11): 'haec autem studia maxime inter se differre non ignoras, quod in his, quibus nunc versor assidue, *rebus* agatur, in illis vero, in quibus tu potissimum a me requiris ut operam consumam, de *verbis* tantum quaeratur; nec te laetet, si stylo operam dedero, animum meum a philosophia, quae hominem sapientem reddit, avocatum iri, quod eodem tempore utraque in re operam ponere nequeam'.

G

theology and ethics. 'Our age, because of an insufficient knowledge of antiquity, has assigned too narrow a limit to grammar. And it was precisely grammar which was held in such a high regard by the ancients that only grammarians were allowed to be judges, and censors of literature.' Thus Poliziano in his *Lamia*.[44] He then proceeded to speak of himself. He contemptuously refused to call himself a philosopher, but reminded his readers that he had, in his capacity of grammarian, written books on law, medicine, ethics and philosophy: 'nec aliud mihi nomen postulo', he added, 'quam grammatici'. For the grammarian, as the investigator of language and speech, seeks the whole of human wisdom in the spoken word. If we take up Poliziano's *Dialectics*, we will recognise that at the very beginning he draws our attention to the fact that there are two different kinds of dialectics. The one 'the highest of all arts, the purest part of philosophy, places itself above all disciplines and is their very crown'. But it is not this kind of dialectics with which Poliziano proposes to deal. It is too distant, too difficult, for it is enthroned on the peaks of Platonic mysteries. On the contrary, the dialectics of which he wants to treat are the arts of speech and of argument, related to grammar. They are a kind of grammar of thought and help us to grasp the structure of thought as expressed concretely in language. Similarly, they help us to understand how our intentions cause us to coin words.

Poliziano's researches into the meanings of words were closely related to those of Valla. His interest in the monuments of legal, scientific, moral, religious and philosophical thought bears witness to his determination to understand original and genuine human attitudes through the monuments they have left behind in history.[45] It was for this reason that he wanted to be known as a grammarian and not as a philosopher—although he considered himself, *qua* grammarian, a true philosopher. As he wrote in *Lamia*, grammar is anything but a sober and poor form of knowledge. It represents, on the contrary, the attempt to reveal in human expressions the human soul. To read the legal writings in their original and intended meaning is to be a true jurist. To be able to read the book of God in its genuine meaning is to be a

[44] *Politiani Lamia, Opera*, II, 302.
[45] *Politiani Opera*, II, 459.

genuine theologian. And finally, real philosophy consists in the thorough reading of the books of the great philosophers. If anyone denies Poliziano the title of philosopher, the latter would reply by pointing to the great classical teachers whom he had understood and written commentaries on. To those who complained of the dry and sterile philosophy of the schools, he replied by proving philosophy to be a form of human communication, the ultimate efficacy of which amounts to a clarification of consciousness. His eulogy of rhetoric—not uninfluenced by that of Gorgias—had something in common with the attitude of the Sophists. Both Poliziano and the Sophists had a firm faith in the importance of human encounters, especially on the plane of morals and politics: 'There is nothing more fertile and useful than to persuade one's fellow-citizens by means of words, so that they perform actions advantageous to the state and refrain from those that are damaging'.[46]

Rhetoric thus appeared as statecraft, as the medicine of the soul, the tamer of the passions—and as such, rhetoric is the most select form of human contact, a happy form of the science of man.

Nevertheless there was always the danger that rhetoric, forgetting its original function, might degenerate into a purely literary performance. It might cease to be concerned exclusively with the organisation of the world of man and be tempted to follow a spurious aesthetic ideal of linguistic elegance. We can trace this kind of transformation when we turn our gaze to Poliziano's great friend Ermolao Barbaro. The latter was only interested in the refined elegance of speech and did not endeavour to reproduce the original intentions of the minds of the men with whom he happened to come into contact. He merely wanted to decorate alien expressions with a *concinnitas*; and thus he was in great danger of betraying the content of these expressions. Whereas Poliziano was always specially intent upon accounting for the exact value of every word and to discover at the same time the most hidden nuances of its meanings, Barbaro merely loved the harmony of sounds, the refinement of phrases and the elimination of every harshness of speech.

Barbaro had started with a justifiable intention, expressed in a letter to Giorgio Merula. He had argued that one ought to avoid

[46] *Angeli Politiani Oratio super Fabio Quintiliano et Statii Sylvis* (*Opera*, II, 384–5).

any separation of the content from the form. Philosophers and jurists, he said, had established such a separation at the expense of form. Barbaro had translated Themistius; and in 1480 he explained his programme to Girolamo Donato, the translator of Alexander of Aphrodisia. Barbaro suggested that one ought to fight mercilessly against 'the plebeian and wooden philosophasters who separate philosophy from eloquence' in order to bring about a 'reconciliation between the philosophy of nature and *studia humanitatis*'. But it so happened that in the end he himself brought about such a separation at the expense of the content, for his horror of barbarism and his cult of *concinnitas* made him a fanatical zealot for stylistic refinements. Thus we can see that with him translation becomes a kind of *exornare* and he finished up by condemning civic life in the name of *litterae*, by defending the view that scholars ought to remain celibate and by formulating his position in the famous expression which might serve as the motto and title of his whole outlook: *duos agnosco dominos, Christum et litteras*.[47]

10. GALATEO AND PONTANO

Barbaro dedicated his translation of Themistius' commentary on the *Physics* to Galateo and requested him with considerable warmth to collaborate with Pontano in a comprehensive propaganda campaign in favour of a complete reconciliation between philosophical and literary studies. Apart from a few effective pages, including especially those numerous passages in which he branded the corruption of the clergy, Galateo's writings were fairly insignificant and lacked any kind of theoretical formulation. In his *De Dignitate Disciplinarum ad Pancratium* he criticised Salutati and placed pure contemplation high above action. The latter, he held, is appropriate for the mob; whereas the former is becoming to the few wise men. In another place he emphasised with equal vivacity the leisurely beatitude of sages and the necessity of avoiding even the bonds of friendship. In a letter of the year 1513 the same Galateo launched an attack on *litterae* but did not shrink

[47] *Barbari Epistolae et Orationes*, Branca ed., Firenze, 1943, II, 90–93.

from making the following splendid exclamation: *in malevolam et improbam animam non intrabit sapienta.*[48]

By contrast, Pontano was a man of completely different stature. It is true that he tended to cultivate astrological studies, and these studies inspired him to both prose and verse works. It is equally true, however, that in his moral treatises he loved to display quite effective variations upon both Aristotelian and Stoic themes. And often enough, in difficult philosophical discussions, he remained content with very general assertions. In spite of these facts he proved clearly that he was aware of the importance of some of the questions that were to move men's minds in the 16th century. Thus he tried in his *Actius* to define the nature of poetry by comparing it to history. He adopted the definition according to which history is a *poetica soluta* and argued that poetry and history had an identical content and that they differed from one another merely in their dispositions. Historical discourse, he said, was more chaste; and poetical discourse more 'lascivious'.

He took the fact that poetry tended to invest both gods and mute objects with speech as proof of the fact that it was incontinent and free from all restraint. 'Both history and poetry have rhythms and figures of speech, but in different ways. They also differ in the order in which they arrange facts for narration. For history follows the sequence of the events themselves while poetry very often begins in the middle or even at the end . . . and attributes power of speech to beings that are mute'. This argument reminds one of Vico. So does another, also from *Actius*, in which Pontano said that language had its origin in the expressions of rural people, the lives and customs of which are reflected in the words they have handed down to us.

Whereas he described poetry as an imitation of nature, he argued that history was mainly rhetoric. In this sense he attributed to it an educative task and expected it to lead to the formation of social morality. Rhetoric, that is the speeches of great men, embody, as it were, the soul of history: 'Those public speeches not only adorn history but represent its soul. On the other hand

---

[48] The works of Galateo, here referred to, are published in *Collana degli scrittori della Terra d'Otranto*, Lecce, 1867, vols. II–IV, XVIII, XXII.

it seems as if rhetoric, in so far as it is inspired and moves, penetrates and shapes the soul, leads back to that original power of
poetry which derived its strength from nature herself.'

The concluding reflections of *Actius*, with their enthusiastic
eulogy of poetry, belong to the finest passages in Pontano's
writings. 'When the poets imagine their pictures and then express
them sweetly, miraculously and magnificently, they teach at the
same time other men to speak. Those who have imitated them, be
it in pleading a cause in a court of law, be it during the discussion
of a law in the senate, be it for the narration of historical events,
have perfected the art of this early kind of free eloquence. In this
sense every mode of expression is derived from history. For poets
were the first sages and expressed themselves in songs and other
rhythms. . . . Hail to thee, oh poetry, most fertile mother of all
knowledge! And hail again! For thou, because of the immortality
of thy authors, truly didst come to the succour of a mankind
destined to death. *Thou didst lead men forth from their forests and
caves.* Through thee we arrive at knowledge, through thee we
can revive and recall in front of our eyes, things of the past.
Through thee we know God; through thee we have both religion
and devotion' . . . [49]

11. Towards a Philosophy of Education

Both Barbaro and Galateo had dealt with educational problems,
even though the latter's ideas on this subject were without originality.[50] Both men had narrowed the concept of *litterae* to mean
rhetoric and had thus deprived it of all concrete value. It had
thus lost a large part of the importance attributed to it by the
early humanists, by whom *litterae* had been considered the
foundation of *studia humanitatis*. Eventually there emerged a
complete separation between *litterae* and *studia humanitatis*; and
by the middle of the 16th century, Sadoleto's nephew, Paolo
Sacrato, who was a student of philosophy in Padua, was able to
write to his father who had exhorted him to practise his Latin: 'I

[49] Pontano, *Dialoghi*, C. Previtera ed., Firenze, 1944, pp. 143, 194, 207, 221,
238–39.
[50] *De Educatione* ('Collana degli scrittori della Terra d'Otranto', Lecce, 1867).
But cp. the letter by B. Acquaviva in A. Croce, *Contributo a un'edizione delle opere di
A. Galateo*, 'Archivio storico per le provincie napoletane', 1937, pp. 20–33).

suppose you know that these two subjects diverge profoundly. I have dedicated myself to philosophy, which treates of reality. But the *litterae*, which you enjoin me to study, treat only of words'. The very things which Salutati and Leonardo Bruni had endeavoured to join had finally been separated from one another. The ideal of humanistic education had been the formation of the complete man through the experience of classical culture. This ideal degenerated into a purely literary training, incompatible with genuine education. The solitary, monkish man of letters who came to replace the man soaked in *humanitas* and filled with social consciousness, saw in *humanitas* nothing but literary elegance.

As we have seen, Bruni had maintained that *humanitas* was a spiritual, nay, the only true, education. And in order to fight all those who had criticised this point of view, he had translated in 1403 the defence of literary studies which Basil the Great had undertaken.[51] Always following Salutati he had then shown that an education in poetry is a kind of rejuvenation, a form of regeneration through beauty in its divine greatness and its objective validity. This education was not a teaching of words, but of things. It was a matter of leading the soul into the whole of reality. *Litterae* confront the soul with an absolute value and sublimate it. The *litterae* are called *humanae* because they help the full development of *humanitas*. Even so one is wont to speak of the *liberal* arts because they have the ability to free man, make him master of himself and place him as such into a free world of free minds.

The whole of Pier Paolo Vergerio's *De Ingenuis Moribus* seeks to show how *litterae*, through their ability to further the conversation between minds across the ages, make the soul capable of absorbing a richer and more all-embracing kind of *humanitas*. 'What is there more beautiful than reading and writing and to get to know the ancient world and to converse with those who will live after us and to appropriate all ages, the past as well as the present?' Thanks to *litterae* the mind unfolds and enlarges itself. And while it enriches itself with untold treasures, it learns to

---

[51] Bruni dedicated the translation to Salutati and stated that with the name of Basil the Great he wanted to repress the vileness and perversity of the critics of *studia humanitatis*.

respect the value of other minds and to live in human society. Wisdom, far from incarcerating itself in an ivory tower 'lives in cities, flees solitude and longs to be of help to as many men as possible'.[52]

We find a similar tenor in Maffeo Vegio's *De Educatione Liberorum*. In this work, *litterae* are not only taken to build a secure bridge of civilised social life across the rushing current of time, but are also considered to inspire us to love our neighbours and to forge the bonds of society.[53]

We find the same attitude in Gasparino Barzizza, the teacher of Francesco Barbaro. But above all we find it in Guarino Guarini, pupil of both Giovanni da Ravenna and Emanuele Chrysoloras. Guarini ran a school in Ferrara which produced men like Pannonio, Ermolao Barbaro, Lamola, Alberto da Sarteano and many others, some famous and some not so famous. They all had rushed to him not only from the most remote corners of Italy, but also from as far away as Crete and Cyprus, Poland and England. Guarini, too, maintained that man is enriched by *litterae* and in a letter to Corbinelli he declared that he admired especially those who managed a harmonious combination of knowledge with an active life. And in a letter to the mayor of Bologna he developed at great length the idea that the muses and the muses alone are a preparation for the life of politics. He wrote that one owed 'no little gratitude to the muses for they have educated you from childhood onwards and they have taught you to exercise control over yourself, over your relatives and over the state. . . . Thus one finds the explanation of the splendid saying by Scipio. When he rested one day from public business and devoted himself to the pleasures of literature he said: "by inaction I am now accomplishing the greatest of deeds".'

In Guarini's school, *litterae* were considered the cause of the development of all civilised energy. For they knock at the doors of the soul in order that the soul may reply: *fores, ut si dicam, pulsatis, quo vel rogatus ad intelligendum pateat additus*. One ought to

---

[52] Cp. the work by Vergerio in the edition by Gnesotto, *op. cit.*, and in the volume *L'educazione umanistica in Italia*. I would also like to refer to *L'Educazione in Europa*, Bari, 1957, and to the collection of texts, translated and illustrated, *L'umanesimo*, Firenze 1958.

[53] For the work by Vegio cp. *Maxima Bibliotheca Veterum Patrum et Antiquorum Ecclesiasticorum*, XXVI, Lugduni, 1677.

read the great authors and re-read them, one ought to learn them by heart and to live with them, *summa cum voluntate*, until soul meets soul beyond the limits set by words. One must weigh up every word and analyse subtly its every meaning so that one can use it finally in its right sense and sound. In this manner, one can discover the spirit in the flesh and find among the ruins of by-gone worlds and in monuments which the passage of time seems to have deprived of their splendour, the light that originally shone in them. Only by this method of philological approximation will we be able to make the mute letters yield their living meaning; *nec verbum ex verbo, sed sensa tantisper exprimes*. This kind of conversation will have an invigorating effect. It will make us wise and mature through the wisdom of the ancients.[54]

To these men, antiquity was indeed not only a field in which to exercise their scholarly curiosity, but also a living example. In their eyes, classical antiquity had achieved a wonderful fullness of life and of harmony and had both expressed these achievements and handed them down in works of art and thought as perfect as that life itself. To come into contact with these monuments and with the minds behind them was like an ideal conversation with perfect men and allowed one to learn from them the meaning of existence. If one opens one's heart humbly to those wonderful works and transforms oneself, as it were, through love into them, one can regenerate oneself by absorbing so much human richness and thus reconquer the mastery over all the treasures of the mind. The entrance into this world, this preparation for an existence worthy of man, was contemplated with a well-nigh religious sentiment. Vespasiano Bisticci wrote that Vittorino da Feltre's house 'was a sanctuary of customs, actions and words'. And in his school the respect for man in his completeness—body and soul—acquired something of a ritual. The formation of man appeared as a form of religious awareness of all those things in man that are valuable and that are aroused and confirmed by the liberal arts.[55]

[54] The works of Barzizza, in the Roman edition of 1728. The texts of Guarino, in the edition by Sabbadini.

[55] Besides the life of Vespasiano da Bisticci cp. Fr. Prendilacqua, *De Vita Victorini Feltrensis Dialogus*, Padova, 1774.

All the documents on Vittorino are now collected in my volume *L'Umanesimo*, Firenze, 1958.

Chapter III

PLATONISM AND THE DIGNITY OF MAN

1. The Crisis of Liberty and the Dialogues *De Libertate* by Rinuccini

IF early humanism was a glorification of civic life and of the construction of an earthly city by man, the last part of the fifteenth century was characterised by an orientation towards contemplation and an escape from the world. The serene eulogies that used to be the dominant notes in Salutati and Bruni were replaced by Platonism with its ascetic tone and by a philosophy conceived as a preparation for death. This re-orientation was determined by the pressure of the political development of Italy. The predominance of princes came to be more and more pronounced. To-day we are inclined to recognise their merits; but during the Renaissance they appeared, even though some of them were tyrants of genius, as oppressors of liberty. In 1478 the Pazzi and their supporters were lynched in the streets of Florence by an irate crowd. They had tried to overthrow the Medici, and the populace replied to the conspirators' clamour for liberty by shouting: 'Long live Lorenzo, who gives us bread!'[1] It cannot be denied that those princes often patronised both poets and writers. But it is equally true that they turned them into courtiers whom it is impossible to imagine capable of clear political thinking.

Today we can assess the formation of the *Signoria* as the result of the elimination of the privileged, rich merchants and nobles. But in those days the emergence of the princes destroyed the enthusiasm for political controversy as well as the strong heartbeat of the city-state. The ideal of social co-operation came to be replaced by the rulership of a prince or Caesar. For the new prince forced everybody from active political life and transformed culture either into an elegant decoration of his court or into a desperate flight from the world.

The humanists were very clearly conscious of a crisis. We get a foretaste of it in the sharp attack launched by Poggio Bracciolini

[1] A. Fabroni, *Laurentii Medicis Magnifici Vita*, Pisis, 1784, II, p. 137e sqq.

in a letter to Scipione Mainenti of Ferrara, written in 1435. He called Caesar a depraved murderer of liberty and praised Scipio, the republican. Guarini replied with a defence of Caesar and then Francesco Barbaro, Ciriaco d'Ancona and Pietro dal Monte entered the foray. In spite of appearances, the controversy was by no means an academic exercise.[2] The glorification of the hero as represented by the historical Caesar was opposed to the defence of the idea that man is truly human only when he is allowed to develop his faculties freely. Machiavelli's invective against Caesar and Caesarism that fills every page of the *Discorsi*, allows us to gauge the feelings that prompted the defenders of liberty. People who look at the founder of the Empire superficially—he remarks—may well admire the splendid power of the ruler. But if one observes carefully the consequences of the tyranny founded by Caesar, one 'will recognise that Italy has been tried severely, afflicted by unheard-of misfortunes, and that her cities have been destroyed and ravaged. One will see the fire of Rome and the Capitol devastated by its own citizens. One will remember that the ancient temples are in ruins and the sacred customs corrupted, the cities themselves replete with vice; the sea full of exiles and the cliffs splattered with blood. One will watch innumerable brutalities perpetrated in Rome and nobility, wealth, ancient honours and above all, virtue, counted as capital crimes. One will find that the liars are rewarded and the slaves rebellious against their masters. . . . And that those who had no enemies are now oppressed by their friends. And thus one will understand very well what Rome, Italy and the whole world owes to Caesar.'[3]

In his old age, Salutati, in his *Invettiva* against Loschi, had praised Florentine liberty as the legitimate heir of Roman liberty. In the eyes of Filelfo the Caesarian destroyer of that liberty was no other than the infamous, venomous and ominous Cosimo de' Medici, who had corrupted the city of Florence and had become a threat to the whole of Italy. The *Commentationes* were a merciless attack on the rule of the Medici and revealed the interests of their author all too openly. Similarly, Alamanno Rinuccini's dialogues *De Libertate* contain a direct and painful condemnation of the new Phalaris, Lorenzo de' Medici, and describe with incomparable

[2] Guarino, *Epistolario*, II, pp. 226–29.
[3] Machiavelli, *Discorsi sopra la prima deca di Tito Livio*, I, 10.

effectiveness the changing patterns of 15th century culture and the profound reasons for the radical changes in the orientation of thought.[4]

Rinuccini's ideal as outlined in his funeral oration for Matteo Palmieri, consisted in a harmonious fusion of the active with the contemplative life. Thus he developed the Ciceronian programme which had been the main theme of the works of Palmieri; we are not born for ourselves, but for family and for our country. These are the thoughts of *De Libertate*. They were repeated by a friend and taken to be a reproach to Rinuccini himself; for Rinuccini was living like an exile in his own country. He had retired to a country house and was sunk in solitary contemplation. Culture, so the reproach ran, should not detach us from life and our place ought to be in the world and among men. Our activities, no matter what they might be, ought always to express themselves through our relations to our fellow-men.

Rinuccini's answer sounds deeply embittered. He replied that liberty was a necessary precondition for this kind of activity, and that a man could only develop himself in a free society. In Florence this was no longer possible, for in that city a tyrant, Lorenzo de' Medici, kept the citizens imprisoned in a net of lies and compelled them either to become corrupt or to retire. Culture had ceased to contribute towards the development of mankind and had merely become capable of offering a refuge and a shelter to those that had learnt to fulfil their political function by a betrayal of their conscience and of truth.

When liberty disappears from social life, man is forced back to another plane. He will turn in on himself and seek the freedom that is rooted in wisdom. As far as morals are concerned, Rinuccini, like the representatives of early humanism, continued to reject Stoic asceticism in the name of an Aristotelian balance. But in the sphere of metaphysical reality he tended, for political reasons, to favour a 'monkish and solitary' virtue. In this way the man who had loved civic life so much, came, with bitter resignation, to regard culture as a refuge, as contemplation and as a preparation for death. He moved thus from a Socratic form of

[4] Alamanno Rinuccini, *De Libertate*, ms. Laur. 'Acquisti e Doni', 216; Ravenna, class. 332. Cp. F. Adorno ed., Editorial Losada 1952: *Lettere ed Orazioni*, V. R. Giustiniani ed., Firenze, 1953.

philosophising and a complete absorption in human problems, to a Platonic level. And as humanism drew closer to Platonism, its attitude to Christianity also underwent a subtle change. So far, Christianity, because of its positive evaluation of earthly existence, had always been taken to be opposed to Stoicism. But now the idea of Christianity began to change under the ever-growing influence of the Plotinian tradition. In Florence, while Savonarola was launching his last fiery invective against the tyranny that had corrupted and devastated everything, the 'divine' Marsilio Ficino sought in his *Iperuranio* a serene harbour to protect him from the tempests of the world.

2. THE INFLUENCES OF THE BYZANTINE SCHOLARS AND THE TRANSLATIONS FROM PLATO

It was at this point that the influence of the Byzantine scholars became noticeable, even though it was not terribly important. For late Greek civilisation had become a mere play upon dry theological formulas, devoid of life.[5] The Greeks who migrated to Italy often gave vent to their contempt for the Latins because of their insufficient scholarship. For those Latins, however, the poets and thinkers of antiquity were alive, and their voices had penetrated their hearts and had provided food for thought. The very thing that appeared to those who had faith in the letter as insufficient knowledge, was in reality often enough a faithfulness to the spirit.

The actual contribution made by Byzantium to humanism consisted mainly in new tools and in precious materials which enriched occidental civilisation. The East was able to provide useful formulas to a western system of thought which had already reached an autonomous maturity. At the same time one must admit that at certain opportune moments men of noble character and of high mind, like Chrysoloras and Argyropulos, like Pletho and Bessarion, showed the way towards a flight from the world to many a desperate soul. In spite of this, people went on searching for answers to the old problems—even in the sphere of Platonic metaphysics. These problems continued to be mainly problems

[5] Cp. G. Pasquali, *Medioevo bizantino*, in 'Civiltà moderna', 1941, p. 289 sqq. For a revision of this judgement cp. now F. Masai, *Pléthon et le platonisme de Mistra*, Paris, 1956, and my *Studi sul platonismo medievale*, Firenze, 1958, pp. 155–219.

of morals, of aesthetics and, at times, of religion; and they always continued to have a human reference. Even in the greatest of the Platonists, like Ficino, Pico and Diacceto, we will seek in vain for an ordered system. We will find instead, again and again, meditations upon man.

Manuel Chrysoloras deserves special mention both as a grammarian and as a translator, and also because he had been the inspiring teacher of Guarini. Similarly, John Argyropulos will live in our memory as he was described by Acciaiuoli, his most faithful disciple. 'By reputation he was a scholar. But in reality he was more: he was a sage, venerable, and in everything worthy of the ancient Greeks.' Argyropulos had indeed provided the stimulus for an investigation of, and commentaries on, the *Nicomachean Ethics*. These commentaries ceased to interpret this work in the narrow terms of social and political problems and of man seen as a political animal. They interpreted the *Nicomachean Ethics* as a final exaltation of the contemplative and separated intellect. And thus the flood-gates were opened and the purest Platonism poured in. In his commentary to the *Nicomachean Ethics*, in which he faithfully explained the teachings of Argyropulos, Acciaiuoli concerned himself especially with the problem of the reconciliation of Plato with Aristotle. This problem was to become a central theme in Ficino's circle and was to occupy people for the whole of the 16th century. It is well known that Argyropulos played a certain part in the controversy between Gemistos Pletho and George of Trebizond about the question as to whether one ought to prefer Platonism or Aristotelianism. This controversy was quite inconclusive, especially as long as it continued to be conducted on the level of gossip, abuse and personal invective. In the end, however, when the noble mind of Cardinal Bessarion entered the field, it yielded a fruitful point. For Bessarion raised it to the level of an essentially theoretical problem. And thus he provided a point of departure for a large part of the highest speculations of the Renaissance.[6]

[6] Cp. A. Della Torre, *Storia dell'Accademia platonica di Firenze*, Firenze, 1902; Pletho, Νόμοι, Alexandre, ed. Paris, 1858; G. Cammelli, *I dotti bizantini e le origini del umanesimo*, I (Crisolora), Firenze, 1941, II (Argiropulo), Firenze, 1943; L. Mohler, *Kardinal Bessarion als Theologe, Humanist und Staatsmann, etc.*, Paderborn 1923 sqq., 3 vols.; B. Kieszkowski, *Studi sul Platonismo del Rinascimento in Italia*, Firenze, 1936. Also, specially on Argyropulos, cp. *Giovinezza di D. Acciaiuoli* and the studies in *Medioevo e Rinascimento*, Bari, 1954.

Pletho had come to Florence in order to participate in the Council. Because of the pressure of urgent contemporary political events, he was deeply concerned to bring about a reconciliation between the Greek and the Roman churches. He wanted to give his Italian friends, who were completely infatuated with Aristotle, some idea of the greatness of Plato. In reality, however, he offered them his own bizarre picture of Plato which was a colourful mixture of Neoplatonism and a reforming prophetism. George of Trebizond, himself a translator of Plato, although an indifferent one, replied by trying to disentangle the ancient philosopher from his modern prophet. Pletho's commanding prophetic attitudes are indeed remarkable. He announced the imminent end of the three great religions, Judaism, Christianity and Islam, and the realisation of the Platonic state constructed according to a conception of the world in which Neoplatonism assumed the role of a ritual and law of life. We have only a few fragments of the *Laws*, for Giorgio Scolario consigned them to the flames. These fragments are nevertheless interesting, for we find in them the dream of a moral, religious and political reformation of mankind. The thinkers of the late 15th century and of the 16th century, down to Campanella, were to pursue this dream. Like Campanella after him, Pletho saw the signs that heralded the new era. And it was for the sake of this new era that Pico della Mirandola and Giordano Bruno, each in his own way, were to fight and to suffer. Apart from this, Pletho was filled with the desire to interpret the ancient legends, myths and visions of poets. In short, he wanted to build up the *poetical theology* which Pico was to promise and which, in a completely different sense, Vico was to furnish in his *Scienza Nuova*.

It is certain that Pletho made as great an impression upon Cosimo de' Medici as Plato had made upon Dionysios. And as a consequence, the tyrant of the Italian Athens was impelled to promote at his court a renaissance of the school of Plato and to invite the son of his physician, the promising young Ficino, to translate and explain Plato.

As far as the delicate question of the superiority of Plato was concerned, Bessarion, in his *In Calumniatorem Platonis*, tried to prove by many subtle arguments that it was after all possible to discover an inner agreement on essential points between the two

greatest philosophers of antiquity. Bessarion was well qualified
for this task, for he was the author of a learned translation of the
Metaphysics and had, at the same time, a deep knowledge of Plato.
He even argued that the time had come for an attempt to be made
to base a Christian apologetic upon the reconciliation of Plato
with Aristotle. It is possible that he was the man who first
suggested to Ficino the road that was to lead to the *docta religio*.

3. The Problem of the Relationship Between Action and Contemplation in Cristoforo Landino

The transformation of thought that corresponded to the new
orientation of life can be traced in one of the most characteristic
works of the second half of the 15th century. Cristoforo Landino,
from Pratovecchio, wrote his *Quaestiones Camaldunenses* in 1475. In
this work Platonism asserted itself in a very lively fashion as a
tendency towards pure contemplation.[7] Already in 1441 the
young Landino had taken part in the poetic contest known as the
certame coronario and had been much admired because of his fine
recitation of *terzine* by Franceso Alberti. Later he became one of
the instructors and counsellors of Ficino who was to mention
him as one of the Platonists. In the *Quaestiones* he praised that
inexpressible something, so characteristic of Platonic inspiration
(*habet nescio quid, quod exprimere nequam*). Thus he had become a
full follower of Neoplatonism. We may be struck, in the Italian
prelude to his lectures on Petrarch, by his eulogies of the vernacular as well as by his enthusiasm for early humanism and for the
points he had culled from Bruni. But in his allegorical commentaries on Virgil and Dante we fully enter that sphere of
poetical theology which was to become so dear to Ficino and
Pico. It was the theology which had already been taught by the
Greek representatives of the Platonic school, who had endeavoured to discover in the poets, especially in the more ancient
ones, a divine revelation, partially hidden by the richness of
images. They had wanted to reach that hidden wisdom towards
which Vico was to direct all his critical powers.

[7] *C. Landini Quaestiones Camaldulenses ad Federicum Urbinatum Principem*, Florentiae,
1480?

In the last two books of the *Quaestiones Camaldulenses*, Landino attempted to discover in the *Aeneid* the ideal history of the human soul and a glorification of the contemplative life. For this was indeed the central problem of his whole work; and, as he sensed, it was a very decisive problem. Its solution would shed light upon the orientation of a whole civilisation. Salutati, though he had admitted, in keeping with medieval tradition, that contemplation is to be rated more highly than action, had projected the beatific vision into heaven. On earth, he had insisted, man is destined for action. But Landino returned quite decisively to the primacy of knowledge and of the contemplative life. Even so he justified contemplation as a necessary basis of action. Like Bruni, he took Cicero for his starting point. But Landino argued that the greatest benefit mankind derived from Cicero did not come from the latter's battle against Catilina or Anthony. For these achievements had made no more than a temporary contribution to the welfare of his fellow-citizens. Much the greater benefit was derived, instead, from Cicero's abandonment of politics. He was of most use when, 'far away from politics, he was entirely concerned with the greatest problems... fixed his eyes on universal reality and tried to determine the goal of man's life.' He was of infinite use to society when he wrote in one of his political treatises a sentence that was to become immortal and that is valid for every human being at all times. It is true that through his prudent action he managed to cope with dangers that threatened at the moment. But the thoughts he expressed in his books are relevant to all ages and we owe to them 'prescriptions for an honest and happy existence not only of his contemporaries but also for those who lived after him. The works of those who did not lead an active life have shown men the road from barbarism and ignorance to gentleness and humaneness.... In conclusion, one can see that those who precipitate themselves into an active life may well be useful; but only in the present and then only for a short span. But those who unveil the mysterious nature of things are perpetually useful. Deeds die with men. But thoughts vanquish time. They are immortal and lead to eternity'. If, in an ideal society, we were to ask the several members which position they would like to have assigned to themselves, 'the sage would reply to the question as to which special service he would like to

H

render to the community, that he would like to be one of those whose purpose it is not to have any one special practical activity but to be completely immersed in the investigation of the last things and to say in his writings what, by nature, is honest and useful'. In such a case he should not be rejected as a man useless and harmful to the community. On the contrary, he ought to be a living example to all men. 'Can anyone maintain that such a man is of no use to his city? Nobody will be able to carry out his task without turning to the philosopher for advice'.

It is obvious that Plato was at the root of Landino's trans-valuation; and, more precisely, Plato's *Republic* and Plato's conception of a wise ruler. At the same time, there is the influence of the view, expressed in the *Nicomachean Ethics*, that theoretical contemplation has a practical value and that the former is therefore the highest pursuit for man. And finally there is the influence of the idea that cultural education has a human and hence social value. Man is a man and a citizen because he possesses culture.

In spite of this, the efforts to bring about a connection between knowledge and action—a connection for which already the earliest humanists had pleaded—were condemned to failure. This failure was due to the insistence upon a divorce of action from contemplation. The purely contemplative man, who was held up as an ideal type and a living example, was a man who did not want to descend into the cave in order to suffer. And thus he had more in common with a scholarly monk than with the Socrates who had fought at Potidea and who had been the educator of Athens.

Landino admitted explicitly that in rejecting the view that the passivity of the best men would leave the state at the mercy of the worst men he had gone beyond the views of the writers of the earlier generation. He believed, with Aristotle, that human development reaches its greatest heights through knowledge. But he failed to notice that that 'earthly god' of whom he was dreaming and who, through his contemplation of the heavens, was to be an example to all other men, was not likely to be worshipped as a god. On the contrary, the ignorant multitude was more likely to kill him should he ever descend into that famous cave. Plato had placed the wise at the head of a miraculous state in which, by the will of the gods, the wise were the rulers and the rulers the wise. These rulers were supposed to have both the means and the power to guide the others. But not even they could avoid descending into the cave and risking their lives. In a very facile way Landino simply assumed that fools would want to be guided and that it would be more pleasurable to be governed than to govern. Anyway, 'even if it is admitted that most people do not desire to be forcibly improved, the wise man will simply close in upon himself and help the rest of mankind in some other way'. Thus we find that Rinuccini's approval of a flight from the world and his willing renunciation of the ideal of full *humanitas*, led, in this case, to the justification of a monkish and solitary existence the educational value of which was postulated, but not demonstrated. Accordingly, with Guarini, the educative power of *litterae* descended from the heights of Plato's Republic to the depths of Rome; and the citizens of the heavenly Jerusalem were struggling amongst the citizens of an earthly Babylon. Their knowledge, though firmly rooted in the contemplation of God, was well adjusted to earthly conditions. Landino, who was well able to emphasise the political value of culture, weakened the latter by relegating it to a literary republic.

It was no accident that the expression *politia litterarum* had meant, at the beginning of the fifteenth century, not an ideal city of wise men but a form of *humana disciplina*, i.e. a complete formation of every man as a whole. Eventually there was to be a real crisis in the civilisation and the life of the Renaissance. This crisis originated at the moment at which the accomplishments of the Renaissance *appeared* to gain human universality but were losing in reality their fullness, for they were becoming alienated from the society in which they had grown. This crisis led to the shift in the meaning of 'literary republic' (*politia litterarum*), and this new meaning was destined to come into its own during the seventeenth century. Salutati, paraphrasing St. Augustine, had emphasised the complete fusion, on earth, of the city of God with the city of man. For the soul always appears in a body and an idea, provided it is a serious one, is always engaged in an *earthly* struggle. Landino, on the other hand, postulated the notion of a wisdom outside human history and free of all temporal or spatial bonds. Thus he began to move in the orbit of Ficino who was the greatest repre-

---

[8] *C. Landini De Vera Nobilitate*, ms. 433 Bibl. Corsini (36, E, 5) fol. 36–7.

sentative of that *pia philosophia*, a 'philosophical peace', which unites all spirits in a super-essential unity that leads towards the abyss of mystical darkness.

But Landino did not always move in the orbit of the Academy which had re-emerged in Careggi. His dialogues *De Nobilitate Animae*, dedicated approximately in 1472 to Ercole d'Este, were in all significant points a reflection of Ficino's views. But in his *De Vera Nobilitate*, in which he described a banquet that took place after Cosimo's death, he treated a subject that had been of great interest to the earlier humanists—aristocracy. He gave a new lease of life to this subject by discussing the problem of an aristocracy that was not due to birth but to deeds. He especially contrasted the Venetian nobility, who owed their pre-eminence to action, with the Neapolitan nobility, whom he considered to be on the point of losing the last semblance of a right to their investiture by their undignified obsequiousness to a king and their utterly vain pride. In plain opposition, Landino even praised commerce and the money acquired by commerce, although he continued to attack usury. 'Liberal commerce . . . advances both public and private splendour, leads many towards wealth and helps the people to fight hunger and cold through their own work. Thus it substitutes industry for inertia.' Commercial entrepreneurs, he concluded, deserve well of the human race and are worthy to be considered almost divine benefactors.[8]

In spite of all this, even his *De Nobilitate* contains an enthuasiastic praise of Ficino, of Ficino's *Docta Religio* and his deep interest in metaphysical and religious problems.

4. MARSILIO FICINO AND THE *Docta Religio*

There is a group of Ficino's writings, more properly described as youthful notes and recently edited by P. O. Kristeller, which are proof of his connections with traditional scholasticism. As late as 1454 and 1455 he was still moving in the circle of a purely technical and scholastic Aristotelianism.[9] 'Moral' humanism, the

[9] P. O. Kristeller, 'The Scholastic Background of Marsilio Ficino', *Traditio*, 1944, II, pp. 257 sq. *Ibid.*, pp. 274–316 there is published an early *Summa Philosophiae* from a Morenian ms. of the Riccardiana Library of Florence (Palagi, 199). Kristeller has given us another noteworthy letter-treatise by Ficino in *Rinascimento*, I, 1950;

development of which we have followed so far, was completely
foreign to him and had not even aroused in him a polemical
attitude towards it. Later on, in the *proemium* to his Latin edition
of Plotinus, addressed to Lorenzo de' Medici, he attributed his
conversion to Platonism to the combined influences of Pletho
and of Cosimo de' Medici. Pletho had suggested to Cosimo to
resurrect the ancient Academy in Florence. A few years later,
Cosimo had charged the young son of his physician, Marsilio
Ficino, with the translation of the whole of Plato, of the Platonists, and particularly of the Hermetic writings. When the translation of Plato was completed, by a mysterious infusion (*nescio
quomodo*), the soul of Cosimo had inspired the young Prince of
Mirandola to prevail upon Ficino to translate the *Enneads* and the
Neoplatonists.[10]

In all probability, Ficino's early Aristotelianism[11] had been
determined by the teaching of Niccolò Tignosi da Foligno.
Niccolò Tignosi da Foligno was an orthodox Peripatetic and an
opponent of Argyropulos' Platonic speculations. But eventually
the connections with Cosimo and the influence of Landino guided
Ficino's interests towards Plato. And in 1456 Landino persuaded
him to compose the four books of the *Institutiones Platonicae* from
Latin sources.[12]

During the years 1456 and 1457 Ficino was occupied with
commentaries on Lucretius. But the few fragments of this work
that have come down to us—the original seems to have been
rather short—are anything but revealing. There are more telling
traces of his sympathy for Lucretius and for Epicureanism in the

pp. 35–42. There is some precise information on Ficino's development in an anonymous *Life*—perhaps the work of Caponsacchi, contained in Palat. 488, Nat. Library,
Florence. It was not known to Della Torre. Kristeller's researches can now also be
found in the collection of studies cited above.

---

[10] *Ficini Opera*, Basileae, 1576, II, 1537–38.

[11] On Tignosi cp. Thorndike, *Science and Thought in the Fifteenth Century*, New
York, 1929, p. 161, 308 sq. Perhaps one ought to see Tignosi's position and the
whole of Florentine Aristotelianism in a different light and thus also change one's
perspective in regard to Ficino. For Tignosi see esp. his *opusculum* in defence of his
own commentaries (National Library, Florence, Conv. C, 8, 1800) Cp. also my *Testi
minori sull'anima nella cultura del Quattrocento in Toscana*, 'Arch. di filosofia', 1951, pp.
1–36.

[12] On the lost *Institutiones*, cp. *Opera*, I. 929 (Kristeller, *Supplementum Ficinianum*,
Florentiae, 1937, I, CLXIII–IV). On the *Commentariola*, *Opera*, I, 933 (*Supplementum*,
I, CLXIII; II, 81). The *De Voluptate ad Antonium Canisianum* in *Opera*, I, 986 sqq.

treatise entitled *De Voluptate* which he wrote as a young man and which was completed towards the end of December 1457. Ficino himself regarded this work as a doxographical compilation rather than as a personal work. In spite of this fact, it is not an insignificant piece; for its centre of gravity is a eulogy of a *voluptas* conceived as an adhesion of the will and a perfect assent of the mind to an ideal object, i.e. to the truth which is appropriate to it and with which it is familiar. The greatest pleasure is therefore to be had when the mind is inherent in its object. Even if it is true, as we read in the Platonic commentaries, that *voluptas* is a form of servitude, this noble pleasure is a real good, for it is a servitude of the soul to an absolutely and intrinsically valuable object. It is a servitude that amounts to perfect freedom; for it is not a passion, but the perfection of an act.[13] By this argument, Ficino was able to rediscover the religious elements in Lucretius; and his idea of *voluptas*, divested of all sensuousness, became the sign of a peace attained through perfect communion with God.

Ficino's first clear expression of an opinion on religion, which was the problem that was to fascinate him most, is to be found in his dedicatory epistle to Cosimo, attached to his translation of Hermes Trismegistos. This translation was completed in 1463 and published in 1471. In this epistle he put forward the thesis which was to recur time and again in all his writings. It was the thesis of the eternal revelation of the Word, of the *Logos*, of a *pia philosophia*. The *pia philosophia* was handed down from the most ancient poets and the Bible, taken up by Pythagoras and Plato and deepened by Plotinus as well as by the writings attributed to Dionysius the Areopagite. In this sense Platonic theology is an exemplary type of *docta religio*. It is a knowledge of one's self through knowledge of God, and *vice versa*, a knowledge of God through a knowledge of one's self.[14]

Influenced by Ficino, the Hermetic poet and philosopher Ludovico Lazzarelli was to explain that the highest, paradisaical felicity, which is the goal of our existence, consists entirely in the self-knowledge that is knowledge of God. More correctly, it is to be found in the knowledge of the Logos that is to be re-dis-

[13] Cp. the commentary *In Convivium Platonis de Amore*, *Opera*, II, 1320 sqq. Cp. also the edition by R. Marcel, Paris, 1956.
[14] *Opera*, II, 1836.

covered in our own selves. It consists in the conversion of every one of our desires from the outside to the inside, in order that we may obtain the quietness in the innermost life of the Word that lives inside our own Self. This achievement is the very process illuminated by Ficino. We cannot grasp the truth with the means at our disposal. The human mind is an eye which in order to see needs a special light, just as in order to see the sun it needs the light of the sun. But the divine sunlight (the Logos) is not revealed unless our mind turns towards it, just as the sun illuminates only that part of the moon that is turned towards it. But such a conversion of the mind is possible only if the mind has freed itself of the illusions caused by the senses and of the mists created by phantasy.[15]

According to Ficino, this liberation is a conversion towards God. It is accomplished with the help of Platonic theology because that theology has succeeded in discovering, under the mists of the poetic imagination in which religious revelation is clothed, the deep meaning of truth. The Peripatetic philosophers are mistaken in their rejection of religion as an old wife's tale. For they recognise only the outward appearance of religion. Similarly, the poets are wrong in always trying to force every metaphysical truth into an image.

In his preface to Plotinus, Ficino explained the motives of his twofold attack with the greatest precision. He argued that philosophy, in the technical sense, had now come to mean no more than Peripatetic philosophy, divided into two opposing schools. There are the followers of Alexander of Aphrodisia on one side; and the Averroists, on the other. Both schools are agreed in their determination to destroy religion. Apart from this, both poets and writers in general are quite incapable of understanding the doctrines put forward by the ancients under the guise of poetry. 'It was the custom of the ancient theologians to clothe the divine mysteries in mathematical symbols and poetic images, lest they be exhibited defencelessly to the gaze of the vulgar'. Ficino propounded his own *docta religio* in opposition to the naturalism of the Aristotelians and the aestheticism of the poets —one might almost say, against the philosophy of the philo-

---

[15] L. Lazzarelli, *Crater Hermetis*, Parisiis, 1505. Cp. M. Brini, 'Archivio di Filosofia', 1955, *Testi umanistici su l'ermetismo*, pp. 23–77.

sophers and the poetry of the poets. His own *docta religio* is nothing more and nothing less than a *pia philosophia*.[16]

Ficino stressed that in our age it was no longer possible for faith to be founded upon miracles. People were no longer prepared to accept miraculous stories at their face value. But Peripatetic philosophy—like exclusively literary criticism—regards religious monuments in general and the Bible as well as ancient theological poetry in particular, as fables. That is to say, as pure phantasy, opposed to reality: *aniles fabellae*. Ficino thus confronted the problem as to the meaning of poetry, and he provided a solution which remained, on the whole, unchanged until Vico. The question was: what is the relationship between a philosophical conception of reality, a total view of life and the images presented in poetry? During the 16th century, the Peripatetics asked the same kind of question when they inquired as to the nature of the things of which art was said to be an imitation.

Under the pressure of strong religious considerations, Ficino began, almost without noticing it, with the assumption that there are two kinds of men. On one side there are the simple and the ignorant, the men who have not been initiated into the sacred mysteries. On the other side, there are those who comprehend the spirit under the letter. These are the philosophers. The Gnostics had been fond of this distinction. It also had been maintained by Averroes. The distinction was based upon the view that all images, like nature herself, hide a soul, a meaning. According to this view it is a pernicious error to content oneself with an image of the phantasy or to confine oneself to a mere physical contemplation of nature, without penetrating to the deeper spiritual layers, i.e., the intentions of the artist. It does not matter whether the artist is human or divine, for ultimately the only artist is the Logos. The error consists essentially in the attempt to separate the surface from the content and to consider it in isolation. There is a similarity between the intuitively apprehended external appearance and the inner movement from which it springs. It is therefore necessary to fathom the source of the appearance in order to understand the appearance. But this source is none other than the light and the wisdom of God. On the other hand, once we have reached the Word, we can immerse

---

[16] *Ficini Opera*, II, 1537.

ourselves in a timeless truth, in that luminousness of which Plato
spoke and which stands beyond discourse and lies outside all
distinctions, because it is the source and root of everything. The
followers of *pia philosophia* derive their inspiration from that
source; for that philosophy has not detached the external symbol,
be it word, measure or nature, from the source of its life: 'factum
est ut pia quaedam philosophia quondam et apud Persas sub
Zoroastre, et apud Aegyptios sub Mercurio nasceretur, utrobique
sibimet consona, nutriretur deinde apud Traces sub Orpheo atque
Aglaophemo, adolesceret quoque mox sub Pythagora apud
Graecos et Italos, tandem vero a divo Platone consummaretur
Athenis'.

Poetry, therefore, is nothing but a veil which possesses the
same expressive force as numbers and symbols, which are means
both for hiding and for translating the divine mysteries. But
underneath the various languages—the natural reality of the
physicists, the mathematical symbols, the poetic images—there
stands revealed a single truth and a single life. It was the singular
merit of Plotinus to have uncovered the deep connection between
the one single root and all those many manifestations. With this
discovery he laid the foundation for a genuine theology. It is
therefore the task of the newer theology to translate Plotinus
and to explain him. Thus the role which Ficino assigned to
Plotinus can only be compared to the role which the physicists of
late scholasticism had assigned to Aristotle.

At the same time, there is also a more subtle argument in
Ficino. Unity, beyond the manifold sensuous manifestations, can
reveal itself only in one single truth. This single truth can assume
many different forms but must essentially and always remain the
same because it is eternally present. If one goes to the heart of the
matter, and this is exactly what the *pia philosophia* intends to do,
one grasps the single truth that lies beyond the many forms in
which it appears. In this way, one can enter into the Logos, the
single soul, and pass beyond all religious revelations, beyond the
songs of the poets, beyond the beauties of nature and beyond all
mathematical harmonies. This single Logos speaks in us; and—
as Lazzarelli, following Plato, was to exclaim in somewhat
extravagant language—we sense it in other souls, in all things, and
in the infinite, for everything is a revelation of God.

Pia philosophia is identical with *docta religio*, the true religion of
the Logos which is the only true religion of Christ. The knowledge of this solidarity of the whole with God signifies both an
eternal radiation of light and an eternal reflection of light. These
reflections and radiations form a circle suffused by love. 'One
cannot see the sun without sun and cannot hear the air without
air; but the eye filled with light can see the light and the sun, and
the ear filled with air can hear the vibrations of the air; even so
it is impossible to recognise God without knowing God already.
But the soul that is filled with God not only ascends to God but
also, being illuminated by the divine light, can recognise God;
and, set ablaze by the divine flame, thirsts for God. For the soul
cannot ascend to Him Who is infinitely high above it unless it is
empowered to do so by the strength of Him Who is above it and
Who is infinite. Thus the soul becomes the divine seal.'[17]

If the question is put in this way, there exists not only a 'deep
relationship . . . between wisdom and religion', but a complete
identity. To break the 'connection between Pallas and Themis'
is to allow superstition and heresy to flourish, for the ignorant,
'like swine', would abuse 'the pearls of religion'. And the philosophers would then become atheists. For if it is heresy to detach
the natural world from its divine roots, one must 'call the petty
cares of the ignorant superstition rather than religion'. *Docta
religio* is therefore genuine philosophy. It consists of a full coincidence of the intellect (wisdom) and the will (priesthood). If one
had asked Ficino to whom he would assign ideal priority, he
would have pointed to the philosopher. For it is 'reasonable to
assume that the men who first used their own reason to discover
divine things or managed to attain to them through God, were
also the first to worship divine things with their will and to teach
their fellow-men the right way to conduct such worship.'[18]

To those who wish to reach truth, the truthfulness of Christianity will reveal itself. For Christianity, provided it is understood
correctly, comprehends in itself and perfects the whole of human
knowledge.

[17] *Della Christiana Religione*, II.
[18] *Della Christiana Religione*, Proemium II.

5. Platonic Theology

It follows from the above premisses that the unchanging, eternal truth expressed symbolically by primitive, poetical theologies, revealed by Christ, and philosophically established by Plato and Plotinus, concerns the unity of the world and the indivisibility of the things that are revealed. Ficino decided to vindicate the truth that everything that exists converges into a unity, against the heretical opinions about the dividedness and about the autonomy of the material world.

The road he chose led through two stages. In the first stage he demonstrated that all divine revelations converge into one single uninterrupted tradition (the *pia philosophia*). The latter, however, does not represent a single, straight historical development, but is a timeless coincidence within the one truth that lives eternally. The second stage is represented by the conception of a single reality which is organised in such a way that only he who reads it off the face of God may claim to know it.

In both stages the road leads from the sensuous image to the inner light. There is an ascent, as it were, from symbol to inwardness; from the expression to the soul. In each case the road leads from what is manifest to the thing that is manifested. In Ficino's view, poetry loses its intrinsic value, for it becomes solely an incarnation of the truth, a sensuous image of the One. But at the same time it is clear that the whole of cosmic reality is seen as a poem by God. It is His language, His sensuous expression, His poetry, the truth of which is not contained in a concept but in the living God Himself and in the human spirit which, given wings by love, becomes one with eternal life.

> *Ut sole attrahitur vapor,*
> *Ut magnes calybem trahit,*
> *Sic flammis rapiar tuis.*
> *Te coniunge michi, Pater;*
> *Mox ad te penitus trahar*
> *Unumque efficiar simul.*[19]

Platonic theology corresponds to poetical theology. The latter is the discovery of a single truth hidden in the depths of the

[19] *Crater Hermetis, loc. cit.*

manifold which is manifest. The former is the systematic explanation of the truth of things arrived at through a re-thinking of the Platonic tradition. For in that tradition the divine is unfolded and has developed itself. But the essence of Ficino's doctrine, as expressed in his most important works, is the conception of the One as the arch-source, expressed in a multiplicity of appearances intuited directly, 'even as all the separate numbers are which, in their original unity, are one single thing. Similarly, different lines that meet in one single centre are, in that centre, one single and individual thing.'[20]

Knowledge, therefore, is an ascent to God. It implies that every appearance of reality is conceived as a moment, a station, a step in the chain of Being. In terms of the ancient, traditional image, to know meant to ascend *via* the radius towards the centre of the circle; or to grasp the inadequacy of things in order to form a notion of the divine adequacy. Each link in the chain of Being is a 'mirror' of God. And yet, each link or each step, if considered accurately, is also imperfect and thus points towards something that is higher and more perfect. Thus all things point towards us men; and men point towards God. 'We ought to get to know things in order to know ourselves. And we ought to know ourselves in order to know God... Why did God construct an order in which we can know ourselves if not in order to understand through self-knowledge that everything good we have is derived wholly from Him?'[21]

The notion that reality is One and the notion that reality is a series of steps, are closely linked in Ficino's thought. They form the foundation of the conception that these various moments are symbols, appearances and *mirrors* of divinity. On the other hand, the single steps in the series of things (*series, ordo rerum*) sort themselves out in terms of a gradual convergence into a full Oneness. They start with pure corporeality in the form of quantity. And then they progress through quality, the souls and the angels, towards God. Thus they converge towards Oneness, which fact alone explains the structure of the world. The world is articulated by a musical rhythm pulsating as *recessum* and *accessum*. 'Even as numerical Oneness is contained in all numbers;

[20] *Ficini Orphica Comparatio Solis ad Deum (Opera*, I, p. 825 sqq.)
[21] *Ficini Ep. lib.* VI (*Opera*, I, 812–13).

and as the point is present in all lines, the divine Oneness, though remaining indivisible, is present in all bodies and minds and connects and ties up all parts of the universe. For this very reason all things converge, mutually adequate to one another, towards one single goal. For they are guided by one single principle. And as one can derive all bodies from one single highest body which moves them all, one can reduce all spirits to one single high spirit which embraces them all, animates the bodies and guides them by means of subject spirits.'[22]

Ficino attributed a special significance to the concept of the mediator, of the μεταξύ; a concept very characteristic of Platonism. This concept belongs to all theories based upon a contemplation of the dynamic Oneness of the world. The return from the multiplicity of beings to the Oneness of Being has always been explained with the help of a mediator. Ficino once remarked that one ought to avoid three errors in one's conception of the universe. The first error is the idea that there is an eternally recurring circularity, through which everything becomes like everything else, and on the basis of which no distinctions other than illusory ones can be possible. The second error consists in the idea that there are several distinct principles of reality. The third error consists in the assumption that there is an infinite process without beginning and without goal.

One can see that Ficino, by exposing the first error, intended to attack the idea of circularity as capable of exhausting the whole of the highest Oneness. On the contrary, he seems to be arguing, the idea of circularity is above the process of becoming—a process which has its beginning in the circle and ends in it. The soul is similar to God and this means that it is a unifying agent, but one that has not itself reached unity. The soul has indeed the task of connecting and of making restitution. Given that God exists in the other world, the soul is the only agent capable of participating in both of the extreme poles of reality. For the soul can connect that which is most similar to God, the pure, angel-like spirit, with that which is farthest away from God, elemental matter. As far as time is concerned, Ficino declared: 'God is above eternity. Angels are entirely in eternity, for their essence and their efficacy endures and the condition of eternity is their proper condition.

---

[22] *Ficini Argumentum in Platonicam Theologiam.*

The soul finds itself partly in eternity and partly in time. For its essence remains always the same without change, without increase and without decrease. But its operation . . . takes place in time. The body is entirely subject to time for its substance changes and its efficacy is such that it consumes time'.[23] Since God is outside the *ordo rerum*, even though He is the meaning of that *ordo*, only a being which is both perfect and not perfect and thus participates in both extremes, is capable of connecting the two extremes. In this way the soul can become the symbol of transcendental Oneness. The connection it brings about is continuously efficacious, albeit never complete.

In this context, Ficino always concerns himself with four themes: light, beauty, love and the soul. These things never exclude one another but depend on one another reciprocally, even though in his various works one may be more emphasised than another. Ontologically speaking, reality is light, a ballet of lights. Reality reaches from the invisible light of God to the darkness of matter in which for all practical purposes light is extinguished. But the God Who is *Deus Lux, abyssus luminum* is as such also *fons formarum*, for light, as the stuff of the universe, transforms itself into something that makes the universe visible and into universal beauty. 'I will reply to you that you are ignorant if you think that beauty is something other than light'. Now that which translates itself visually and intellectually into symbols of light, expresses itself for all practical purposes in terms of warmth and of love. 'For since warmth comes from light there is an enormous warmth . . . which we will experience as ardour of the will rather than as an intellectual illumination.'[24]

Thus the soul, like the whole of reality, translates both its knowledge and its capacity of being known, into terms of light. But it expresses its deepest essence in terms of love and warmth. The more light is light, the more unreachable it is; just as love is the more invincible, the higher it is. 'The more God transcends us through the light of His intellect, the more He penetrates us with the ardour of His will. For there is nothing more highly above us than God; and nothing more deeply within us. The more glaring His light, the more incomprehensible it is to the

[23] Ficino, *Sopra lo Amore*, Rensi ed., Lanciano, 1914, p. 121.
[24] *Ficini Opera*, I, 706–16; *De Sole et Lumine*, I, 965 sqq.

intellect. But the mightier its heat, the more certain the will.'
Our desire for knowledge cannot be fulfilled if it is directed
towards the understanding of an infinitely higher reality. It
cannot conquer it, for such a conquest would amount to an
incarceration of the infinite in circumscribed limits. Every
attempt to confine God within things is condemned to failure.
But if we cease to be captivated by the world's external facets and
concentrate ourselves upon ourselves, we may discover our
Selves and all other things in God through love. And then,
instead of being closed up, we will become totally open: 'In
such a case it will become apparent that first of all it was God
Whom we loved in all things in order that we might later be
able to love the things that are in Him. We worship the things
in God mainly in order to be able to grasp our Selves. And
loving God, we have loved our own Selves.'

We are dealing here with a radical conversion (*circuitus*,
restitutio). By such a conversion it becomes possible to rediscover,
beyond the confines of this world, the dynamic processes of the
universe. One starts from the visible, external facts, turns away
from the things that are known and caught within the confines of
actuality and finally ascends to the sources themselves. Or, more
correctly: we dive into the divine stream and conquer the truth
by allowing ourselves to be conquered. 'The light of God, since
it goes far beyond the limits of human reason cannot be understood in any way by man's natural intelligence. But it is loved;
and loved, it is fused into us by grace. It is truly thus: the soul,
once it is afire with love, shines more splendidly, penetrates more
deeply and enjoys in greater beatitude, the more it burns. For
this reason Plato used to say that one ought not to point at the
light of God with the finger of reason, but that one ought to
accept it in the clear serenity of a devout life.'

It is the task of beauty to cause this conversion. In this crisis
the visible clarity of the light lights the fire of love and thus a
status is turned into a *circuitus*. Ficino said that 'eye ache' was the
beginning of love. For in such a case the object we are contem-
plating passes from passivity to activity. It begins, in accordance
with nature, to respond to our action by an action of its own.
And this 'amounts to a certain attraction between the two on
account of the similarity of their natures'. This is the case, for

instance, when the lover's eye stares at the beloved and remains captivated, or when the hunter becomes the prey. For love causes us to turn from active, or at least apparently active, beings into passive ones, into humble and devout servants. 'The sun attracts leaves and flowers. The moon moves the waters and Mars the winds . . . similarly, each of us is drawn along by his own desire'. Our salvation, therefore, consists in letting ourselves be overcome by Him Who is true beauty and highest beauty. We will find our own Selves once we have become His totally devoted servants.

Passion, provided it results from suffering the effects of the good, is man's true education. For such passion draws (*e-ducit*) man's divine essence out. If the beloved object is good, it will draw the lover to itself and thus towards the good. In this way the lover becomes the passive victim of the beloved and everything that is good in the lover is brought out. This, according to Ficino, is the educative purpose of Socratic love. For Socrates, the wise and good Socrates, was 'loved more by the youths than he loved any of them'. He was a mid-wife because he educated, i.e. drew out. And he accomplished it in a 'gay' manner because he allowed himself to be loved. 'The city does not consist of stones but of men. It is necessary to tend men like trees while they are young and to guide them to bear fruit. One cannot improve them by laws. We cannot all be a Solon or a Lycurgus. Few men have the authority to make new laws; and fewer obey the laws that have been made.' The only fruitful method is the method of Socrates. Socrates loved God and became His devout servant. Inspired by the love of his fatherland 'he did not become a lover of young men but aroused *their* love instead'. By this method he educated them to be good, to draw goodness out. He educated them, by his mediation, to become servants of God through the gaiety of love. He behaved like that genuine Love which we believe we are seeking: all along, it is Love that seeks *us* and conquers *us*. Love, as Plato said, has wings; for it gives wings and helps us to fly.[25]

Ficino's theology resolved itself in terms of poetry, beauty and love.

[25] Ficino, *Sopra lo Amore*, p. 153 (cap. XVI).

6. Pico della Mirandola and the Attack on Rhetoric

Ficino's philosophical development appears to have taken place along a straight line. In the first instance it was conditioned by a youthful but not too inhibiting Peripatetic scholasticism. After that it came to be orientated, by Lucretian considerations, towards humanism. A little later there was a peaceful parting of the ways and a development towards constant fidelity to Plato. The stages of Pico's philosophical development were much more complex. They bear witness to incessant and troubled labours and to an endeavour to satisfy a curiosity which vacillated between the problems of nature and the relations of man to God. Pico had been educated in the cultural atmosphere of Paduan Aristotelianism, in the school of Vernia. But he soon enlarged his horizon by taking in both Arabic and Hebrew Peripatetic philosophy, for he was in touch with Elia del Medigo, a very erudite Jew, a scholarly student and translator of Averroes. Elia del Medigo was deeply aware of the conflict between the demands of his faith and his inclination towards Aristotle and his commentator. Elia believed that it was possible to avoid the conflict either by a brutal application of the doctrine of 'double truth' or by stressing those mystical themes that had trickled from Neoplatonism into Averroism. There was, for instance, the idea that felicity is something that arises at the conjunction, at the moment of contemplative encounter, of the human and the divine. In this way an agreement between Elia and Vernia was possible; and Pico's religious demands could be accommodated.[26] Pico himself was by no means insensitive to the charms of literary humanism. But he remained too subtle a connoisseur of scholasticism and Peripatetic philosophy ever to be led astray by the all too easy and ambiguous solutions of a rhetoric which, by the end of the 15th century, had divested itself of all human reality. The *litterae* which had initially endeavoured to be an expression of a complete

---

[26] The Latin opuscoli of Elia del Medigo are in the appendices of the Venetian editions of the *Fisica* of Jean of Jandun (e.g., Venetiis 1546). The long letter to Pico (Paris, Bibl. Nat., lat. 6508, fol. 71–82) in G. Pico D. M., *De Hominis Dignitate*, etc., Firenze, 1942, pp. 67–72. The letter of Barbaro to Elia, in *Epistulae* of B., *ed. cir.*, I, 87–90. On the cabbalists ('Li libri di Mitridate') see the almost unknown letter by Pico of 1489 (Paris, B.N., Autogr. Rotschild, no. 252).

I

humanitas appeared diluted to the point of an empty formalism, devoid of any interest in truth and life. In 1485, in a letter addressed to Ermolao Barbaro, Pico gave a clear indication of how conscious he was of this separation. The letter was entitled *De Genere Dicendi Philosophorum* and is a veritable manifesto against that degeneration of rhetoric which had led to the worst kind of nominalism of the *calculatores* of Oxford. Pico argued that the new philology, which had emerged as a new philosophy in that it had been a critical search for human concreteness, had by now degenerated into a *scientia nominum* and was opposed to a *scientia rerum*. It had petered out into a cult of empty forms which was bound to lead to the veiled kind of scepticism that was apparent in the present moral crisis.[27]

A careful study of Barbaro—instructive in more ways than one—reveals how he intended to combine philosophy with rhetoric. He began his dedication of his translation of Themistius to Sixtus IV in 1480, with a praise of *litterae*. He explained that *litterae* alone distinguished men from beasts; that he had not provided a literal translation *sed libere et translationibus et figuris et tropis usi sumus ad morem romanum*. He wanted his translation to bear witness to a living Latinity, a sort of lively competition with Themistius himself. He contrasted the alleged spirit of the Latin language with the spirit of the author and compared his own thoughts and requirements with those of Themistius. He considered that translation was not mere slavish fidelity but a sort of sporting test. Barbaro attacked his predecessors sharply for having prostituted texts in a barbarous manner to their own requirements. But he himself did much the same. And while it is true that he did not use Cicero in order to present Aristotle, he did not hesitate to make use of Aristotle in order to propagate his own Ciceronianism.[28]

This is the point which Pico took up. He castigated the far too frequent distortions of the relationship between *res* and *verba*. In

[27] For Pico's letter, see *Filosofi italiani del' 400*, pp. 428–45. Barbaro's letters are in Branca ed., *op. cit.*, I, 84, 100, 101 sq. An interesting document, hitherto unnoticed, on the relations between Pico and contemporary scientists is to be found among the writings of the physicist and physician Bernardo Torni, Professor in Pisa between 1476 and 1496 (ms. Ricc. 930, fol. 26 r–31 r). There is an important contribution to the relations between E. Barbaro and the logicians in C. Dionisotti, *Ermolao Barbaro e la fortuna di Suiseth*, Miscellanea Nardi, pp. 219–53.

[28] Barbaro, *Epistol.*, I, p. 8 sqq., 12, 14, 96.

this way he started a controversy which was to continue, basically without changes, until well into the seventeenth century. One of Pico's beautiful letters is an eloquent defence of pure thought and of the dignity of research. 'We have become famous, Ermolao, and therefore we will live in the future. True, not in the schools of the grammarians where children are taught, but in the academies of the philosophers and the assemblies of the wise, where one does not discuss the mother of Andromache and the sons of Niobe and similar fatuous matters, but where discussion centres upon the principles of matters human and divine.' This letter is at the same time a denunciation of all literary men who have degenerated into empty grammarianship and who have forgotten the human significance of communication and who have lost, in consequence, their human dignity. We can certainly agree with Pico's description of the thinker as incessantly *anxius*, as never satisfied and never content with easy rhetorical formulations. But we feel that Pico carries his polemics too far and that he goes further than his own premises warrant when he, too, separates wisdom from eloquence. For in his attack on *ornaments* he is almost prompted to separate the word from its root; or, more correctly, to assume that such a separation can be made. Sforza Pallavicino was to give an answer to this question. He took Pico as his starting point, but also made use of Famiano Strada's and Agostino Mascardi's observations on how to write history. In his *Trattato dello stile* Sforza Pallavicino had written: 'It is the task of philosophy to communicate the truth in its plainest form. It is therefore not permissible to distort, by enlargement, her face or, by movement, the eyes of the spectator'.[29] This means that thought should not be separated from the word that is adequate for its expression. One ought, however, to separate the ornament, i.e. degenerate rhetoric, from thought. Pico himself was aware of the deep moral importance of this problem. 'People who do not care for literary form are not civilised. People without philosophy are not human. Eloquence without wisdom can still be useful. But inane eloquence is like a sword in the hands of a fool: it can do nothing except damage.'

[29] Sforza Pallavicino, *Opere*, Milano, 1834, vol. II, p. 586. The orations by Mureto of the middle of the sixteenth century are interesting; and so is especially the seventh oration by Carlo Sigonio, *De Studiis Humanitatis* (Lugduni, 1590, pp. 97–115).

Philosophy, understood as philology, had aimed to draw attention to the spiritual and intimate roots of words. It had tried to grasp words without detaching their inner meaning from them. But rhetoric, completely detached from the world of human feelings, transformed speech into a purely formal game. Such games occasion joy and give power and, in their abstract formality, are a standard unto themselves. But they introduced an ominous divorce of the realm of ideas from the realm of *litterae*—a divorce which turned the philosopher into a dreamer, and the man of letters into a courtly mountebank. Although he was not fully conscious of this, Pico attacked rhetoric as a kind of pseudo-logic and pseudo-poetry. He insisted that there was no such thing as a doctrine of the pure forms of expression; for there were no pure forms of expression into which one simply could pour a philosopher's meditations or a poet's song. He remarked: 'You may object that if my view were correct, one ought to praise statues not on account of their form but on account of the material; or that if Choirilos had chosen the same subject as Homer, or Naevius the same subject as Virgil, they too would have been great poets. But are you not aware of the absurdity of the analogy? I too maintain that the value depends on the forms of expression and not on the content; for a thing is the thing it is because of the form it has. Only, one ought to add that the form of poetry is utterly different from the form of philosophy.' For this very reason it is absurd to clothe Aristotle in a Ciceronian coat. In 1497 a disciple of Ficino and a follower of Piagnoni, Giovanni Nesi, published a work entitled *Oraculum de Novo Saeculo*. In this prophetic tract he glorified the eloquence of Savonarola whom he described as the 'Socrates from Ferrara'. His arguments were based upon the theories of Pico and they went to prove the value of an eloquence which did not consist in the addition of ornaments to plain speech, but in an effective, naked expression of the soul.

It was no accident that the philosopher's demands were connected with the appeals of the Dominican friar of San Marco. For Savonarola's appeal, too, was a moral one. He appealed to seriousness and sincerity in philosophy and condemned *littérateurs*, grammarians and all people interested in words by themselves, detached from their meanings.

7. MAN

In 1487, Pico, the wealthy Lord of Mirandola, summoned a
kind of international assembly of philosophers to Rome. In
order to introduce the public discussion he wrote an oration.
But this *Carmen de Pace* was more like a manifesto or an appeal than
like an inaugural lecture. It had been composed in a moment of
religious enthusiasm. The oration was indeed written while the
author was deeply occupied with the study and the explanation
of Gnostic and Hebrew texts and of cabbalistic mysticism. He
was also engaged in the writing of a treatise on beauty and love,
debating these questions with Ficino. The oration itself was
dominated by two themes. There was, first, a discussion of the
central position of man in the universe; and, secondly, the notion
of the deep and intimate agreement among all sincere manifestations of human thought.[30] The first subject is the one that has
become the more famous one—so much so that eventually the
whole oration took its title from it: *De Hominis Dignitate*. The
theory which Pico advanced is really noteworthy. He argued that
every existing reality has its own *nature* by which its behaviour is
determined. Thus the dog will always behave like a dog; and a
lion, like a lion. Man alone has no nature which determines him
and has no essence to determine his behaviour. Man creates
himself by his own deeds and thus he is father of himself. The
only condition he is subject to is the condition that there is no
condition, i.e. liberty. The compulsion he is subject to is the
compulsion to be free and the compulsion to choose his own
destiny, to build the altar of his own fame with his own hands or
to forge his own chains and convict himself.

Manetti had spoken of man as the creator of the world of art.
Ficino had spoken of the horizon of a multitude of worlds. But
for Pico the human condition consists in not having a condition
and of being a genuine *quis*. Man, therefore, is not a *quid*, but a
cause and a free act. Man is everything because he can be everything: animal, plant, stone—but also angel and 'son of God'.
For this reason he is the image of God and similar to God. He

[30] See the whole oration in *op. cit.*, pp. 102–45. In the meantime I have come
across what was probably the original version of the famous discourse contained
anonymously in Palat. 885 of the Nat. Library of Florence: cp. *Notizie intorno a G.P.*,
'Riv. di storia della filosofia', 1949, fasc. 3).

is cause, freedom, act; in short, the outcome of his own behaviour.

Pico thus pointed at the idea of an existence in which all essence was both gathered and dissolved. This kind of existence had one condition only: free choice. It was bound to lead to the notion that man is a person among persons, and ultimately, a person, vis-à-vis the highest Person. It was also certain to lead to a conception of the superiority of will and love over all abstract knowledge. Hence Pico's originality. Nesi, who almost worshipped Pico, wrote: 'You are the image and likeness of the eternal God . . . the more perfect, the more effectively you represent your own model. You depict it through love rather than through doctrine. His image shines in you more strongly through love than through speculation. God is more pleased with the man who loves Him than with the man who knows Him. But since he loves Him he is loved back.' Pico himself, in a letter to Manuzio, asked why we should, in vain, seek with our reason the things we can reach joyfully in a single moment by love. And Lorenzo de' Medici was to echo this idea in verse: why should we seek to capture God *in* us when, by love, we could 'enlarge' ourselves through Him?

8. THE PEACE OF PHILOSOPHY

The second theme touched upon by Pico in his oration was *peace:* the Pythagorean notion of the concord of all thinking and the Christian notion of redemption from every single manifestation by the *logos*. There is a great antithesis between the philosophies of Plato and Aristotle, of Avicenna and Averroes, of St. Thomas and Duns Scotus. It exemplifies the clash between 'separateness' and unity, between transcendence and immanence, between nature and spirit. Pico sought to overcome this antithesis by insisting on the unity of all human thought. Human thinking, he explained, emphasises now one aspect, now another; now one problem, now another. At first sight these appear to exclude one another. But on second consideration they turn out to evoke one another and to imply one another. This *concord* is postulated, according to Pico, by the unity of truth, the continuity of speculation, the uniqueness of the Lord, the identity of the divine illumination. He discovered single instances of this concord in something that amounted to a critical history of philosophy. Such a critical history, he held, ought to illuminate the magic of concord by explaining the multiplicity of the different attitudes. The concord which thus stands revealed as the result of philosophical thinking is nothing other than one of the appearances of the concord that is also revealed in religious tradition and manifest in the reality of the whole universe.

Pico did not hesitate to appropriate the old idea of a parallelism between nature and Scripture, according to which both were considered as the books of God. They are written in different signs, but have the same course. The cabbala was nothing but a perfected kind of philology with the help of which the genuine meaning of the Bible could be deciphered. Similarly, the natural sciences are an instrument which enables us to grasp the inner meaning of things. In the *Heptaplus* the different worlds, i.e. the different levels of reality, appear as so many worlds that dovetail into one another. They correspond to one another and can be interleaved. They appear as a multiplicity of different perspectives, distinct and separate in themselves, but wound up with one another and conjoined in man; for man participates in all of them. Ficino's concept (or rather, the concept frequently used by Ficino) of man as the meeting-point or nodal point of the universe, is taken up by Pico in the light of his thesis that the human act is free. And hence it is transformed into the idea that all aspects of the universe and all levels of reality converge and are concentrated in human knowledge. This philosophical peace corresponds to a universal world pacification. For, through the efforts of the human mind, the various aspects of reality are woven together in human society. Thus man is an earthly god—not because he is impertinently seeking to arrogate to himself the throne of the true God; but because he is, like God Himself, a pure existence capable of becoming the point at which all other beings meet. Through his knowledge he can participate in them all.

It can be seen that Pico intended to stretch the conception of philology to its utmost limits. In this he has much in common with Campanella, in spite of the fact that the latter was to take up his cudgels against him. Pico took it that philology was a true philosophy; and thus assigned it the task of reading all Scriptures and writings and of understanding them—the divine and sacred ones as well as the natural ones. For even the natural ones he considered to be divine and sacred: God reveals Himself in the water and the sand of the oceans as well as in the stars on high. *Caeli enarrant gloriam Dei.* God is a poet and therefore a creator. We must always trace the author in His works, humbly grasping His spirit. And thus we are in harmony with Him, participating, as it were, in His works.

Since in this connection we are spontaneously reminded of Campanella, it is important to add that Pico's views, like those of Campanella, point to the realm of practical life. Pico was indeed led to demand that the unity of truth and of all thoughts ought to be embodied in a single *ecclesia* which was to comprise the whole of mankind. In the writings of Nesi we find his prophecy: *Mahumetanos ad Christianam fidem vobis adhuc viventibus adsciscendos. Ovile tandem omnium unum, pastorem unum.*[31] This statement dates from the year 1497 and was made at the time of Savonarola's prophecies. But we know that the young Prince of Mirandola had conceived the plan of translating his dreams of a universal peace into practice. Shortly before his premature death, he had indeed decided to become a preacher and reformer. Christianity was to him the authentic and perfect expression of the true faith which alone illuminates man's conscience and which is sealed, with clear signs, upon the whole of the universe. Long before Campanella, Francesco Sansovino was to picture, on the island *Utopia*, the worshippers of the one 'occult and eternal deity'. 'By a miracle' these worshippers had all suddenly been converted to Christianity, as if Christianity were the necessary complement to their own views.[32]

9. THE ATTACK ON ASTROLOGY

Even though it may be possible to connect Pico's enthusiastic love for certain mystical and occult matters with his youthful and rather vague interest in everything that was mysterious, imponderable and primitive, one will have to admit that, in the last analysis,

[31] *Oraculum de Novo Saeculo.* For Nesi see the Zibaldone Magliab. VI, 176 and the orations in the mss. Magliab. XXXV, 211 and Ricc. 2204. Cp. *Desideri di riforma nell'oratoria del Quattrocento*, in 'Belfagor', I, 1948, pp. 1–11.

[32] Francesco Sansovino, *Del governo et amministratione di diversi regni et republiche così antiche come moderne*, Venetia, 1578, c. 197 r and sqq.

both cabbala and the magic are closely related to humanistic 'philo-logy', at any rate in its deeper and more comprehensive meaning. Its deepest meaning was indeed the search for a contact with 'nature', the latter being understood, in a polemical sense, as something that is opposed to the crystallization of a tradition. The matter with which Pico was most deeply concerned was the discovery, on every level of reality and in every perspective, of those directives which he had discovered in man. He imagined that the rhythms which had been grasped in human concepts would eventually reveal themselves as radiating also throughout the whole of the universe.

That this is so, is proved by his final attack on astrological prediction. This attack made it clear that Pico was opposed to any kind of more or less explicit occultism. It also became the occasion of another and clearer attempt to define the relationship between man and nature. For in the meditations on love these relations seemed only too easily submerged and confused. It seemed too much as if the unity of the universe, the meeting point and the circle of love, had swept the concept of man away; for both body and soul had become too enmeshed in the universal process, be it a necessary or a capricious one. True, in these meditations man had been represented as the centre, or even as the horizon. But in so far as he had thus become a passive receptacle, he had become an abbreviated formula, a *microcosm*. Ficino, in exploring these trains of thought, had eventually been obliged to transform the primacy of man into a status that was really completely inferior to that of things. And thus man, the mirror of all things, had become dissolved into the fortuitous processes to which all things were subject. For example: the liver follows the move-ments of the planet Mars and reproduces them and is subject to diseases. Temperament therefore depends on the stars and deter-mines the character of man according to the stars. Only other stars or the miraculous power of animals, stones or herbs, can combat those initial influences. Man may well be a microcosm and a mirror of the universe; but for that very reason he amounts to nothing. For thus he is not only not more than a stone but actually less than a stone. He is not free, but subject to com-pulsion, i.e. to whatever he is mirroring.

Pico's glorification of man is, in the last analysis, nothing but an attack upon the idea of the microcosm, *tritum in scholis*. He wanted to stand the theory that man is the centre of the universe on its head in order to arrive at the other theory that man extends into the universe.

The attack on astrology, however, contained more than this. It comprised in fact a precise conception of a regular, rational and ordered process of nature which excludes, because of its own intrinsic orderliness, any possibility of an irregular influence of something that is less dignified upon something that is more dignified; e.g., of darkness upon light. In the emergence of the forms towards God, the heavens, and, for that matter, the rest of the world of elements, find their place in a sphere that is beyond human consciousness. Nature is order—a manifold but harmoniously regulated unity. Causality, conceived as the rationally intelligible, logically definable link between all things, is the expression of this harmony and this unity. All astrological prediction is based on some kind of determinism; and more precisely upon a determinism which claims that the inner life is dependent not only upon bodily changes but, through the body, upon celestial configurations associated with the images of pagan deities. This determinism, moreover, substitutes for the beautiful and divine harmonies of causality a complex of fictitious and accidental correspondences. Pico does not deny that everything in the universe is physically connected with everything else. It would indeed be impossible to insist on such a denial. But he does deny that the stars occupy a determining and privileged position as if they, and they alone, were powerful enough to condition the vicissitudes of all our lives and, in general, of everything that happens in the sublunar sphere—i.e. human character, the destiny of kingdoms and even the rise and fall of entire systems of religions. With great acumen, Pico spotted in this kind of astrology a more or less disguised revival of ancient astral cults.[33] He felt that the real reason why certain influences were being attributed to Mars and Jupiter was not because an investigation of radiation had in fact proved them as the effective authors of

---

[33] For the texts of Pico, of Savonarola, of Pontano cp. my edition in two vols. of *Disputationes* by Pico, Firenze, 1946-51. On p. 16, there is a facsimile of the original of *De Rebus Caelestibus* by Pontano from Vat. lat. 2839.

such influences, but because the corresponding deities on the pagan Mount Olympus had possessed those qualities. He considered that the alleged effects of the stars had been derived from their names, or, more correctly, from the deities who had lent their names to the stars in question, rather than from the stars themselves.

Savonarola was, in questions of morals and religion, extremely sensitive. He saw very clearly that the attack on astrology had an essentially apologetic function. In this sense he developed his own activity parallel to that of Pico, even though he left the philosophical and scientific angle obscure. We must insist that Pico, in spite of Pontano's criticism, and in spite of the objections raised by such professional astrologers as Bellanti or by such fine minds as that of Pomponazzi, did not have the slightest intention of weakening the premisses of the science of nature. On the contrary: he presented himself as the defender of an ordered and rigorously causal conception of the universe. He denounced not only the incessant scientific mistakes made by astrology but also the abuse of analogy and the arbitrary intrusion of religious influences upon the course of natural events. And finally, he exposed the disorder that had resulted from astrology's application of the laws of physical causality to the realm of human consciousness. For these laws are only valid for attempts to determine the soul's horizon; but are incapable of explaining free acts. At the threshold of the soul, the law of nature *sistit pedem et receptui canit*.[34]

10. THE BEGINNINGS OF PLATONIC APOLOGETICS

As mentioned above, Pico della Mirandola raised problems that burst the framework of Ficino's Platonism. To begin with, his familiarity with Scholasticism, of which he made no secret, enriched his thinking with various themes. There was one point, however, on which the followers of Savonarola, to whom Pico felt himself tied more and more closely as time went by, agreed entirely with those of Ficino. Both groups had deep religious aspirations. If one reads through the philosophical writings of

[34] On the tragic figure of the astrologer Lucio Bellanti and his political activities cp. N. Mengozzi, *Un processo politico in Siena sul finire del secolo XV*, 'Bollettino Senese di Storia Patria', 1920.

Savonarola, one will discover in them nothing but the traditional themes of Thomism. In spite of this, he appeared to the citizens of Florence as a prophet—for his message reached them in the period of ferment occasioned by the ideals of regeneration and reform that had accompanied the dawn of humanism. His message fell on receptive ears especially after human and practical action appeared to have failed and the desire for miracles, for mystical revelations and total rejuvenation had become strong. Pico himself saw to it that all his works as well as his life itself appeared to the public as an appeal. His friend Nesi, a follower of Ficino, saw Savonarola as a new Socrates. To Nesi, Savonarola had the same divine inspiration and was driven by the same demon and the same reformatory zeal. The *new century* was about to begin and the world would transform itself politically, and, above all, spiritually. In 1497 he exclaimed: *Mahumethanos ad Christianam fidem, vobis adhuc viventibus, adsciscendos. Ovile tandem omnium unum, pastorem unum*. Ten years earlier he had used both Hermetic and Platonic literature, made fashionable by Ficino, to compose a baroque and over-ornate oration *De Charitate*, the climax of which was a deeply emotional invitation to a mystical union with God. 'I transform the lover into the beloved and the beloved into the lover. The lover becomes the beloved because the lover, dying, lives in the beloved. And the beloved becomes the lover, for he learns to know himself in the lover and gets to love himself through the lover. And while he is thus loving himself in loving the lover, he loves the lover who himself has become the beloved.'[35]

In the dialogue *De Moribus* there was still a faint echo of the early, political and civic speculations of humanism. But now there is no question that there is complete obedience to Pico's appeal: *evolemus ad Patrem*. And there, in the *pax unifica*, Poliziano's proposal becomes valid: *tibi silentium laus*!

Girolamo Benivieni transferred his effusions of love to the religious sphere. In the commentary to his lyrics he transformed the prose of Pico's early years into phrases of Christian enthusiasm. On April 11th, 1484, Giovanni Mercurio da Correggio had

---

[35] There is a different tone in *De Moribus*, ms. Laur. plut. 78, 24, where moral research is praised at the expense of physics. As far as Savonarola is concerned, his small treatise dedicated to Ugolino Verino (*Apologeticus de Ratione Poeticae Artis*) is of special interest.

preached a sermon on Hermetic *renovatio* in the streets of Rome. Ludovico Lazzarelli, a poetic philosopher, had praised that sermon as the work of a miraculous new prophet. In 1488, Hermes Trismegistos was depicted in a mosaic in the Cathedral of Siena. And Egidio da Viterbo, who became a cardinal in 1517, envisaged the triumph of Platonic theology as a return of the golden age and began to erect, upon the basis of Platonism and the cabbala, an apology for Plato. Through the efforts of Cardinal Seripando, these apologetics were destined to remain an effective force right down to the time of the Council of Trent.[36]

From the school of Valla to the Hebrew studies of Pico, humanistic philology, concerning itself with the interpretation of the Scriptures, had prepared the way for a major critical offensive. The *Platonic Theology* had made its own contribution to the same end. By insisting upon the mystical union with God in the deeper and hidden reaches of the soul, it became the prelude to the revival of religiosity that took place during the 16th century. And by providing a justification for all sorts of diverse kinds of religions, it prepared the way for the growth of toleration. Similarly, Savonarola had tried to establish on earth a community worthy of man. His death at the stake, in 1498, signified, for all practical purposes, the complete collapse of a not inconsiderable part of this humanistic programme.

[36] G. Benivieni, *Commento sopra a più sue canzone, ecc.* Firenze, 1500; Cp. Lazzarelli, *Bombix*, Aesii, 1765; for *Epistola de Admiranda ac Portendenti Apparitione Novi atque Divini Prophetae ad omne Humanum Genus*, cp. P. O. Kristeller, 'Annali Scuola Normale Superiore Pisa', 1938, pp. 237–62 [*Studies*, pp. 221 sqq.]

All the same, reading the text made available to me by the courtesy of Delio Cantimori, I am inclined to think of influences other than hermetic 'theological' ones, i.e. of magico-astrological influences. [The text of the *Epistola* in M. Brini, op. cit., pp. 34–50]. For Egidio da Viterbo see *Egidio da Viterbo e la metodologia del sapere nel Cinquecento*, 'Pensée humaniste', *cit.*, pp. 185–239; *L'anima e l'uomo in Egidio da Viterbo*, 'Arch. di filosofia', 1951, pp. 37–138; *I fondamenti metafisici della 'dignitas hominis' e testi inediti di Egidio da Viterbo*, Torino, 1954.

CHAPTER IV

PLATONISM AND THE PHILOSOPHY OF LOVE

1. FRANCESCO CATTANI DA DIACCETO AND ORTHODOX FICINIANISM

IN the *Discorsi* by Count Annibale Romei of Ferrara, certain 'ladies and knights' are introduced to Francesco Patrizi in order to discuss, for seven days, questions of philosophy. On closer inspection we find that the subjects talked about are beauty, love, honour, duelling, nobility, wealth and literature. Romei's work is a true reflection of the sum total of the arguments which people in non-scholastic circles loved to discuss. In these somewhat mannered discussions the vigour of the Platonic opposition to academic Aristotelianism was gradulaly extinguished.[1] Questions of metaphysics came to be left to the specialists; but the cultured public could roam freely in the field of moral and aesthetic speculations which furnished an occasion for *littérateurs* to exhibit their incredible virtuosity in stylistic refinement. The subject of love is always to be found in the centre of such discussions, and its philosophical importance was treated in the rarified prose of many writers in varying shades of sentimentality. Benedetto Varchi's first public lecture in the Florentine Academy contains the following sentence: 'Everything that is good, be it of the soul or the body, comes, has come and will always come from love and from love alone. That is, everything good which people have had in any place at any time or from anything has always been had, is being had now and will always be had by love . . . Love is the first and main cause of the movements of the heavens. And the movement of the heavens results in the earth's standing still. All things have their birth, their growth and their maintenance from the movement of the heavens, as father; and from the stillness of the earth, as mother. This is true for living things as

[1] Annibale Romei, *Discorsi divisi in sette giornate*, Verona, 1586. For the connections between philosophy of love and Petrarchism cp. L. Baldacci, *Il petrarchismo italiano nel Cinquecento*, Milano-Napoli, 1957.

well as for plants and animals and for those that are lacking in life such as all those things under the sky that are neither animal nor vegetable. Yes, not only the things that have their origin in God and in Nature are due to love, but also those that are created by human speech and by the work of man.'[2]

In another place, Varchi himself indicated his sources apart from Plato: Ficino, Pico, Diacceto, Bembo and, finally, the *Dialogue of Philo the Jew*, a work in three volumes by Leone Ebreo. But his most eloquent eulogy was reserved for Diacceto whom he held up as a 'mirror not only of civic life but also of the speculative life', and he considered that Diacceto's influence had been the strongest of all. Diacceto continued the most orthodox Ficinian tradition. 'Everything we are', he wrote, '—if indeed we are anything—we are because of Marsilio Ficino.' To him, Ficino was *quasi familiaris . . . daemon* who, even after our death *nostro ore loquetur*. He admitted, however, that together with Ficino, Pico had provided a great stimulus, for the latter had attempted to reconcile Plato with Aristotle in the general framework of Christianity. Aristotle, the teacher of the civic virtues, had prepared mankind for the higher flights of contemplation.[3] In his preface to a course of lectures on the *Nicomachean Ethics* he wrote that Aristotle 'is an efficient guide for he has prepared for us, in his ethical writings for Nicomachus, with an exquisite wealth of thoughts, the road by which we can reach the highest grade of virtue. Indeed, whoever enters the temple of true virtue will meet in the foyer the civic virtues dealt with in this work. The liberating virtues, on the other hand, belong to the purified soul. They are the apex of life and they will follow later.' But, according to Diacceto, we can approach the deity already in this life by a total commitment to the circle of love which is the universe.

'We say that God is the beginning, the middle and the end. By 'beginning' we mean that everything stems from Him; 'middle' signifies that everything turns towards Him; and 'end' means that everything is donated by Him for the sake of ultimate perfection,

[2] Benedetto Varchi, *Opere*, Trieste, 1859, II, pp. 531 sqq.; cp. pp. 496 sqq. (*Dell' amore, lezione una*); pp. 816 sqq. (*Vita di Francesco Cattani da Diacceto*).
[3] For Diacceto cp. *I tre libri d'amore, con un panegirico d'Amore; et con la vita del detto Autore fatta da M. Benedetto Varchi*, in Vinegia, 1566; *Opera omnia*, Basileae, 1563; For other MSS, Magliab. XII, 47; and P. O. Kristeller, *Francesco da Diacceto and Florentine Platonism in the sixteenth Century*, 'Miscellanea Mercati', Città del Vaticano, 1946, vol. IV, pp. 260–304. (*Studies*, p. 287 sqq.).

which consists in union with Him. This much had already been hinted by the Pythagoreans when they said that the Trinity is the measure of all things. The same idea was indicated by Orpheus when he said that Jupiter was the beginning, the middle and the end. And for this reason Dionysius the Aeropagite said that in this way God is pure splendour to those who have been illuminated, pure perfection to those who are perfect, deity to those who have been deified, simplicity to those who are simple, unity to those who partake of unity, life to those who live; in short: God is the essence of all things that are. For God is the beginning and the cause of all Being, of all life. And therefore every created being, whether it is eternal or mortal, whether it is rational or angelic, can exclaim with the Prophet: 'Lord, the splendour of Thy countenance is signed upon us'. In this circular convergence of the universe there arises the beauty of the material world; and it arises through the intrinsic connection between unity and multiplicity as well as through the perennial movement in which everything proceeds from itself to itself. And this movement is *erotic*: for everything is aware of its insufficiency, but, at the same time, has a profound thirst for sufficiency. 'A marvellous beauty emerges in material bodies through the connection by which so many diverse and contrary, though mutually friendly, things form one big living organism. And if it be permitted to compare big things to small things, one may say that the world resembles a man.' For man is placed in the centre of the universe, at the point of universal convergence. He reflects eminently the twofold nature of love, which is simultaneously a lack and a sufficiency. In this sense, beauty is the visible expression of the harmony of the One-and-Many, and the soul is the living 'junction of the universe'. Man's being consists in making himself a man; and even so, love is an incessant striving towards a goal. Man and love are concepts that are knotted together in the universal rhythm which appears, externally, as beauty. These concepts could be conceived neither in terms of pure multiplicity nor in terms of absolute unity. They are formed at the frontier. And their formation at the frontier creates the presupposition that makes the existence of the two realms thus separated possible.

Though beauty itself is not in God, it shines as God's light in the spheres of angels and of nature. It is the seal of animated life;

externally, a revelation of universal deification and of the movement of all things towards God. It is goodness made visible. 'Beauty is a *grace*, it is a radiation of goodness which, as soon as there is the slightest stirring of it, becomes visible like the colour on the surface of things. Thus it becomes an object to be seen . . . as an accident'. In a good Platonic manner, Diacceto stressed the *visual* character of beauty and emphasised at the same time its extrinsicality, its externality ('in the manner of an accident'). Inwardness and intrinsicality are life ('a great nursery, impregnated by the seeds of all things'). But beauty is appearance; it is a blossom ('a bloom of goodness'). Beauty is also a starting point and, at the same time, both a veiling and an unveiling of the secret of good conduct. (Beauty . . . is the gate-keeper of the most secret mansion wherein dwells divine goodness.')

2. THE PROBLEM OF GRACEFULNESS

Having reduced the problem of love to the problem of beauty, Diacceto was compelled to dwell on a subject which, in that epoch, was one of the favourite topics for discussion: gracefulness, charm. Towards the middle of the 16th century, Tomitano, a very learned man, wrote that 'beauty without gracefulness is like a fishing-line without a bait'. He understood by gracefulness something that was added to the object, something that was artfully superimposed; in short, something artificial. This concept draws our attention to the two most important theoreticians of gracefulness, to Castiglione and Della Casa. These men treated of gracefulness in connection with the problem of a perfect human education. Castiglione introduced the concept of *informality*. He explained that informality is art so artfully perfected, that it dissolves all artificiality. It is a human achievement which seems to be similar to the divine, creative achievement: 'true art is what does not appear to be artful . . . and one ought to endeavour to hide it and this ought to be one's only endeavour'.[4]

Della Casa, too, tried to describe the meaning of such gracefulness more precisely. He thought that gracefulness is now synonymous with beauty and now with something else. Gracefulness adheres to beauty like a sort of sign that makes beauty

[4] Baldassar Castiglione, I, 26 (Cian ed., Firenze, 1894)

K

acceptable. 'Man should not . . . content himself with making
things good, but should also endeavour to make them appear
graceful. For gracefulness is nothing else but a kind of light
which radiates when things are in their appropriate order, when
they are adequately fitted together and connected with one
another. Without these appropriate measures goodness is not
beautiful; and beauty, not graceful.' This measure is a 'certain
sweetness' which manifests itself in all comportment. In this
view, both grace and charm are reduced to the sphere of the will
and of endeavour. In short, they are reduced to an art that
appears, when perfect, to be natural.[5]

> 'E quel che 'l bello e 'l caro accresce a l'opre,
> l'arte, che tutto fa, nulla si scopre.'
>
> (xvi; 9, vii–viii)

> 'And that which beauty most, most wonder brought,
> Nowhere appeared the art which all this wrought.'

Thus Tasso. Later writers were to develop the same topic.
But they were to emphasise the idea of movement and were to
seek beauty in motion. This interesting conclusion was attributed
in Romei's dialogues to Patrizi: 'gracefulness consists for the
most part in the suave and charming movements of the body; for
as long as a body stands without motion, grace is not apparent.
If I were to express my opinion, I would say that gracefulness is
nothing but a certain lightness and agility with which the body
obeys the instructions of the soul.'[6]

For these reasons, gracefulness was considered to be 'the
flower of beauty'. This means that true and perfect beauty
consists in the way in which spiritual movements manifest themselves in bodily movements. An unknown writer, Alessandro
Sardo, expressed himself more clearly. He was the author of
treatises on morality and on aesthetics. In his *Discourse on Beauty*
he maintained that 'gracefulness, charm and beauty, or, to speak
with Dante, gentle appearance', are human properties which
signify that the intellect, i.e. the rational and spiritual element in

---

[5] Giovanni Della Casa, *Galateo ovvero de' costumi*, Firenze, 1707, p. 75.
[6] Romei, *Discorsi*, pp. 13–14.

man, had been poured into 'the material body'. Gracefulness
radiates because of the liveliness of the mind, because of the
quiescence of sensations; because of chastity, seriousness, modesty,
affability and . . . also because of knowledge of causes and knowledge of the sciences.'[7]

In this way, under the guise of grace, Ficino's conception that
beauty is something spiritual, was emphasised. The appeal to
artificiality, moreover, stressed the value of human *art*. There is,
however, no reason for thinking that these treatises always upheld
the distinction between gracefulness and beauty. Often enough
they felt no more than an unconscious need for such a distinction.
In the famous concluding remarks to the *Cortegiano*, Castiglione
compared beauty with 'a flow of divine goodness . . . pouring
itself over all created things, like the rays of the sun'. He finished
up by stating that gracefulness originates when this divine ray
finds in its material receptacle a 'certain gay harmony of different
colours, supported by light and shade and by a measured distance
and by limits of lines'. In this case the divine ray 'adorns and
illuminates the subject upon which it falls with a marvellous
splendour and a marvellous grace—as if it were a ray of sunlight
that passed over a beautiful vase wrought in pure gold and
adorned with precious stones'. We should note in this explanation
that this perfection is based upon the encounter between material
elements, arranged according to geometrical proportions ('a
measured distance and limits of lines') and according to formal
elements ('the flow of divine goodness').[8]

Bembo's thoughts, on the other hand, were much more
confused. In his third book of his *Asolani*, he attempted to define
beauty with the help of the concept of charm: 'beauty', he wrote,
'is nothing else than a gracefulness which has its origins in the
appropriate proportions and the harmonies of things. This
harmony makes the subject the more attractive and graceful the
more perfect it is. As far as man is concerned, beauty is an
accident, both of the soul and of the body. For even as the body
is beautiful if its members are well proportioned, so the soul is
beautiful if its several virtues form a harmonious whole. They
partake of beauty in proportion to the gracefulness and appro-

[7] Alessandro Sardo, *Discorsi*, Venezia, 1586, pp. 13–14.
[8] Castiglione, *Il Cortegiano*, p. 409.

priateness of their members'. Bembo's insistence upon harmony and *appropriateness* seems to echo the formula, proposed by Diacceto, that beauty consists in the unity of the manifold. The same formula was firmly reiterated by Della Casa.[9]

In spite of the fact that most writers tended to define gracefulness in terms of beauty, there are also treatises in which beauty was subordinated to gracefulness. Thus Erizzo, for example, explained beauty as a kind of gracefulness. 'Beauty is nothing but a certain gracefulness which fills the emotions with pleasure, and the knowledge of which stimulates love.'[10]

It would be possible to collect a large number of very fine, but often over-subtle remarks, about the beauty of women from the extremely rich literature on that subject. In this kind of writing there can be no doubt of the eminence of Firenzuola. His work contains pages in which feminine beauty is considered exclusively in relation to sexual functions and explained as nature's clever invention for the purpose of procreation. Then there are pages of extremely refined reflections in the Platonic tradition.[11] He, too, tried to make use of the concept of the body as an instrument. The beauty of the body, he argued, was proportional to the degree to which the body was able to serve the soul; to the degree, that is, to which the body was 'transparent' and spiritualised—or at least, prepared for the spiritual life.

'Take two candles of the same quality and same size and let there be no difference of any kind between them. Put them into two lanterns, one with more transparent glass than the other. You will then see that the candle in the lantern with the more transparent glass gives a more beautiful light than the other. What is the cause of the difference? The make of the lantern.' The author of the argument, however, has nothing to say about the relationship between the inner, divine light and the apparatus in which it is placed. He does not enlighten us at all when, in an effort to explain the objective conditions of gracefulness, he tells us that 'gracefulness' consists in hidden proportions and in a hidden

[9] There are strange developments of the theme of Oneness in the *Opere* of Giulio Cammillo, Venezia, 1560, 2 vols.

[10] For S. Erizzo cp. the letter, pp. 627–35 in Ruscelli, *Lettere di XIII uomini illustri*, Venezia, 1560.

[11] For Firenzuola cp. *Ragionamenti* and *Discorsi* (*Opere*, Firenze, 1848, vol. I, pp. 81–131; II, pp. 239–80; 281–305).

measure of which we can know nothing from books, of which we can have no knowledge at all and of which we cannot even form an idea. And hence we can say of it, as we are wont to say of things we do not understand, it is a *'je ne sais quoi'*. Firenzuola may well have been right in attacking the 'rays' and 'other quintessences'. But he did not succeed in working out a more unambiguous view of his own.

As a matter of fact, when people discussed love, i.e. the effects of beauty upon man, they were compelled to isolate its objective conditions. And it was then that the problems emerged in the guise of the concept of gracefulness. In the prevailing Platonic context it was generally taken for granted that 'beauty is a certain ray or act of God which penetrates into all things'. Or, if one wants to employ the phrases of Brucioli, beauty was considered the imprint of 'God's face' upon things. But a more precise investigation cannot avoid the question: why is it possible to notice in some things 'a certain gracefulness' which 'moves the soul . . . and which is pleasing'; and why is it that from other things such gracefulness is absent?[12]

Much later, Niccolò Vito di Gozze, in his *Dialogo d' Amore detto Antos*, was to say, in the spirit of Plato, that 'beauty is prepared for gracefulness by three factors; that is, by order, by the mode and by the form or the species'. It seems that he was looking for an extreme of precision—even though he cited his source. He even went further when he insisted upon purely quantitative assessments like 'meter, measure, proportion . . . of the parts', and such things like 'due quantity' and 'appropriate lines'.[13] But he did not go beyond the Platonic concept that matter had a mathematical appearance.

At bottom, Diacceto had indicated the general line that was to be taken up in a hundred and one different variations. This line consisted of the argument that beauty is something spiritual. He had explained that beauty consists in the sensuous perception of an inner bloom—that it is a revelation and an outward appearance of an inner value, that is of an intimate process of moral significance. It is goodness that reveals itself as beauty. The body,

[12] Antonio Brucioli, *Dialogi della naturale philosophia e humana*, Venezia, 1544, c. 105 v.
[13] Niccolò Vito di Gozze, *Dialogo della bellezza detto Antos secondo la mente di Platone*, Venezia, 1581, p. 22 (cp. his theological writings in Urb. lat. 499–500).

instead of being an impediment or a barrier, can become the
adequate means or the instrument of such a revelation. It can
become transparent and allow the inner light to show and thus it
can become the latter's exemplary expression. This expression is
especially appropriate for the eye—for beauty emerges when
something becomes visible. 'For the eyes are transparent and
spiritual bodies. They are not made of coarse, flesh-like substance'.[14]
The intimate participation of Being in the divine (i.e. in goodness)
is the objective condition which causes beauty to appear sensuously and which enables us to perceive it. In 1557, in a letter, the
well known philosopher Giulio Castellani attacked official culture
so hostile to the arts, as follows: 'These people do not realise how
much their criticism of art implies a contempt for philosophy.
The one differs from the other only in name. For the one as well
as the other teaches us the honest and virtuous life'.[15]

Federigo Luigini attacked the matter on a different level. He
devoted a whole book of his treatise *Della bella donna* to the
question 'what role is to be attributed to what is inside'. For it is
true, as Firenzuola had said with so much perspicacity, that the
ugliness of the soul is likely to discolour the face. And equally
it is true 'that the beauty of the face is a sure sign of a sound soul
and a clear conscience.'[16]

3. THE METAPHYSICS OF LOVE

The men who were to take part in the debates of the Orti
Oricellari had begun to form their groups in the school of Diacceto.
Among those who were to discuss politics there was Niccolò
Machiavelli. There was also Giovanni Rucellai and Alessandro
de' Pazzi, the translator of Aristotle's *Poetics*; Giovanni Corsi, the
biographer of Ficino; Donato Gianotti, the politician; Antonio
Brucioli, a supporter of the Reformation, translator of the *Politics*
and a prolific compiler of dialogues on physics, metaphysics and
ethics in which he pretended to reproduce, without any originality, the above mentioned Florentine debates. One could also
mention Francesco de' Vieri, or Verino the First, the official

[14] On eyes and vision cp. Mario Equicola, *Di Natura d'Amore*, Venezia 1525.
[15] Giulio Castellani, *Opuscoli volgari editi e inediti*, Faenza, 1847, pp. 74–78.
[16] Federigo Luigini, *Il libro della bella donna* (in *Trattati del '500 sulla donna*, Bari,
1913); Firenzuola, *Delle bellezze delle donne*, I; also Varchi, *Della bellezza e della grazia*
(*Opere*, II, pp. 733–35).

representative of the tradition of Ficino. He was to be succeeded by Lapini da San Giovanni who, when teaching in Pisa, consolidated his exposition of Plato and Aristotle with mathematical theory and philological knowledge. Verino the Second was to derive much benefit from these explanations for as late as the end of the century he was still engaged in 'reasoning' and in 'discourses' about the *Ideas about Beauty and Love*.[17]

But this whole academic tradition was suffused by an aesthetic vision of reality. According to this vision, reality is nothing but manifest beauty; or, as Francesco Giorgio (Zorzi), a friar minor from Venice, was to proclaim with inspired enthusiasm: it is nothing but music. His *De Harmonia Mundi Totius Cantica Tria* is a work as enormous as it is curious. It was published in Venice in 1525, full of Hermetic, Platonic and cabbalistic lore and aimed to represent the architecture of the whole universe as music. He considered the universe to be the face of God. It is governed by numerical laws and could therefore be interpreted solely in terms of numbers. But numbers can assume many different guises, such as vocal rhythms, physical laws and orderly moral actions. Giorgio's goal was to reduce everything to musical concepts. This was to be done by emphasising the harmonious proportions of all relationships, the perfect measures and the musical beauty of the cosmos. For practical purposes he was concerned with the discovery of a series of numerical combinations. Such combinations were the favourite theme of the cabbalistic Pythagoreanism which had begun with Pico and which one can find in the compilations of Alessandro Farra, covered with a veneer of fascinating mysteriousness. In fact, it was to survive right down to the middle of the 17th century. This cabbalistic Pythagoreanism was eventually to nourish the conviction, so effective in the science of the age of the Baroque, that the whole universe is a system written in mathematical formulae.[18]

Jehudah Abarbanel (Leone Ebreo) was another thinker who responded to 'the prayer of the divine Mirandola', by composing, in scholastic style, a treatise *De Caeli Harmonia* which has unfortunately been lost. But his vision of the world under the signs of

---

[17] The list of Diacceto's pupils is in Varchi, *Opere*, II, p. 818.
[18] Alessandro Farra, *Tre discorsi*, Pavia, 1564. On the value of Giorgio cp. Nardi, 'Acta Congr. Schol. Intern'. Romae, 1951, pp. 625–6.

beauty and love has nevertheless come down to us in his *Dialoghi d'amore* which, though written at the beginning of the 16th century, were published only in 1535. It is without doubt the master-piece of this literary genre.[19]

In the second dialogue, Leone Ebreo sang a hymn to universal harmony. 'Even though celestial beings know nothing of bi-sexual reproduction, they are not devoid of perfect and reciprocal love. . . . If you contemplated . . . the correspondences and the concordances of the motions of the celestial bodies . . . and if you knew the number of the celestial orbs that make the various motions necessary . . . you would witness such a miraculous correspondence and concord . . . that you would remain stupefied by these events as well as by Him Who ordained them.' In this argument love is by no means a purely human bond. It is, on the contrary, a universal bond that comprises and vivifies the whole of the universe without distinction. Even the elemental 'non-sensory beings, like metals and certain kinds of stone' have a natural knowledge of the goal of their existence and a natural affection for it. They move in the big ocean of Being, each towards its own port 'as if it were its very own and longed for abode'. Leone Ebreo discovered everywhere the incessant pulsation of life in all things and used his phantasy in order to provide images for the sympathy and friendship that reigns supreme in the cosmic order. Thus he came to speak of heaven and earth as if they were living beings that celebrate their marriage and find their satisfaction in perfect love. 'Through such mutual love the material universe is united; and the world is adorned and sustained. Earth or matter loves heaven as if he were a beloved spouse or a lover or benefactor. And the things that are loved love heaven as if he were a benevolent father or a devoted guardian'.

With the help of astrological fables this poetical philosophy of nature was invested with mythological images. And the poet-ical philosophy of nature, in turn, was used to uncover the hidden meaning of classical myths which amounted to nothing more than the vision of the ever changing interplay of the forces of nature. There is such a complete fusion between man and nature, that it

[19] I have used the works of Leone Ebreo in the edition of S. Caramella, Bari, 1929.

is quite impossible to say whether man dissolves himself in the universe or whether the universe is being humanised. Nature receives a face and becomes rather more than Campanella's temple of God. It becomes God's work of art—a work of art in which He himself is alive and which is animated by Him. There is a God Who is an inexhaustible fountain of love and very different from Aristotle's God, Who was supposed to be closed in on Himself. On the contrary, this God is an over-abundant effusion of life. 'The goal of the cosmic order is the unitary perfection of the whole of the universe. . . . And since this is the law of the universe, the intelligence will find greater bliss in the motion of the celestial orbs . . . than in its intrinsic essence, which consists in mere contemplation.'

Supreme wisdom, therefore, is not to be found in refined syllogisms but in a form of ecstasy, in the divine kiss and the death of one's humanity by which one is re-born in God. 'Such was the death of the blessed ones: they contemplated the divine beauty with extreme longing, and thus their souls were converted to it and left their bodies'. In the universal circle of love, God is not only the loved One and the One towards Whom everything tends. He is also the supreme lover. He 'produces and governs the world with love and ties it to Himself'. His love, however, is not a desire which seeks fulfilment. It is rather a complete gift. 'God does not seek union with creatures as lovers seek union with the persons they love. He seeks, instead, to unite creatures with His divinity in order that such union may make them perfect and that the creator's effect upon His creatures be immaculate.'

If it is true that love is the essence of the world, and beauty its appearance, then 'beauty is gracefulness. For gracefulness makes itself known to the soul and fills it with such delight that the soul responds with love'. According to the theory of the followers of Ficino, beauty is the blossom of goodness. It is the expression of an inner event capable of evoking in the onlooker a similar emotion. The onlooker thus becomes willing to *suffer* its effects. For, as Leone Ebreo remarked, there are two kinds of love. There is a love which is the daughter of desire. It is blind and restless and has its origin in want. It expresses itself in violence and uncontrolled desire for possession. 'The other love is the love that generates the desire . . . it is perfect and true love . . .

it is the father of desire and the son of reason'. But this reason is an 'extraordinary reason' which no longer enjoins man to seek his own preservation but which obliges him to offer himself and to give himself entirely to the beloved—to confound and confuse himself with the beloved lover in the active, cosmic process. Leone Ebreo made a magnificent comparison. 'He who lives according to common reason', lives like a tree which has plenty of foliage but is sterile, because it has exhausted itself. But he who lives in love, collaborates with the fertile stream which animates the universe, 'from the first cause that creates everything to the last created thing'. Thus he consents to the infinite love of God.

4. THE FASHION OF DISCUSSIONS ON LOVE

Leone Ebreo had injected deeply religious elements into his philosophy of love. He had, in fact, derived much from the same sources to which Jochanan Alemanno, a correligionist of his and a man closely connected with the Platonic culture of Florence, had owed so much inspiration for his commentary on the *Song of Songs*.

Side by side with these high-minded speculations on love, there flourished, however, a completely different kind of literature. It consisted mainly of academic orations and 'beautiful questions', as Castiglione called this kind of social conversation. Then there were the so-called 'scruples' for the removal of which such masters of discussion as Equicola and Calandra were famous. Calandra, in a book which has been lost, examined 'whether it be more difficult to simulate a love that is not felt than to dissimulate a love that is felt'. The book consisted of the discussion of sixty-nine such questions. It was written at the beginning of the 16th century. Towards the end, in 1588, the Academy of Ferrara issued a printed programme to invite people to participate in a debate on God's love for His creatures—the sort of thing it is, how it is distributed, whether God loved the angels more than men, whether he loved an innocent more than a repentant man, a virgin more than a courtesan, and how God could love and hate simultaneously. It would take us too far to trace the development which had led to this kind of abstract and sterile academic discussion. Various preoccupations and different kinds of literary interests had combined to produce it. In Bembo's *Asolani*, written at the turn of the century and published in Venice in 1505, *Amor* was still praised, very impressively, as the motive and the stimulus of every human progress and of all human civic life. 'Love succeeds where the teacher's cane and the father's threats fail; and where neither the flatteries nor the rewards of art and effort, cleverness and instruction succeed . . . For love, like the sun, vivifies and ennobles everything. Love teaches to speak and to keep silence and teaches courtesy.' Love is the power that moves the universe, quickens and quietens it. Castiglione, at the end of the *Cortegiano* exclaimed: 'You are the sweet bond of the universe, the mediator between things heavenly and things earthly. Through you the highest beings descend with gracious effect and take over the direction of lower things. And by guiding the senses of mortals towards their own origins, you cause them to be connected with the higher beings.'

In his *Raverta* (1544), Giuseppe Betussi enlarged upon the theme of the *beautiful beautifying* god and demonstrated that the Trinity was identical with beauty: God the Father is the source of beauty, the son is beauty itself and the spirit is beauty in its objective manifestation. Later on, in his *La Leonora* he treated of beauty as an externalisation of inner harmony. In 1547 the courtesan and poetess Tullia D'Aragona discussed the infinity of love. And in this connection we also ought to mention Equicola, Speroni, Doni, Franco, Varchi, Sansovino, Gottifredi as well as Nifo and Patrizi. The poets joined hands with the philosophers but did not manage to transcend the narrow confines of traditional questions. Similarly Tasso, following the advice of Antonio Montecatini who had a predilection for strange Peripatetic-Platonic syntheses, sought his inspiration, of all places, in the *Trattato dell'amore* by Flaminio Nobili, published in Lucca in 1567. This work repeated all the banalities of the moralising literature of the time on honour, nobility and similar matters, and thus reproduced the worst commonplaces of Ficinian thought.[20]

[20] A collection of *Trattati d'amore del Cinquecento* has been edited by G. Zonta (Bari, 1912); but this collection fails to show how this genre became more and more banal. A good list is to be found in P. Lorenzetti, *La bellezza e l'amore nei trattati del' 500*, Pisa, 1920, pp. 165–75 ('Annali della R. Scuola Normale Superiore', XXVIII); but there are both minor and major omissions, e.g. Nifo's *De Pulchro* and *De Amore*, Lugduni, 1549. On p. 91, Nifo expresses great respect for Equicola. For the *Trattato dell'amor humano* by Nobili see the edition by Pasolini, Roma, 1895, which

As against this, the researches into 'the sayings and designs of love, commonly called *imprese*', are much more interesting. They are obviously connected with the aesthetic discussions of the age of the Baroque and stimulated Vico to similar reflections. Here we must mention how Giovio and Domenichi toyed with descriptions of the 'inventions' sported by cavaliers in order to 'reveal one part of their generous thoughts'. But it was Girolamo Ruscelli who insisted on discussing the problem of their value and their significance. Ruscelli had no great intellectual qualities and was mercilessly ridiculed in Tasso's *Minturno*. But he was well educated and had a very wide range of interests. He immediately connected the problem of those 'inventions' with the problem of language in general by pointing out that the visual sign, since it expressed the *intention* more appropriately than a word, was a universal means of communication. For words are defined individually and hence have variable meanings. 'But the representations and the forms of things . . . have universally a natural air. And since it is so natural and universal to communicate by signs (*dimostrar per segni*) one is led to suspect that the verb "to teach" (*insegnare*) is derived from this method of communication'.[21]

5. THE RECONCILIATION BETWEEN PLATO AND ARISTOTLE

The Platonic wave which rolled over the whole of the 16th century, entering into the realms of literature and drawing along poets no less than philosophers, was anything but intolerant of

reproduces also Tasso's marginal notes. But the following work deserves longer discussion: Guido Casoni, *Della Magia d'Amore* . . . *Nella quale si dimostra come Amore sia Metafisico, Fisico, Astrologo, Musico, Geometra, Aritmetico, Grammatico, Dialetico, Rettore, Poeta, Historiografo, Iurisconsulto, Politico, Ethico, Economico, Medico, Capitano, Nocchiero, Agricoltore, Lanifico, Cacciatore, Architetto, Pittore, Scultore, Fabro, Vitreario, Mago naturale, Negromante, Geomante, Hidromante, Aeremante, Piromante, Chiromante, Fisionomo, Augure, Auruspice, Ariolo, Salitore e Genetliaco* . . ., Venezia, 1951. Cp. E. Zanette, *Una figura del secentismo veneto. Guido Casoni*, Bologna, 1933.

[21] *Raggionamento di Mons. Paolo Giovio* . . . *sopra i motti, e disegni d'arme, e d'amore, che comunemente chiamano imprese. Con un discorso di Girolamo Ruscelli intorno allo stesso soggetto*, Milano, 1559, p. 54 sqq. Cp. Ludovico Domenichi, *Regionamento nel quale si parla d'imprese d'armi, et d'amore*, Milano, 1559.

Aristotle. After all, the author of the *Nicomachean Ethics* considered pure contemplation the highest kind of human perfection; and in this he was in full agreement with Plato. It is no accident that the Neapolitan Peripatetic, Simon Porzio, in a dialogue dedicated to Tasso and named after him, exclaimed with reference to the purely theoretical sciences that 'their goal is an exalted one. It lies either in contemplation or in the knowledge of truth. When truth is found, the intelligence comes to rest in its own felicity. Moreover, this discovery links the intellect to God and makes it, as the Platonists are wont to say, the colleague of the divine intelligences.' Nifo, the follower of Averroes and Crisostomo Jovelli, the Thomist, move along the same lines. Jovelli described Platonic ethics as *mediam inter peripateticam et christianam*. Similarly Figliucci, Platonist and disciple of Ficino, translator of the *Phaidros* and commentator of Aristotle's *Ethics*, followed in the same direction. And the Peripatetic Antonio Montecatini, who was a professor in France and a friend of Patrizi, declared, on the occasion of the publication of his commentary on the *Politics*, that it was impossible to understand Plato without Aristotle.[22]

But there is no point in dwelling on the legion of second-rate commentators. The case of Francesco Piccolomini, who was for a long time a professor in Padua and whose 'abundant erudition' was praised by Tasso, is much more characteristic. His 'writings represent a veritable ocean of knowledge'. They are a real encyclopaedia of all the philosophical sciences and betray a tendency towards a certain kind of Aristotelian orthodoxy. In one place he even criticised Pico's attempt at a reconciliation between Plato and Aristotle. But between the years 1557 and 1590 there were published in Venice and in Bâle the *Discussions on the Soul* and the *Platonic Contemplations*. They were alleged to have been written by Pietro Duodo and Stefano Tiepolo, but were in reality the work of Piccolomini. They are suffused by a genuine Platonic passion. And Piccolomini himself explained in his *Academicae Contemplationes (in quibus Plato Explicatur et Peripatetici*

---

[22] *Chrysostomi Javelli Canapicii. . . . Opera*, Lugduni, 1580, II, 269 sqq. Felice Figliucci, *Della filosofia morale libri dieci sopra i dieci libri dell'etica d'Aristotele*, Venezia, 1552. Cp. *Il Fedro, ovvero il Dialogo del bello di Platone tradotto in lingua toscana per F.F.*, Roma, 1544; *Antonii Montecatini In Politica, hoc est in Civiles Libros Aristotelis Progymnasmata*, Ferrariae, 1587–94.

Refelluntur) that reconciliation was impossible for the very reason that Aristotle is nothing but the approach to the serene and exalted peaks of Platonism.[23]

Peripateticism—and this is by no means the only example— was on the point of turning the course of history upside down. It began, as it were, to concede to Aristotle the earth as a kind of foothold the better to rise to the Platonic heavens, in the unearthly vision of which the ideals of the *Nicomachean Ethics* were finally capable of realisation. The most orthodox form of Platonism, however, in any of its various shades, sought a secret link between philosophy, science and religion. Verino the Second, for instance, worked out the 'true doctrines of Plato which agreed both with Christianity and the teachings of Aristotle.' These doctrines were to be grounded upon the triple agreement between Plato and faith, Plato and Aristotle and Plato and Hippocrates.[24]

Verino's treatise appeared in 1589 in Florence. But the argument that Platonism was a *philosophia perennis* had already found its outspoken defender in Agostino Steuco da Gubbio's ten books *De Perenni Philosophia*. Their author had conducted a lively attack against the Lutheran and Calvinist Reformation and had gone back to the essential points of Ficino's Platonism.[25] In his view, Luther and Calvin had strongly emphasised the gulf between the human and the divine, the incomprehensible distance of God and the misery and nothingness of man. Hence, human stupidity and divine folly, philosophy and faith, had remained unreconciled. The separation of heaven from earth cannot be overcome. And the Protestant insistence on the alleged impotence of man vis à vis God seems to be a confirmation of the sad vision that mankind amounts to nothing in action and thought and can achieve something only through the flame of faith, the grace of

[23] *Petri Duodi . . . Peripat. de anima disput. lib. VII*, Venetiis, 1575; *Stephani Theupoli . . . Academicarum contemplationum lib. X . . .*, Basileae, 1590. F. Piccolomini, *Universa Philosophia de Moribus*, Venetiis, 1583; *Libri ad Scientiam Naturae Attinentes*, Venetiis, 1600; *Compendio di scienza civile*, Roma, 1858. In the Platonic literature of the sixteenth century there are the noteworthy translations (*Apologia, Eutifrone, Critone, Fedone e Timeo*) and commentaries (*Fedone*) by Erizzo (Venezia, 1574).

[24] *Vere conclusioni di Platone conformi alla Dottrina Cristiana et a quella d'Aristoteles*, collected by Messer Francesco De' Vieri called Verino the second, Firenze, 1589. For Verino cp. also *Ragionamento de l'eccellenze et de' più meravigliosi artificii della magnanima professione della Filosofia*, Firenze, 1589.

[25] *Augustini Steuchi Eugubini De Perenni Philosophia Libri X*, Lugduni, 1540.

God. By contrast, the Platonic solution showed how *eros* was able to transform ifself into *charitas*. This solution, therefore, was capable of restoring man's confidence in himself by demonstrating his similarity with God and by explaining love as a divine gift which makes it possible for man to offer himself to God. These are the elements which appear to Steuco the only sound means for a new apologetic—provided always that it will be possible to forge a more solid link between priestly and philosophical tradition, between the love of God and an enlightened reason.[26] Hence the idea of a perennial light living in the souls of men, all clear and pure in the first Adam, then made almost opaque by sin, and thence handed down with ever greater precision and comprehended with ever deeper consciousness. Already Roger Bacon had elaborated the idea that in primitive times there had been a perfect knowledge. Steuco connected this idea with the notion that the truth comes to be discovered gradually and is finally fully confirmed in the second Adam. He also considered that the changing relationship between the darkness of ignorance and the light of knowledge corresponds to the moral and religious rhythm of sin and redemption.

Although Steuco had no conception of progress, he postulated that in the beginning all human thought and the object of that thought had been one and indivisible. For Adam was present at the creation and had witnessed God's creative activity. He felt God, as God was creating him. One may conclude, therefore, that the first knowledge was an immediate knowledge of the absoluteness of creative activity (*dum nascerentur, a Deo se creari cernerent.*) Steuco is quite explicit on this matter: the most original revelation consisted literally in the immediate consciousness of the creation of the world. In this respect it differed profoundly from all laborious thinking and inferring. The subsequent dispersion was a double dispersion. There was a material dispersion, in a spatial sense, into the various regions of the world; and a spiritual dispersion into a multiplicity of languages. And for this reason sin found its tangible expression in distance. The closer nations are to the original cradle of mankind (Steuco referred to Chaldeans, Armenians, Babylonians, Assyrians,

[26] *De Perenni Philosophia*, pp. 77–78; also pp. 561–62.

Aegyptians, and Phoenicians) the longer truth manages to maintain itself among them, even though it is true that owing to the way in which this original wholesome knowledge came to be obscured, it became *fabulosa, et scyrpis et latebris absconsa*. And thus we come full circle, back to Ficino's idea that all poetry contains an original, primitive theology. To speak with Vico, we may say that an astute exegesis of mankind's poetic productions reveals that mankind has an essentially uniform language which is the expression of the essential identity of all beliefs.

Thomism had insisted upon the unity of truth. To Steuco this unity is both revealed and demonstrated by the existence of a *philosophia perennis*. 'All men have been naturally agreed that there is nothing higher than religion. They have always been driven instinctively to this conclusion by that reason which distinguishes them from animals. . . . The whole of philosophy, prompted by that same reason, has established that true goodness coincides with the goodness promised by that faith. . . . Plato, Aristotle and many others have recognised this goal so clearly that it seems almost a miracle that they should have been able to recognise by their reason the very things which, later, the heavenly messenger was to reveal.'

This idea of a general agreement among all philosophers was centred upon the synthesis between Platonism and Aristotelianism. Like many other themes, it was to be reiterated in the academic orations by countless minor characters. Most of them were as noisy as they were inconclusive, like the 5197 theses of Jacopo Mazzoni of Cesena, printed in 1577 in Bologna.[27] Mazzoni was to occupy himself later with literary problems—so much so that, at times, he denied ever having had those youthful enthusiasms. With him we enter the age of Galileo. For Mazzoni's relations with Galileo were cordial. There were other Platonists like the Sicilians Pietro Calanna and Giovanni Viperano; or Tommaso Giannini of Ferrara; or Paolo Beni who wrote not only a commentary on Aristotle's *Poetics* and glosses to the *Timaios*, but also

---

[27] *Jacobi Mazonii Cesenatis de triplici hominis vita, activa nempe contemplativa et religiosa, methodi tres, quaestionibus quinque millibus centum et nonaginta septem distinctae, in quibus omnes Platonis et Aristotelis multae vero aliorum Graecorum, Arabum et Latinorum in universo scientarum orbe discordiae componuntur, quae omnia publice disputanda Bononiae proposuit,* Anno salutis, 1577; *Jacobi Mazonii Cesenatis in almo gymnasio pisano Aristotelem ordinarie, Platonem vero extra ordinem profitentis, in universam Platonis et Aristotelis praeludia, sive de comparatione Platonis et Aristotelis,* Venetiis, 1597.

a treatise to prove that Tasso was superior to Homer. But the Platonism of all these men was of little value.

In the end the old problem of the agreement among the philosophers was lost sight of in historical compilations or erudite manuals. And Platonism itself, having satisfied the thirst for courtly conversation, dissolved itself, at worst, into a vague atmosphere of literary escapism, and became at best the occasion for learned dissertations.

6. THE SCEPTICISM OF GIAN FRANCESCO PICO

At the very beginning of the 16th century, Gian Francesco Pico, the nephew of Pico della Mirandola, had predicted the final failure of all attempts at a reconciliation of the different philosophical movements. Gian Francesco Pico was a thinker of very considerable stature and a follower of Savonarola. There was a touch of tragedy about his personality. For his life was suspended, as it were, between the scaffold of Savonarola and incessant family feuds—in the course of one of which he was finally killed. No wonder that he borrowed from the scepticism of Sextus Empiricus in order to destroy philosophy to make more room for religion.

On one side, he joined his uncle in attacking false prophets. He inveighed against Maghi, Necromancers, Geomancers, Astrologers and Cheiromancers and so forth. But on the otherside he firmly believed in the cognitive value of prophecy, that is in the divine light that flashes in the human soul while the intellect is vainly trying to grope its way in the treacherous darkness of rational discourse. 'For our reason, the last of the intelligences, proceeds from potency to act and errs frequently in its conclusions and inferences. It is greatly impeded by the accidents that surround the essences and by the unknown differences between things.' The light that shines in the darkness, however, bursts forth suddenly like a divine gift. It has no continuity, but comes and goes. In this way the encounter and the miraculous accord between imagination and reason, which make it possible to divine the future, are brought about.

These arguments of the *De Rerum Praenotione* contain the criticism of philosophical knowledge which constitutes the scaffolding

L

of the edifice of his own thoughts.[28] He considered human knowledge to be an intuition. This intuition is either tied to the senses
or soars up to the sublime form of prophecy in which the
intelligible is miraculously linked to the sensible. But this
correspondence is a gift, a *grace*, a divine condescension. For in
such a case, things that lie beyond the realm of man express
themselves in forms that can be grasped by man.

As discourse, philosophy is a rational process. It claims to
arrive at the truth by the unaided strength of natural reason. If it
were possible for philosophy to meet the demands that are made,
it would exhaust a large part of religion. The deepest meaning of
Christianity would dissolve itself in smoke if the theory of the
pia philosophia were true; that is, if there were an essential agreement between the philosophers of antiquity and Christianity.
But then Christianity would also lose its fundamental value. The
apologetics of Platonists—or, for that matter, of Aristotelians,
Plotinians and Pythagoreans—pretend that there is a continuity,
where in reality there is a chasm. And by such a pretence, they
prevent salvation. Gian Francesco Pico insisted that the philosophers do *not* agree with one another and that reason by itself is
therefore *not* sufficient; and that the superrational certainty of
revelation towers above the web of lies produced by rational
inference as well as above the total insufficiency of all human
researches.

Giovanni Pico della Mirandola had taken the agreement
among philosophers as proof of the truth of their teachings.
But Gian Francesco wrote that 'it occurred to him that it is more
acceptable and more useful to propound inconclusive philosophical doctrines'.

Classical antiquity, which most of his contemporaries praised
sky-high as the ultimate in perfection, was represented by Gian
Francesco Pico as a culture grown out of the wildest kinds of
contradictions. He believed that the only redeeming feature in
the crisis of reason and in the failure of the absurd attempts of

[28] Most of the works of Gian Francesco Pico are collected in the 2nd volume of
the Bâle edition, 1573, of the works of his uncle. Cp. also *On the imagination* by G. F.
Pico of M., the Latin text, with an intr. and an English transl. and notes by H.
Caplan, Cornell Univ. Press, 1930. For the controversy on imitation cp. Giorgio
Santangelo, *La polemica fra P. Bembo e G. F. Pico intorno al principio d'imitazione*,
'Rinascimento', I, 1950, pp. 323–340. Santangelo has also republished the texts,
Firenze, 1954.

classical man was the constant light of the Word of Christ. But his *Examen Vanitatis Doctrinae Gentium et Veritatis Disciplinae Christianae* is not only a criticism of human knowledge which can, as has been done, be compared with Montaigne. It is also a wholesale destruction of the whole world of human values, of that *regnum hominis* so dear to the Renaissance. And as such, it inclines one to think that it anticipated Pascal. With philosophy, there fell *litterae*, the arts, grammar, rhetoric and mathematics. Man by himself is nothing—or rather, he is error and guilt. Religion alone, understood as a total surrender of the self to God, *sine lite, sine dissensione, sine vago et anxio discursu*, is capable of restoring truth and peace to man. To this faith without limits there corresponds the gift of divine grace.

Gian Francesco Pico was fully aware of the danger that humanism might frustrate the deepest and the most instinctive reactions and aims of man. He was to exercise a strong influence upon the intransigent and anti-philosophical attitude of the Lateran Council of 1517 and did not hesitate, on the occasion of a controversy with Bembo on the problem of imitation, to question even the literary value of humanistic form.

CHAPTER V

ARISTOTELIANISM AND THE PROBLEM OF THE SOUL

1. Pietro Pomponazzi

O N another plane and in a very different atmosphere, there took place a complete renewal of those sciences that were derived from Aristotelian premisses—be they of the Averroistic, the Alexandrian, the Thomistic or the Scotist type. It is undoubtedly very difficult to keep the different currents apart and to follow, separately, the developments due to Themistius and to Simplicius and to distinguish them from the above mentioned well known and more obvious influences. At the same time, Platonic considerations played their part—so that the traditional view that there was a clear opposition between a Platonic Florence and a Padua committed to Aristotle and Averroes seems completely untenable. At the same time, it cannot be denied that encounters, in so far as they did take place, were due to the fact that different roads crossed and that themes originating in diverse regions, converged upon one another. This is particularly true if one directs one's attention to that characteristic subject, the central position of man. For this subject is common to Ficino's *Theologia Platonica* and to Pomponazzi's *De Immortalitate Animae*.

Pietro Pomponazzi was the most important of the Aristotelians of the 16th century. He was the successor of Vernia, of that *Nicoletus philosophus celeberrimus*, who was as famous as he was unproductive. In 1488, when he was still a very young man, he received a call to Padua to lecture together with Alessandro Achillini. Later he was to succeed to Achillini's chair in Bologna. According to the testimony of Giovio, Achillini had been Pomponazzi's teacher. Achillini, though less brilliant and less profound than Pomponazzi, was a thinker of considerable quality. He was a follower of Averroes and seems to have resorted openly to a most characteristic expression of the formula of 'the double truth'. He declared indeed that, as far as the intellect was concerned, he would choose 'from two false opinions (in respect of faith) the one that seemed the more probable, i.e. the one that was held by Averroes'. It is evident from his writings that he was wont to treat of the customary scientific, medical and logical subjects, always giving preference to the one which was made obligatory by the Universities, the subject of the soul. He considered the assumption that the human intelligence is a form of the body, a dangerous reduction of the spiritual principle to the bodily principle. He believed that a complete *separation* of the one from the other was the only secure way of defending the autonomy of thought. On the other hand, he saw in man the living conjunction of a particular body and the intelligible universal. Hence 'man was the peak of the material world for in him things material and things immaterial were so united that he stood revealed as the link between the higher and the lower spheres'. Pietro Trapolino, another teacher of Pomponazzi's, always standing on firm Aristotelian ground, reached much the same conclusion. Trapolino wrote the inevitable commentary on the problem of the soul. Following Aristotle and Averroes, he emphasised the mediatorship of the intellect—a *separate* form and yet, at the same time, the principle that animates matter.[1]

This atmosphere provided the background for Pomponazzi's own researches. He reached the conclusion that man occupied a central position in the Universe. This conclusion was indistinguishable from the conclusions of Ficino and Pico; but it was arrived at by another route. Padua did not provide a fertile soil for explicitly humanistic essays of the literary kind. Whenever they were attempted, they degenerated easily into dry grammatical investigations. It is true that Vernia praised Barbaro for his translation of Themistius and perhaps also because of his

[1] The works of Achillini are collected in the Venice edition of 1508. The commentaries of Trapolino are in manuscript. Cp. B. Nardi, *Appunti sull'averroista bolognese Alessandro Achillini*, 'Giornale critico della filosofia italiana', 33, 1954, pp. 67–108. For Pomponazzi, cp. the Venice edition of 1525; for *De Fato* and for *De Incantationibus* the Bâle edition of 1567 by Gratarol. There is now a critical edition of *De Fato* by R. Lemay, Lugano, 1957. For *De Immortalitate*, cp. Morra's edition, Bologna, 1954. For *Dubitationes in IV meteor. Arist. lib.*, see the Venice edition of 1563. As far as the lectures are concerned, only those on the soul have been edited by Ferri in 1877. They are now being studied systematically and the important ones published by B. Nardi, 'Giornale critico della filosofia italiana', 1950–6. Cp. also *Il commento di Simplicio al 'De Anima' nelle controversie della fine del sec. XV e del sec. XVI*, 'Archiv. di filosofia', 1951.

interest in logic. But neither Barbaro nor the elegantly erudite Niccolò Leonico Tomeo, a friend and protegé of Bembo, were able to find any response outside a narrow circle of pure and exclusively literary men.[2] As against this, the scene was dominated by the discussions of Occamists on formal logic and on physics. As a young man, Pomponazzi was completely captivated by discussions of this sort. The debates of the followers of Scotus, among whom Trombetta, an effective controversialist, stood out, were equally lively. And finally, there was no lack of Thomists who, at a certain moment thought they could count Pomponazzi among their number. At least, Crisostomo Javelli of Casale, a Dominican, was to bemoan Pomponazzi's attitude after the latter had published his *De Immortalitate* and considered it a kind of treason: 'many people devoted to you . . . are surprised that you have turned your back on Thomas who is a most sound guide for you and for me'.

As a matter of fact, Peretto was not a slavish adherent of either Aquinas or Averroes. Contarini mentions him as a critic of the latter while another pupil noted in his exercise book the ridicule that has been heaped upon *isti fratres truffaldini, dominichini, franceschini vel diabolini*. He considered that philosophy was not a dogma, but a difficult search, and he was fond of comparing it to the vulture that nibbled at the liver of the chained Prometheus. He described philosophising as an incessant discussion with one's self—a sort of combat, likely to lead to heresy: *oportet enim in philosophia haereticum esse qui veritatem invenire cupit*. For this very reason he ridiculed the authors of glosses, the slavish adherents of other philosophers, in short all those people whom Galileo was to describe as the mouthpieces of other people's opinions.

One can easily understand, therefore, that Speroni saw in Pomponazzi a severe critic of all those people who, relying solely on their knowledge of the language, had dared to 'lay hands' on the books of Aristotle 'pretending to explain them in public like any other work of literature'.

Like Achillini, Pomponazzi had begun by dealing with problems of physics and of logic. Thus he had taken up the

---

[2] Tomeo collected his *Dialoghi* in 1524 (ed. Venezia) and the *Opuscula* in 1525. The philosophical writings of Contarini are collected in the Venice edition of 1588.

question, first dealt with by the English Occamists and discussed later by the philosophers of Paris and in Italy by Gaetano di Thiene and by Marliano. That is, the question as to the relationship between qualitative and quantitative variations (*de intensione et remissione formarum*). But the work that was to occupy his mind most, because of the discussions that were to follow it, was a work published in 1516 in Bologna. It was concerned with the attempt to solve the problem of immortality by the sole method of pure reason. The great themes of the 15th century had been man, man's double nature and man's central position in the universe. Ficino himself had devoted his masterpiece to the great problem of immortality. Pomponazzi devoted astringent analysis to this problem and connected it with his clear conception of the natural order of things. 'Nature,' he once remarked, 'proceeds in steps. Plants have a little bit of soul. Next come those animals that have senses of touch and taste, but merely a very undifferentiating power of imagining. Then come those animals that seem so perfect that they almost appear to be endowed with reason: they build their homes and organise themselves in communities. They have something like a real state, like the bees, for example. There are many men who, in so far as reason is concerned, cannot compete with those animals.' This conception of continuity implies the conception of mediatorship, i.e. of rings that are joined to one another and that make a synthetic whole. 'There are animals that stand between plants and other animals, e.g. the sponges of the ocean. The latter are fixed to plants, but, unlike plants, they have sensations like animals. Then there is the ape, of whom one cannot say whether he is animal or human. And similarly, there are rational souls that are suspended between time and eternity.'

As far as this last point was concerned, it did not escape Pomponazzi that his conception of this middle position of the soul had an entirely new character. For this middle position was a position not between two levels of nature, but a position on the frontier between nature and supernature. Hence his efforts were directed towards an attempt to understand what the meaning of the soul's participation in supernature might be. For he rejected the Platonic as well as the Averroistic notion of a *separation*, even though, like the Averroists, he had no presuppositions. There were, to him, too many links between sensation and understanding; and the latter cannot be explained without reference to the former. 'If the essence with which I feel were different from the essence with which I understand, how could I, when I feel, be the same person as I, when I understand? It would be ridiculous to suppose that one is dealing in fact with two people joined together, whose cognitions happen to correspond to one another'. Thus he contemptuously discarded not only the notion of a strict separation but also of any kind of a merely 'occasionalistic' correspondence.

It was therefore natural that Pomponazzi, in his opposition to both Averroists and Platonists, should have drawn closer to St. Thomas. For Thomas had clearly emphasised that in man, matter and form are intimately suffused with one another. On the other hand, the influence of Alexander of Aphrodisia, who had stubbornly defended the view that the intellectual light and God are identical, is very much less apparent than people have often supposed. But his contemporaries, especially alert opponents like Javelli, liked to think that there was no real difference between Pomponazzi and the great Thomist Tommaso da Vio. According to Javelli, as far as the problem of the soul was concerned, it was not possible to distinguish between the two men.[3]

Nevertheless, Pomponazzi was critical of Aquinas; for the latter had inferred, from his premises, that the soul is 'truly and absolutely immortal'. Whereas the truth of the matter, according to Pomponazzi, was that to man, immortality is merely 'not proper'. For the intellect can only be partially separated from the body in that its functions are only relatively independent. If Pomponazzi spoke metaphorically of the *perfume* of immortality, he did so in order to indicate to man what he ought to long for, what he ought to seek—an ideal goal. But he did not mean to say that immortality is a human property. For to say this would have been absurd and contradictory. In the ascending line of nature, man is the peak. But where Pico saw man as the last frontier of nature, worshipped by all the rest of nature as something superior, Pomponazzi placed man well inside the limits of nature and merely took it that man aims beyond those limits. But often

---

[3] *Quaestiones Subtilissimae super Tres Libros Arist. de An.*, Venetiis, 1552, fol, 131; See Thomas De Vio, *Scripta Philosoph.*, I, Roma, 1938.

enough man does not even strive to surpass those limits! And
frequently we find bitter reflections like the following: 'If you
consider the inhabited regions of the earth, you will find that
almost all men are beasts rather than human beings. Rational
beings are very rare among them. But even those who are rational
beings, are so not absolutely, but only by comparison with the
rest who are wholly beastly; just as women are never really wise,
but appear so only in contrast to those women who are particularly stupid.'

In Pomponazzi's view, therefore, it was not possible to think
of a complete separation as the Platonists had done, and of an
immortality that presupposed an autonomous life of the soul.
He saw the soul as a mediator, as a kind of horizon to the realm of
nature. And for this reason he found it impossible to separate it
from the reality of which it forms the limit. If one were to
separate the soul from it, one would distort it and render it
completely unintelligible. For the soul's activity always requires
a sensuous element.

The rejection of immortality, or at least of the rational
certainty of immortality, cannot, however, shake the foundations
of ethics. Virtue and happiness are intimately connected with one
another. In fact, they are simply two different aspects of one and
the same reality. They constitute an inner harmony. They are
destroyed by vice which turns man into a beast and deprives him
of all joy. 'Who, therefore, no matter how mortal he be, will
prefer a vice that makes him into an animal and into something
worse than an animal?'

In spite of all this, Pomponazzi's thought did not manage to
reach a really unequivocal conclusion. It ended with a *neutral*
problem and repeats, in respect to the problem of immortality,
more or less what St. Thomas had said about the problem of the
eternity of the world: 'Those who proceed along the path of
faith will remain firm and sound.' In his *De Nutritione*, Pomponazzi's most radical work in which someone, exaggeratedly, claims
to have discovered traces of pure materialism, we can find the
following assertion: 'I believe that it is true, according to Aristotle, that the souls not only of plants and of insects, but also
of all those things that are act in regard to an inferior matter, are
divisible. And this is so in spite of that (revealed) Truth, of which

Aristotle knew nothing, that the soul ought to be considered absolutely indivisible. The latter view, it seems to me, must be accepted by faith, and not by natural reason. . . . The church, on the other hand, is neither based upon the stupidity of philosophers nor on human reason which is altogether lost in fog, but on the Holy Ghost and the indisputable evidence of miracles. And we must not abandon these sacred propositions either because of reason or because of the words of Aristotle.' It is difficult to say whether Pomponazzi, here, was sincere or ironical. Or did he, perhaps, only want to emphasise the paradoxical possibility of appealing, beyond all earthly limits, to an act of faith?

2. THE CONTROVERSY ABOUT IMMORTALITY

It would take too long to follow in detail the endless discussions occasioned by Pomponazzi's small book. It was publicly burnt in Venice and preachers fulminated from pulpits against it. It was attacked by Ambrogio Fiandino, Bartholomeo di Spina, Crisostomo Javelli, Fornari, and, above all, by Gaspare Contarini and Agostino Nifo.[4] Pomponazzi replied to these attacks in his *Apologia* and his *Defensorium*. The main attacks were all directed against Pomponazzi's denial of the possibility of separate substances. Reason, it was stated, leads to the knowledge of first principles and recognises the forms that are completely detached from matter. By this activity it proves that the theory that there can be no thought without sensual images, is false. Moreover, in so far as the intellect is a pure capacity of understanding it follows that it has no link with anything extended; and hence, that it is not divisible. It was no accident that Contarini recalled Avicenna's famous argument of 'the flying man' which had also been dear to Ficino and which was meant to demonstrate the pure spirituality of the soul. Nifo, on the other hand, referred to the celestial intelligences, the existence of which had been admitted by Pomponazzi, and considered them extrinsic and assisting agents, in a typically Platonic sense.

It has been known for a long time that Nifo was both confused and loquacious. Already Varchi thought that 'he used to chat,

---

[4] For Nifo cp. *De Immortalitate Animae*, Venetiis, 1525. *De Intellectu*, Venetiis, 1527 and the commentary on *De Anima*, Venetiis, 1503.

without the slightest sense of judgement, not only about this matter but about a thousand other topics. He said not only the things that happened to cross his mind, but also those that happened to be on his tongue. He behaved like this not so much because of his character, but because of his very great reputation and his incredible authority.' He owed this reputation and authority to a truly unlimited erudition and to a productivity which invaded every field even though the results remained only too often very poor. In the discussion on the problem of the soul he first showed himself to be a pupil of Vernia. Then he came under the influence of Averroistic doctrines only in order to end up by paying homage to the Platonic view of separation. Historically speaking, however, his function was not to express the one or the other doctrine—the content of which nobody could clearly ascertain anyway—but in the breadth of his know-ledge and in the way in which he provided an ideal link between the schools of Padua and Bologna and those of Florence and Pisa; and later also with those of Salerno and Naples. Hence his fame rests not so much on the opinion of philosophers as on his appear-ances in the writings of men of letters such as Galeazzo Flori-monte, surnamed 'good old Galateo', or Toquato Tasso, for instance, who dedicated two of his dialogues on pleasure to him. In these dialogues, Tasso brought out well the mundane mind of this easily intelligible populariser—or, as Plato would have said, of this pedlar of philosophy. 'I am a philosopher,' Tasso made him say, 'but unlike Socrates, I have not walked about until my feet hurt. Like Scipio, I have accustomed them to slippers and to the comforts of the Greek schools.' Averroism meant to him an appeal to open-mindedness rather than a solid and defined point of view. Hence he was for ever ready to dilute it until it turned into a conventional form of Platonism. For that matter, such a Platonism was much more suitable to the fashionable assemblies which Nifo preferred anyway to the stale air of the academies.

Simone Porzio, though preoccupied by similar problems, had a very different temperament. He taught both in Pisa and Naples, and was on friendly terms with the bizarre and learned Giovan Battista Gelli, shoemaker, writer and philosopher, who combined the Hermetic inspiration of the Ficinian tradition with the stern rigour of the purest Peripateticism.[5] Porzio was really opposed to the view that the soul can be separated. For this reason he fought against Averroists and Simplicians and charged Alexander of Aphrodisias with identifying God with the light of the intellect. He held that the intellect, in spite of the nobility of its function, is an *opus naturae*. Aristotelianism, provided it is understood correctly, means nothing more than a firm fidelity to nature. It amounts to man confining himself to the limits set by nature. With these views Porzio came into opposition to Jacopo Antonio Marta (a pupil of Nifo's). Marta carried on a controversy with Porzio, and later also with Telesio, for he was determined to keep on trying to find a support for religion in Aristotle.

Although several valiant attempts have been made, it is really impossible to distinguish systematically between the various movements of opinion about the problem of the soul. Although there is constant talk about Simplicians, Averroists, Thomists and Alexandrists, it is not possible to establish the differences between the followers of Themistius, Simplicius, Averroes or between those of Alexander, Avicenna and St. Thomas. We have mentioned above that to some, Pomponazzi appeared to be an orthodox follower of Alexander of Aphrodisias; and that to others like Javelli da Casale, who was a Dominican and a sort of Platonist, his position was identical with that of De Vio, the greatest Thomist of the 16th century. The truth of the matter is that these descriptions of Pomponazzi are so many labels and have no more than a purely polemical significance. Take, for example, Giulio Castellani. Castellani identified himself with the views of Porzio and declared at the same time that he shared the ideas expressed in the commentary of Alexander of Aphrodisias and of Pomponazzi. And although he cherished the views of Ficino and Plato, he tried to imitate Vincenzo Maggi, an orthodox Peripatetic. At bottom, Castellani's efforts amount to no more than an attempt to assign to philosophy the task of a precise psychological investigation, free from all religious considerations, of the development from sense experience to pure thought. His criticism was directed in fact against the Simplicians of Padua and against the

---

[5] *Simonis Portii Neapolitani De Humana Mente Disputatio*, Florentiae, 1551 (the Italian translation by Gelli is in a MS of the National Library, Paris). The *opuscoli* of Porzio with the *Apologia* by Marta, were published in Naples, 1578.

Averroists in so far as these men argued in favour of a separation, in the Platonic sense, of the spiritual or intellectual world from nature. He did not even exempt from his criticism his own kinsman, Pier Niccolò Castellani, for the latter's translation of the Plotinian *Theologia Aristotelis* had helped, so to speak, the propagation of the theory of separation.[6]

On the other side one can observe that the Averroists, in the eyes of the followers of Alexander of Aphrodisia, inclined too much towards transcendence—for they, at times, owing to the hold a certain kind of Platonism had on them, extended the separation even to the possible intellect. But, in the eyes of the Thomists, these same Averroists appeared as the defenders of free and critical thought. Varchi, who had a great weakness for Averroes, when discussing the problem of the soul, remarked as follows: 'This problem is not only, by its very nature, highly doubtful and controversial; but it has also been treated by so many people in a most obscure manner and in so many different ways that not even those who have studied it for years dare speak of it with any sense of certainty. One might almost say that it is the sort of problem of which those who know most are least bold to speak.'

3. JACOPO ZABARELLA

The problem of the soul tended to become more and more complicated in more ways than one. It had first arisen as the question whether it was possible to prove the immortality of the soul by pure reason. As time went by, it forced people to attempt the solution of epistemological and psychological problems. This is not the place to report on the many subtle shades the problem tended to assume in the hands of the all too many professors who either had their lectures printed or left them behind as manuscripts, like the strict Averroist Zimara, like Bacilieri or Bernardi of Mirandola, or Passero the Simplician, surnamed Genova. Then there was the great Pendasio; there was Burana, Vimercati, Montecatini, Vito Piza, Piccolomini, Cremonini, Liceti and a host of minor, less well known characters. It is much more

[6] G. Castellani, *De Humano Intellectu Libri Tres*, Bononiae, 1561. Cp. Varchi's 'Sulla creazione ed infusione dell'anima razionale', *Opere*, II, pp. 311 sqq.

rewarding to follow the major steps of the discussion with Jacopo Zabarella. He wrote them down and commented on them in a masterly fashion.[7] In his opinion, the basic opposition between Plato and Aristotle had found its repetition in the opposition of Alexander to Averroes. According to Averroism, the soul is a *forma assistens*. This means that it is in itself a perfected reality, an act in an act. '*Forma assistens* is a form which is to be found associated with an object for the purpose of guiding it. But it is not only separable but also separate, and completely different from the matter to which it gives being, just as the pilot of a ship is separate from the ship because his being is alien to the essence of the ship'. As against this, the followers of Alexander take the soul to be a *forma formans*: in the ship it is the very nature of the ship, and in man, the very species that lives inside each concrete individual. In short, Zabarella is of the opinion that the controversies about the problem of the soul which were taking place within the Aristotelian universe of discourse, were simply repeating all the difficulties originally inherent in Platonism. For genuine Aristotelians were fighting Platonists disguised as Aristotelians.

A similar invidious equivocation appears in regard to the problems of the intellect. For as far as the intellect is concerned, the Platonic separation reappears in order to detach now one, now the other intellect, so that the soul is rent asunder and the separation reaffirmed. If we follow the Averroists and take the possible intellect to be separate, we are compelled to see the act of understanding as *transiens* or accidental, at least as far as man is concerned. It will certainly not appear to be *immanens* or essential to man. This is so even though the Averroists speak of an objective connection between intellect and man; for, they say, one can only know through the bodily senses. But, Zabarella objects, this would mean that, since the pilot sees the ship, the ship is not only seen, but is itself seeing. It is equally impossible to argue in favour of a separation by insisting that the intellect thinks of *universalia* that are completely detached from all matter. To say that they are detached, is to say that they are abstract; and to say that they are abstract, is to say that there is a separation *secundum operationem* and not *secundum esse*. And this amounts to saying

[7] *Jacobi Zabarellae de Rebus Naturalibus libri XXX*, Venetiis, 1590.

that in man there is an activity which can be distinguished from organic changes but which is not separate from them. One may, therefore, say that the soul *is* the pilot, though not in the sense that it is separate from the body, but only in the sense that it governs the organs, changes and guides them as a unity immanent in the organism—as the element which makes the organism what it is. The separation of which Aristotle had spoken, therefore, is not an absolute separation in the Platonic sense, but merely a way of referring to a relationship. The process of acquiring knowledge is an autonomous process in the course of which one rises without external interventions from mere sensations to purely intellectual apprehension.

It would be vain to search for something approaching to Zarabella's clarity in any of his successors. His sense of logic was certainly not shared by Piccolomini who kept vacillating between Aristotle and Plato. He confessed himself a supporter of the former; but, secretly, he was in love with the latter. Nor was the famous Cesare Cremonini da Cento, Zabarella's equal in logic. Cesare Cremonini da Cento was a pupil of Pendasio. He was a friend of both Tasso and Patrizi and a colleague of Galilei, and displayed an admirable and proud stubbornness when he defended his faith in rational research against threats, intrigues and criticisms. He made the following reply to the Inquisition: 'As far as my mode of expression is concerned, I do not know how I could ever promise to change myself. One man has one form of expression; another man has another mode. I cannot and do not wish to retract my exposition of Aristotle; for this is the way in which I understand him.' He also disagreed with the Averroists' conception of the soul as a *forma assistens*; but he, like Nifo, remained content with the vague description of the soul as a form which uses the body like a tool. Liceti was equally insignificant. His weakness in speculation became all the more apparent when he managed to acquire some kind of fame through his relations with Galilei.[8]

In conclusion, one can note that the lengthy discussions on the problem of the soul and the intellect, which make up most of the Italian Aristotelian movement, only managed to twist the Platonic theme, but not to alter it. The soul is the extreme point of nature. But the great question is whether as such it is part of the world of nature and therefore mortal and subject to all physical vicissitudes, or whether its activities in the fields of ethics and of knowledge and its double essence, place it in a position that is irreducible to the pure and simple plane of nature. This problem, which appeared both as a problem of ethics and as a problem in the theory of knowledge, was in reality a metaphysical problem. But it so happened that Aristotelianism found itself in a very insecure position. It was perforated, so to speak, and endangered not only by the Platonic elements which were immanent in it; but also by the Neoplatonism of the Arabs and by Christian interpretations. Thus it was impotent to develop the logical consequences of that naturalism which was, after all, its main foundation.

4. THE RELIGIOUS PROBLEM IN ARISTOTELIANISM

On the whole, Aristotelianism proved more fertile when it invaded fields other than those of the classical problems to which it was customarily confined. It was indeed most fertile in the fields of logic and of methodology, of morals and politics. The Aristotelians showed genuinely subtle minds in sincere descriptions of reality and in a faithful adherence to facts. Pomponazzi, for instance, was at his best in his *De Incantationibus* and his *De Fato*. Both treatises were works of uncommon daring and of undeniable profundity. In spite of this they are much less famous than his *De Immortalitate*. In the *De Incantationibus*, Pomponazzi discussed the question of the supernatural and the possibility of the interference of external forces with nature. And similarly, Machiavelli, in a famous section of the *Discorsi sulla prima deca di Tito Livio* investigated the various religions from the point of view of their practical and political efficacy. From an exclusively earthly standpoint he considered man's devotion to heaven as a purely mundane phenomenon, highly interesting because of its undeniable and far-reaching effects.[8]

In many senses, Pomponazzi's mind was akin to that of Machiavelli. Both directed their gaze entirely upon the earth.

[8] For the texts on the soul by minor Aristotelians cp. E. Renan, *Averroës et l'averroisme*, Paris, 1852. F. Fiorentino, *Pietro Pomponazzi*, Firenze, 1868; K. Werner, *Der Averroismus in der christlich-peripat. Psychol. d. späteren Mittelalters*, Wien, 1881. L. Mabilleau, *Étude historique sur la philosophie de la Renaissance en Italie: C. Cremonini*, Paris, 1881; B. Nardi, *La fine dell' averroismo*, in 'Pensée humaniste' op. cit., pp. 139–151. Cremonini, *Quaestio Utrum Animi Mores Sequantur Corporis Temperantiam.*

They saw in man a marvellous builder; but nevertheless nothing more than an earthly creature confined to the earth. They admitted that, as far as the beyond is concerned, the possibility of faith cannot be excluded. But such a faith is without basis and entirely devoid of reason. And rational research can take it only into account in so far as it can become the cause of concrete phenomena that affect our earthly lives. Machiavelli considered these effects of faith in the sphere of politics; and Pomponazzi investigated them from the standpoint of logic, psychology and physics. Pomponazzi asked himself indeed in which way the religious factor affected human nature and tended to modify it. And similarly he wanted to know what value one ought to attribute to the assertion that supernatural causes have miraculous effects. In his *De Incantationibus* his answer is extremely clear: 'It is possible to justify any experience by natural causes. There is no reason that could ever compel us to make any perception depend on demonic powers. There is no point in introducing supernatural agents. It is ridiculous as well as frivolous to abandon the evidence of natural reason and to search for things that are neither probable nor rational.'

There is no difficulty in reducing all miraculous interventions to the realm of natural causes. Or, to be more precise, these interventions are no more and no less miraculous than all other causal connections. Miracles can no more be explained than it is possible to explain why the raven's croak is supposed to herald a misfortune or why a certain herb can cure a disease. It is typical for Pomponazzi to think always in the following terms. Everything belongs to the rational order which we know about through experience; and in this order everything except explanation itself can be explained. And therefore he leaves, in the last analysis, a way open to God. He considers that the stars and religious symbols have purely natural effects. The same is true of magic formulas and astrological pictures. The only difference is that 'the cross is effective solely as the sign of that Legislator Whom also the stars respect'.

A similar paradox is to be found in his *De Fato* which he placed in the centre of the conflict between the contingentism of Alexander of Aphrodisia and the doctrine of universal necessity of the Stoics. Here too Pomponazzi seems, at first, to have decided

M

in favour of the Stoics, only in order to reject Stoicism in the end in favour of the view that the wise man, 'a terrestial deity', has the fullness of freedom. For the few wise men are placed above the rest of human animals, dominated as they are by the laws of nature. For the wise men transform damnation into redemption. Thus they transcend nature and irremediably loosen up its solid compactness.

In his dialogue on rhetoric, Speroni, who was tied in many ways to Peretto, contrasted the solitary philosopher, deeply immersed in metaphysical contemplation, to the 'civic' orator. Thus he distinguished, without being aware of it, between a scholastic, traditional conception of philosophy as systematic metaphysics and active thinking, deeply rooted in life and determined to change life. Pomponazzi, though he never rendered a full account of it to himself, followed the path of active thinking.

CHAPTER VI

LOGIC, RHETORIC AND POETICS

1. LOGICAL AND METHODOLOGICAL PROBLEMS

THE occupants of University chairs were expected to provide clarification of psychological problems—for every serious metaphysical and religious question was tied up with them. But logical discussion, too, stood in the centre of public interest. In these discussions we find on one side the orthodox Aristotelians and on the other all those whom the pursuits of rhetoric and grammar had caused to feel the need for some kind of discipline of thought. Such a discipline, they hoped, would make possible a closer adherence to concreteness. In the *Massimi sistemi* Galilei made Salviati, on the first day of the debate, express a condemnation of formal logic: formal logic is a mere 'tool' which has, unfortunately, become an end in itself. 'Logic is the organ with which one philosophises'; but 'one cannot learn to play the organ from those who build organs, but only from those who know how to play organs. Thus one can learn to write poetry by the continuous reading of poems; and one can learn to paint . . . by persisting in drawing and painting. Similarly, one can learn how to deduce, by reading books which contain deductions, that is, from books on mathematics; but not from books on logic'. In short, there is no point in discussing abstract schemes of how a logical argument ought to be conducted. These schemes remain empty and sterile. This argument amounted to the condemnation not only of a certain method, but also of a philosophy; and more precisely of the dumb and hateful philosophy of which one might say, as one says of faith, that without works it is dead. And by 'works' Stefano Guazzo meant, in this connection, the posession of fertile knowledge, capable of leaving an effective mark on civil 'conversation'.[1]

---

[1] *La civile conversatione del Sig. Stefano Guazzo, gentiluomo di Casale di Monferrato, divisa in quattro libri . . . nouvamente dall' istesso autore corretta e . . . ampliata,* Venezia, 1586, pp. 16, 19, 24. For Guazzo cp. also *Lettere*, Torino, 1591.

In short, logic was supposed to be a conscious criticism of thought in action. Long before Galilei, Alexander Piccolomini had eloquently maintained the same thing. He had written often and at great length on logic and had always advocated that 'all sciences ought to be studied together, as if they were mixed up with one another; so that any one was always a necessary prerequisite for any other.'[2] For this reason, 'although, following common opinion, one can always regard any one of the sciences as the principal one, every science will become more perfect if, having studied it, one also studies those that come after it.' Piccolomini never tired of reiterating that it is useless to chase the 'superfluous and petty little problems' of the Occamists. For he held it to be senseless to carry on debates for debating's sake. 'For this reason I often feel pity for those who, not so very long ago, used to exercise themselves in *litteris* without being able to approach truth. Truth can only be reached on a straight and proper path. Never on crooked and long paths. And truth can never be reached by those who seek it in order to doubt and quarrel, but only by those *who seek doubt in order to find truth*.' With this statement he emphasised the inventive moment as against the demonstrative one; and, in the last analysis, subtracted from the value of logic. According to another pronouncement by Piccolomini, logic was to be relegated to a question of demonstration and proof, while other sciences were to have a monopoly of invention and description. When, in a small work of the year 1547, he examined the validity of mathematics, he ascribed to logic proper the two functions of resolution and of composition as methods of proof. He also insisted that logic can lead to discoveries only by accident. As against this, a man like Varchi, treating of methodology, considered it in a much more comprehensive sense: 'by this name,' Varchi said, 'I understand Topics . . . that is, genuine invention, as well as Juristics, that is, demonstration'. Thus he had described logic in general as 'the science or art, or better, the faculty which alone points the way towards all other sciences and arts'.[3]

[2] Alessandro Piccolomini, *L'istrumento della filosofia*, Venezia, 1560; *Della institution morale libri XII*, Venetia, 1582, pp. 125, 133.
[3] A. Piccolomini, *In Mechanicas Quaestiones . . . Comm. de Certitudine Mathem. Discipl.*, Romae, 1547, p. LXXIII; see Varchi, *Opere*, II, p. 797.

On the whole there was a general disapproval of the subtleties of the Terminists whose prestige had remained high right down to the time of Pomponazzi. But from then on, people's attention came to be directed more and more towards invention, and the analytical and dissecting methods were emphatically considered to be the proper means for obtaining definitions. We need consider, for instance, only the *Trattato dell' istrumento e via inventrice degli antichi* by Sebastiano Erizzo. Erizzo was a writer much given to Platonic thoughts and in his treatise we will find the following solemn affirmation: 'Through division we find what is most important in things, i.e. their essential differences, the sum total of which makes up their definition'. But there is more: *dissection* is the only means of invention, he wrote. And it is no accident that he appealed to Galen and the natural sciences. 'One must not stray from this path, i.e. from the idea that division is both the instrument and the way, and is, in fact—the Greeks called it method—the inventor of all things. One can certainly deny that it does not lead to invention'.

Similarly, Giacomo Aconcio in his booklet *De Methodo* appealed to Galen, to experience, to the principle of utility and to the necessity for the overhaul of ancient and insufficient schemes. It is significant that he too preferred the analytically dividing process as the sole effective instrument of discovery.[4]

2. ZABARELLA AND THE PADUAN CONTROVERSIES

Varchi, in the above mentioned lectures, considered the effort to decide whether logic is a science or an art, a vain one. This, however, was not the opinion of the Paduan teachers. One of them, Zabarella, reached quite interesting conclusions in this respect. For more than half a century, the Paduan Professors, when they were writing their commentaries on Aristotle and Averroes, had been trying to determine the processes of thought that led from effects to causes and from causes to effects. Tomitano, a highly respected grammarian and rhetorician, had insisted that in the natural sciences all reasoning is from effects to causes; and

[4] S. Erizzo, *Trattato dell' istrumento e via inventrice degli antichi*, Venevia, 1554; *Lettere di XIII uomini illustri*, pp. 620–25; Giacomo Aconcio, *De Methodo e Opuscoli*, G. Radetti ed., Firenze, 1944, p. 166.

that inferences from the universal to the singular (in syllogisms) are employed only in the systematisation of knowledge already acquired. The force of all constructive investigation and research consists in regressive thinking, which is nothing else but induction. We can see therefore that Tomitano gave a very clear formulation of the rhythm analysis-synthesis, so dear to Galilei.

Zabarella was a pupil of Tomitano's and as a logician he was repeatedly involved in controversies. First, we ought to mention those with Francesco Piccolomini of whose uncertain position, halfway between Plato and Aristotle, we have already spoken. Zabarella distinguished between *method* and *order*. By *method*, which he considered to be the more important of the two, he meant the inventive factor; that is, the transition from what is known in experience to the unknown cause. By *order*, on the other hand, he meant no more than a simple and secondary process of justification. To Piccolomini, however, order was fundamental; for it reflects in us the structure which God has imprinted on things. And this structure is reproduced in human thought. In a similar vein, Varchi, when he compared *order* to *method*, said that 'the seeds of all arts and all sciences are implanted in us, as are their principles, by Nature, and he who wants to learn or teach must follow them.' In other words: logic has not only a metaphysical basis, but all our reasoning processes presuppose the existence of the objective pattern of nature.[5]

As against this, Zabarella not only clung to the theory that there was a difference between actual invention and demonstration —a difference which had also been emphasised, as we have seen, by Alessandro Piccolomini—but also denied that logic is a science. By this he meant to reject the view that logic has reality as its object. According to him, logic is a technique, a human art, designed to lead to the establishment of scientific knowledge. He insisted that 'logic refers to secondary or derived notions, to terms which are our own inventions and which need not exist. These terms are not necessary things, but contingent ones. For this reason, they cannot be an object of science, for science concerns itself only with necessary things.' Men have created

[5] Cp. Zabarella, *Opera Logica*, Frankfurth, 1608; Fr. Piccolomini, *Universa Philosophia de Moribus*, Venezia, 1594 (cap. XIV–XXIV, *De Doctrina Ordine Apologia e Comes Politicus*); Persio, *Defensiones*; Petrella, *Quaestiones Logicae*, Patavii, 1571 e 1576; for Varchi cp. *Del methodo*, *Opere*, II, pp. 796 sqq.

logic by creating secondary and derived concepts. For this reason, logic occupies a place analogous to that of grammar.

On this very point, Zabarella was forced to conduct a lively controversy with an old logician, Bernardino Petrella. Or rather, he had it conducted for him by one of his students, a certain Ascanio Persio. On Petrella's side, the controversy was continued by a pupil of his, one Giulio Marziale—unless this name was only a pseudonym for Petrella. Petrella maintained stubbornly that logic is a science and that its subject matter does not consist of terms but of pure concepts. Hence its subject matter consists not of secondary, derived knowledge, but of first order knowledge. It is very instructive to watch Petrella's difficulties in finding a transition from those reified concepts to the world of physical reality. Indeed, he found this transition to be impossible and in the end he was left with a circular argument about analysis and synthesis suspended in abstract and empty formulations. As against this, the process of logical reasoning was for Zabarella a means to reach, beyond mere terms, the entities signified by the terms. The method of logic endeavours to guide all thinking, including physical and metaphysical research, and to supervise the progress of discovery that starts with what is known, and aims at grasping the unknown. It is no longer a question of the analysis and synthesis of abstract knowledge, but of a transition from facts to their causes, and *vice versa*, from the causes to the facts. It is not a question of geometrical reasoning in which the subject contains the predicate, but of *hunting* for concepts in terms of which logic explains the methods and ruses employed by wise men. Method, therefore, is nothing else but the technique employed in hunting the unknown. And this method or technique of hunting has a double rhythm. There is first a dividing inference, an inference from effect to cause; and, secondly, a constructive inference which helps us to discern how a certain cause produces a certain effect. Thus every entity is discovered in the secret relationship in which it stands to itself. In this way it is grasped in its depth and illuminated. 'Induction does not prove one thing by another. In a certain sense, every thing reveals itself through itself. And since every thing is better known as a particular than as a universal (for as a particular it can be grasped by the senses), induction is a process of reasoning that proceeds from the thing to the thing. It starts with a knowledge of the particular thing in its most obvious appearance and leads to the thing in its most dark and hidden aspect. In this way, induction not only leads to the principles of all things but also to the fundamentals of scientific knowledge, which are usually said to be undemonstrable.' It is impossible to give a clearer account of logic as an inner movement through which a thing is understood in relation to itself and in reflection. And, at the same time, Galilei's method could not have found a clearer explanation. In the 66th lesson of his *Dialettica*, recorded by his pupil Troilo Lancetta, Galilei's opponent Cremoni gave the following definition: 'The method of composition begins with principles and advances towards the knowledge of things. The method of dissolution, however, begins from the end and advances towards a consideration of those things that must have occurred for those ends to have been brought about.'[6]

3. LOGIC AND RHETORIC: MARIO NIZOLIO

There can be no doubt that Zabarella was a philosopher of penetrating intelligence. But in spite of his acumen, he remained much more captive to tradition than a grammarian like Mario Nizolio. The latter wrote a work of four books *De Veris Principiis et Vera Ratione Philosophandi* which purported to be no more than a refutation of Maioragio. But in fact it amounted to a destruction of the last vestiges of the old Atistotelian logical systems and endeavoured to trace the living processes of effective thinking by grasping its rhythm and by following it, unencumbered by ideas that have become crystallised and by artificially invented universals. It was no more than an attempt, albeit an attempt that was to earn the admiration of no less a person than Leibniz. But this attempt was designed to describe the pulsations of reason in their relation to things and to man and to show the unity of the process underlying both linguistic communication and all forms of cognition. According to Nizolio, one ought to begin by freeing oneself of the fictitious superstructure—*universalia stulta et inepta*—and to rediscover the purity of man as well as that of things in the untouched virginity of linguistic expressions. For

---

[6] *Caesaris Cremonini Centensis . . . Dialectica, addita in fine singularum lectionum paraphrasi a Troylo de Lancettis,* Venetiis, 1663, p. 89.

these expressions are nothing but a spontaneous translation of the fundamental relationship between man and the world [7]

It is necessary to keep in mind Nizolio's initial declaration. He had spoken of the vanity of all researches that bear no relation to morals, politics or economics—that is, to the 'mundane sciences'. It is all the more necessary to keep this declaration in mind if one reads, in his *First General Principles of Philosophising*, that the knowledge of Latin and Greek must stand at the root of all science. For to him these languages are the concrete and exemplary expressions of the original direction in which the human mind first moved in its search for knowledge. Hence we see that the recommended study of rhetoric and grammar is an attempt to get into touch with the actual movement and unfolding of the inner human mind, with its rhythms and actual processes. All this amounts to a material, rather than a formal, logic. Indeed, these arguments are immediately followed by a criticism of metaphysics. The latter, it is alleged, busies itself with an empty truth and remains completely indifferent to researches that are concerned *de utilitate et de pertinentia rerum*. Metaphysics proceeds as if it were possible to speak of truth regardless of all concrete and human conditions. But in fact, only the latter make truth true.

To his mind, the reading of the great classics is the only genuine philosophical education there is. And such reading must be both continuous and penetrating in order to lead to a comprehension of their words. In this way it becomes, at the same time, a comprehension of the discourse common to all men. This goal can be reached only through experience because one is moving here on the terrain of a completely autonomous, free, human creation. Through the effort to assimilate to ourselves the consciousness of other men we will discover our innermost secrets as well as the whole meaning and value of man in all his

[7] M. Nizolio *De Veris Principiis et Vera Ratione Philosophandi contra Pseudophilosophos Libri IV, in quibus statuuntur ferme omnia vera verarum artium et scientiarum principia . . . et praeterea refelluntur fere omnes M.A. Majoagii obiectationes contra eundem Nizolium*, Parmae, 1553. It is well known that this work was republished by Leibniz with an introduction and notes, in Frankfurth, 1674. (*Antibarbarus Philosophicus, sive Philosophia Scholasticorum Impugnata Libris IV de veris*. On Nizolio, cp. P. Manutius, *Epistolarium libri V*, Venetiis, 1561, cc. 35–36. *De Veris Principiis* by Nizolio, now in the good edition of Q. Breen, 2 vols., Roma, 1956; on N. see Breen and the two essays by Paolo Rossi, in *La crisi dell'uso dogmatico della ragione*, ed. by A. Banfi, Milano, 1953, and *Testi umanistici sulla retorica*, 'Archivio di filosofia', 1953, pp. 57–92.

relationships. For this effort is a kind of civil and sociable conversation. The appeal to the classics does not contain so much as an ambiguous hint that we should abandon our own freedom; for it is indeed nothing but a means to rediscovering our *own* liberty. Nizolio's fourth principle emphatically stressed the complete independence of all research, for truth itself requires such independence. The senses, thought and experience are the only true teachers and they stand high above every author and also high above both Plato and Aristotle.

The scientific comprehension of reality does by no means amount to an escape into the nebulous realm of universals. On the contrary: it amounts to a firm attachment to particular realities, understood in their inner relationships to themselves and to other particulars of the same species. Nizolio joined an eternal controversy when he contrasted the comprehension through which reason grasps *simul et semel, singularia omnia cuiusque generis*, to the power of abstraction which invents fictitious entities. This kind of comprehension, instead of losing itself in the clouds of abstraction, remains closely attached to the senses and to consci-ousness. In short, he tried to replace Aristotelian logic by a new logic, supposed to correspond to the actual movements of human inwardness and to represent them consciously. The study of the poets and of language in general makes one conscious of live expression For all real motions of the soul are translated into language and are thus the cause of language. The study of language, therefore, enables one to enter into the depths of the world such as it is revealed in its relations to man. In this way the new logic, far from allowing itself to be coined in accordance with mathematical processes, is meant to be founded upon the actual processes through which the human mind communicates with other minds and comprehends reality.[8]

4. RHETORIC AND *La Civile Conversazione*

Nizolio's attitude had been formed by the whole of the accumulated experience of humanism. It had been an essential part of this experience to believe that since man needs a human world it is necessary to formulate a human logic that would apply to human and social communication and conversation. Thus

[8] *Op. cit.*, I, 7. Cp. III, 7, the definition of *comprehensio*.

attention had been drawn to language as the exemplary manifestation of mankind. Stefano Guazzo, in his dialogues on *La civile conversazione*, the first edition of which appeared in 1574, argued as follows: 'Nature herself has given man the power of speech. But certainly not in order that he converse with himself. ... It was given to him so that he could use it as a means of communication with others. You can see that we are using this tool in order to teach, question, negotiate, deliberate, improve, discuss and judge. Also, in order to express the emotions of the soul. All these are means by which men can come together and love one another.' Language, however, is not only a method of tying society together. It is also the living communication of human knowledge, the instrument through which science is realised and handed on: 'One cannot acquire scientific knowledge if it is not taught by others. ... Conversation is not only an advantage but also a necessary condition for the perfection of man.'

Dialogue between men is the beginning and end of all knowledge. In such dialogue, our knowledge is tested and our souls are awakened and stimulated to fruitful research. In fact, the whole concept of humanity exhausts itself in this concept of conversation, in this dialogue, in this speech which gathers in itself the concrete meaning of the life of the mind. 'The solitary man deserves the Hellebore as much as the madman. And if one examines the etymology of the word 'man' (in Greek, according to the opinion of some scholars, it is supposed to mean 'together') one will find that nobody can be man without conversation. For he who does not converse with his fellowmen can have no experience; and he who has no experience has no power of judgement; and he who has no power of judgement, is not far from an animal.'[9]

In Guazzo's modest but well formulated treatise, taken here as an example, the problem of the relationship between rhetoric and philosophy, between formal logic and the various living ways by which truth is discovered and communicated, is taken for granted. Nobody saw and illuminated this problem as clearly as Speroni who had not been a pupil of Pomponazzi's for nothing.[10] In his *Dialogo delle lingue* he approached the problem of Latin and Greek.

[9] Stefano Guazzo, *La civile conversazione*, Venezia, 1586, p. 14.
[10] Sperone Speroni, *Dialoghi*, Venezia, 1552, c. 110 sqq.

He asked himself whether the study of formal logic ought not to be replaced by the study of the classical languages, since the latter alone were sufficient for the discovery of the truth. It is 'as if the spirit of Aristotle, like the ghost in the bottle, were held captive in the Greek alphabet.' But he was aware of the fact that such a substitution would amount to no more than the substitution of one formalism for another. *Humanitas* had meant the rediscovery of thought by means of words. And more precisely, as far as the classics were concerned, it had meant the rediscovery of the highest thought by means of the most scrutinised verbal expressions. But the corruption of *studia humanitatis* had led to the very erroneous belief that a language 'by itself had the ability to signify the concepts of the mind'. Hence there had arisen the error that the Latin and the Greek languages expressed, as they stood, in definitive form, the logical structure of all thinking. The same thing had happened to Aristotelian logic. As long as it had been a living thought, it had been valid. But once it had come to be frozen into a rigid scheme, it became dead and useless. And now the same thing was happening to the classical languages. They were being separated from the original intentions of the mind and therefore became useless.

It was natural, however, that Speroni, in defending the *humanitas* of the vernacular, should be fully aware of the fact that the position of rhetoric as the art of persuasion, when compared with logic as the philosophy that possesses the norm of truth, is a problematical one. The simplest and the most widely held solution of this problem was the one propounded by Tomitano to the Academy of the *Infiammati* of Padua of which Speroni was the president. Tomitano had argued that 'the perfect rhetorician and poet requires philosophy', for philosophy searches for the truth which the rhetorician is supposed to divulge 'with elegance' in a persuasive manner. He is to do this by sweetening the rim of the cup of therapeutical medicines with attractive juices.[11]

Speroni himself started from a similar position and explained rhetoric as the beautification of speech: rhetoric is meant to make concepts more agreeable. Rhetoric, therefore, comes into the

[11] B. Tomitano, *Quattro libri della lingua toscana . . . . ove si prova la filosofia esser necessaria al perfetto oratore e poeta con due libri nuovamente aggiunti di precetti, necessari allo scrivere e parlare con eleganze*, 3rd ed., Padova, 1570. (The Venice edition of 1546 contains, after the second book, a noteworthy paraphrase of Aristotle's *Rhetoric*.)

category of art and is destined to beautify truth for educational purposes. Thus Speroni compared rhetoric with painting: 'the words originate from the mouths of people, even as the colours originate from herbs. But the grammarian is the assistant of the orator; it is he who smoothes and decorates the words, even as the painter's assistant smoothes and decorates the colours. In this way the master of rhetoric, when he comes to painting a full picture of the truth, can make a speech in his own manner and deliver a discourse.' But it does not suffice for the painter to see nature and its truth: it is necessary for him 'to familiarise himself thoroughly with them' in order to express their mute soul. Even so, the rhetorician needs to know the '*je ne sais quoi* element of the truth in question'. He has to know something of the truth which speaks to us and which dwells in our heart 'like the thing which God implanted in the beginning in our souls and which our souls naturally strive to know.'[12]

At this point, Speroni moved a step forward and ascribed, mindful of the ending of Plato's *Phaidros*, to rhetoric and poetry the function of awakening the soul and of thus calling truth into being. In this respect he ended up by considering rhetoric not so much a mere decoration of truth and subordinate to the latter, as an annunciation and intimation of truth; or, better, as a guide to the truth—as a guide which makes truth articulate. As far as the philosopher is concerned, he observed, he may well consider rhetoric and poetry like the dessert that comes at the end of a meal. 'But for those who are not philosophers but would like to become philosophers, the two above mentioned arts are like flowers that delight to blossom before the fruits (i.e. the sciences) mature. Their minds are longing to bear fruit; and, therefore, when spring comes they delight in their flowers.'

The human function of rhetoric consists in education, in teaching, in changing a mere intuition into a clear idea, in persuasion and in giving form. 'It would be vain if we tried to teach without delighting. . . . And by delighting, such is the power of pleasure, we acquire the power to persuade'. Persuasion amounts to an active participation in reaching the truth. Persuasion is a warm and heartfelt cooperation and an ideal kind of conversation. Only when the word succeeds in persuading 'is it possible to win

[12] S. Speroni, *Dial. della Rhettorica* (*Dialoghi*, Ven. 1596, c. 130 sqq.).

a true victory. Such a victory is based not on force . . . but on grace, bestowed on us by the audience. . . . And truly, the man who tries to agree with the whims and the pleasures of the audience, no matter what the subject, is a good orator. In this he will differ from the philosopher who will insist on talking on the subject.'

Even though these words were meant as praise of the philosopher, they amounted, in reality, to a praise of the orator. For the latter occupied himself not with the detached and scientific contemplation of nature but with civic, human and concrete conversation. It is therefore not surprising that Speroni, when he asked himself whether the commonwealth ought to be ruled by the philosopher or by the orator, did not hesitate. The laws 'of a state change all the time. They change their form and appearance according to the times, the place, the utility and according to their own and extraneous forces.' The laws are not deities. They are human products which have been elevated to the position of idols. Therefore, the wise ruler ought not to be guided by rigid and universal norms. He ought to understand 'rationally' what happens to be required by the circumstances. 'It is rational that our states should not be governed by firm, demonstrable and for all times secure, sciences; but by rhetorical, changing and variable opinions. For such are our laws and we ought to be governed by prudence.' In the end, this was nothing but a fully conscious and justified version of Guicciardini's appeal in favour of the *particular*, in opposition to Machiavelli's regard for the universal and the rigidly necessary. It sounded indeed as if one were reading the famous passage of the *Ricordi*: 'It is a great error to speak of the things of this world in an undifferentiated and absolute way, as if they all obeyed rules. For all things exhibit differences and exceptions, because there is a great variety of circumstances. And because of this, they cannot all be measured by the same standards. These differences and exceptions are not described in books. They have to be taught by one's power of judgement.'

5. THE PROBLEM OF LANGUAGE

The search for the value of rhetoric and the tendency to contrast rhetoric, because of its concreteness, with philosophy, did not lead so much to a condemnation of philosophy as such, as to a manifest dissatisfaction with a certain type of scholastic philosophy. It was certainly based upon the confidence that human realities would have to be approached by means other than those of Scholastic philosophy. It is therefore no surprise that the most sensitive men of letters, the disciples of the profoundest of the humanists, in their love of concreteness, began to defend not the use of Latin but the vernacular. For the insistence that one ought to preserve Latin was based upon the idea that human society never changes and is subject to a rigid norm. But human society after all is subject to movement, development and life. The classical authors, once they had been studied in Greek and in Latin and once they had helped to lead men back to true *humanitas*, were the very authors who would demand, in the name of *humanitas*, that Greek and Latin ought to be abandoned. In one place, Speroni made Pomponazzi say that an Aristotle, interpreted with a genuine understanding of his real meaning in a Mantuan dialect, would be a much more genuine Aristotle than the Aristotle provided by someone who had failed to penetrate beyond the external form of the text, with glosses in Greek. As a result, there was an apparent reversal of the defence of the vernacular. It spread in the course of the 16th century, especially among those people who had derived their income from the study of *litterae*. These people now demanded, in conformity with the attitude of the ancients, the right to express themselves in a manner adequate to their own feelings. Even though this is not the place to examine the rich literature in which the problem of the vernacular was endlessly discussed in all its different aspects by Bembo, Caro, Trissino, Varchi, Castelvetro, Muzio, Tolomei and many others, it is necessary to mention at least the precise statement by Varchi. According to the latter, the vernacular is a new language which, when compared to Latin, 'ought not to be considered a corruption but a new birth'. The Gothic languages are barbarous only as long as they are in fact erroneous deviations from Latin. But they are by no means 'as barbarous as some people like to think', provided they are regarded as the births of new languages.

These men went to learn, in order to conduct the controversy against the moderns, in the schools of the ancients. But in the end it was in those very schools that they learnt to respect modernity, the achievements and significance of which acquired new value and strength in the light of earlier achievements.[13]

6. POETRY

Neither Vincenzo Maggi nor Bartolomeo Lombardi, when they wrote their commentaries on Aristotle's *Poetics*, had the slightest hesitation in maintaining that poetry ought to serve morality. They even went so far as to reduce poetry and poetics to ethics.[14] Platonists like Patrizi, Francesco Piccolomini and, above all, Jacopo Mazzoni, asserted that poetics is a kind of civic discipline. And Patrizi was not afraid to declare that the *Poetics* was the ninth book of the *Politics*. As against this, the most orthodox Aristotelians reduced poetry to logic and, like Varchi, expressed the belief that 'dialectics, logic and poetry . . . amount to much the same thing. There is no substantial difference between them and they are distinguished from one another only *per accidens.*' They went even further: since poetry 'forms a part or a species of logic, it is not possible to be a poet without being a logician. The more skilled a man is in logic, the more perfect a poet he is likely to make'.

In both cases poetry was considered a tool. It was taken for granted that poetry has both educational and moral tasks. If Platonism regarded beauty as a means to an ascent to God, Aristotelianism regarded it as a means to moral education and intellectual clarification—something like rhetoric or like an aid to logic. It is necessary to keep this in mind when one contemplates the broad interest with which the 16th century received the *Poetics* of Aristotle. In the first instance, Aristotle's work was circulated in a Latin translation by Giorgio Valla (1498). Later the original text was published. And later again, there appeared both Latin and Italian translations by Pazzi, Segni, Maggi, Vettori, Castelvetro and Piccolomini, complete with notes, explanations and paraphrases, not to mention the many treatises by Vida, Trissino, Daniello, Giraldi, Muzio, Varchi, Minturno, Scaligero, Tasso and a host of minor writers.

[13]Benedetto Varchi, *L'Hercolano, dialogo . . . nel qual si ragiona generalmente delle lingue, e in particolare della Toscana, e della Fiorentina, con la correzione . . di Lodovico Castelvetro, e la Varchina di Girolamo Muzio,* Firenze, 1846.
[14] *In Aristotelis Librum de Poetica Explanationes,* Venetiis, 1560. The writings of Varchi are in the edition cited above, *Opere,* vol. II.

Even though there was no end to the Platonic discussions about beauty, Aristotelianism tended to guide aesthetic interests into the sphere of 'communication' or human conversation. It did this by asking what the proper subject of poetic representation was and by investigating the practical function of writing poetry. The almost completely unknown Alessandro Sardo defined poetry thus: 'a poet is a man who writes about fictitious things and who amplifies true ones, reducing them to the perfection pertaining to the quality that is proper to the subject chosen for exhibition'. And many other writers, to whom poetry was a kind of imitation, expressed themselves in much the same way. Varchi said that poetry imitates, 'i.e. imagines or represents in order to amend or correct life', without labour but with 'very great delight'. In order to effect this sort of representation, it is necessary for the poet to know something about everything. Above all, he ought to be a scientist. 'A poet ought . . . to have knowledge of the arts and the sciences . . . and he ought to be at home in geography, astrology, theology and in all other sciences'. Thus Bernardo Tasso, to whose mind the poet was to have a universal education in all spheres of knowledge in order to be able 'to distribute those treasures with the utmost order and clarity, with purpose and with the aid of pretty words'. He considered this necessary for adorning the human mind with good habits.[15]

He propounded these thoughts in a most agreeable manner by availing himself of 'the erudite Robortello, of our most judicious Vincenzo Maggi and of the excellent Pier Vittorio'. But it was precisely here that he struck the greatest problems. For it was not enough to repeat, as most people had been wont to do, that the essence of poetry, as of all art, is the 'imagination or representation' of all reality, the mixing of invention with truth. (*Addit ficta veris, aut ficta veris imitatur*, Scaligero said). Similarly, it is not enough to falsify the epigram *imitatur ut doceat*. For the problem is precisely to determine what kind of imitation poetic imitation is. Poetic imitation appears to be a sort of creation of images of things. But these images represent things not as they are, but as they might be or ought to be, simultaneously serving

[15] Sardo, *Discorsi*, p. 76; Varchi, *Della poetica, Opere*, II, 685; Bernardo Tasso, *Ragionamento della poesia*, in *Opuscoli inediti o rari di classici o approvati scrittori*, vol. I, Firenze, 1845, p. 174.

the purposes of delight and of education.[16]   This, at any rate, was the carefully worked out formula at which Scaligero finally arrived. In this conclusion he had availed himself of the treatises by Capriano, Leonardi, Minturno and, above all, by Castelvetro. All these writers had flogged the old subject of the parallelism between history and poetry and had inquired into the specific nature of poetic imitation. What, in fact, is the imitated object? There was a frequent appeal to the classical example of Zeuxis who had derived the picture of a beautiful girl from the observation of several models, each one of whom had exhibited a different perfection.

Among others, this idea was used by Giulio Cammillo. In his *Discorso sopra Hermogene*, published by Patrizi and acclaimed by Tasso, he considered that the peculiar mark of poetic imitation was the unity that resulted from the synthesis of man's separate appearances in one definitive, single form. Hence, the poet is the man who assembles several separate pieces in such a way that there is not just a heap of elements, but a living unity, an organism. As Giraldi Cintio remarked: 'It seems to me that one might compare the bodies of poems with the composition of the human body'.[17] It has often been observed that the 16th century regarded poetic imitation as an attempt to represent the organic life of reality. It is important to stress, however, that the discussion did not stop there. It endeavoured also to reach some precision as to the differences between the pure imitation of what is, and poetical works that went not only beyond historical truth but also beyond reality itself. The example of Zeuxis furnished the idea that art, by creating a visible object, expresses sensually what is distributed, as it were, among many things. 'To imitate something that is perfect, is to imitate the perfection of a thousand different things by assembling them into one thing.' The synthesis of separate elements into one single picture seemed to represent organically in one single, real, object, the whole of life. It manages to do this by elevating a single individual creature above the ordinary. For this reason, it is necessary for art to reach

---

[16] *Julii Caesaris Scaligeri Poetices libri septem*, Apud Petrum Santandreanum, 1594, p. 2; Cp. B. Weinberg, *Scaliger versus Aristotle on Poetics*, 'Mod. Philol.', 1942, pp. 337–60.

[17] M. Giulio Cammillo, *Opere*, Venezia, 1560, vol. II, p. 111; G. B. Giraldi Cintio, *Scritti estetici*, Milano, 1864, vol. I, p. 20.

continually towards the divine and the miraculous. 'All phantastic images, like Saturn, the Titans, the Giants, the Centaurs, the Sirens, the Tritons, the Cyclops and Perseus are suitable for poetry. For poetry has to state things that transcend man's nature in a miraculous manner . . . It must speak of the inanimate things of which the Gods avail themselves, as if those things were possessed of senses . . . It must mention universally and in an extraordinary manner things that are incredible . . .' But at the same time, it is always necessary to pass from divine beings to the most concrete ones and to allow the divinely absolute to descend to the sphere of the humble and the well defined: 'One ought not to appear to be saying those things oneself, but . . . see to it that the speech in question appears to be the speech of the gods'.[18]

7. GIROLAMO FRACASTORO'S *Naugerius*

The examination of the Aristotelian concept of imitation as the basis of poetic activity and of the probable as its object, served the purpose of representing art as a form of human education. But when the points of departure for such examinations were Platonic ones, the arguments moved in a different direction and led people to emphasise the fact that beauty, as the sensuous expression of goodness, is a liberating force, an ascent of the soul to God. It is difficult, of course, to distinguish a Platonic theme from an Aristotelian one, let alone to contrast the one with the other, especially if one wants to go beyond mere premises to actual examples. For the idea of imitation points to something which is beyond appearances, to a universal form, to an eternal value, crystallised in a sense expression and thus made visible. And similarly, the idea that art has a liberating function, leads one into the sphere of *eros*, that is, of an education towards the divine.

Bernardo Tasso, having praised the good fortune of the century that had discovered 'Aristotle's *Poetics* in which the art of poetry is taught', declared nevertheless in the end, quoting Plato, that the purpose of poetry is to decorate human minds with beautiful and refined manners and various virtues. Poetry does

[18] Giulio Cammillo, *Opere*, II, p. 119; cfr. I, p. 219.

this through the agreeableness of its fables, through the pleasing quality of words arranged in a most beautiful order and through the harmony of verses. It was easy to pass from this moralistic and magisterial point of view to the Platonism of Torquato Tasso. The latter put formulations into the mouth of Minturno (in a dialogue dedicated to him) which are worthy of the strictest Ficinian orthodoxy. First, he put forward the theory that 'beauty is a victory of form over matter'; or better, that it is 'the appearance or the picture of goodness'. Then he proceeded to define the concept of beauty in such a way that it excluded all possibility of contamination with matter. 'For this reason I am surprised at Nifo and the other Peripatetics who place beauty in matter. For matter, by its very nature, is extremely ugly and formless. Indeed, matter is ugliness itself. And if it were true that beauty is to be found in matter, beauty would be inside ugliness, as if it were its object. But this, it seems to me, is very unbecoming. For beauty ought to spring from beauty, as a flower comes from a flower'. Thus beauty fled from all human contacts and did 'not allow itself to be described or to be defined by place or time or matter or words'.[19]

Tasso, naturally enough, did not adhere to this extreme view for any length of time. Indeed he compromised by announcing that beauty consists in the harmony of elements that are dissimilar —that beauty is an imperfect sign of an uncreated unity which lies beyond beauty.

But there was one thinker who was able to fuse the Aristotelian theme of imitation with the most subtle Platonic ideas into one harmonious whole. In his *Naugerius sive de Poetica Dialogus*, Fracastoro declared clearly that the poet does not imitate things, but *forms*; and that it is in this way that he realises the ultimate reality of the thing and the most complete and most perfect manner.

In general, the authors of treatises on poetry were wont to understand art in either of the two following ways. They either considered art, in a Platonic sense, as an invitation to an escape into the heavenly spheres of forms; or followed the worldly

---

[19] Bernardo Tasso, *loc. cit.*, pp. 174, 179; Torquato Tasso, *Il Minturno ovvero della bellezza, Prose filosofiche*, Firenze, 1847, 413. Cp. *Discorsi del Poema Eroico*; (*Discorsi*, II, Venetia, 1587, c. 10 r).

spirit of Aristotle and held it to be a human education, preferably an agreeable one. As against these views, Fracastoro, in spite of the fact that even in him there are undeniable reminiscences of the pedagogic view of art, inclined to the belief that art is its own purpose and has its own norms. No matter what subject is treated, poetry will always treat it poetically; for it is the nature of poetry to be poetical. It is therefore inappropriate to consider any one subject to be proper for a poet: *omnis materia poetae convenit*. The only thing that is really appropriate for a poet is the art of the beautifully measured expression, that is, the ability to articulate the *form* by clothing it in beauty and thus realising its freedom of expression and the completeness of its meaning. The poet neither invents nor falsifies; he sees and expresses the *form* in its visible beauty.

The systematic precision with which Fracastoro treated the contradictory theories and the way in which he managed to reconcile them with one another, explains the success enjoyed by his dialogue. He started with man's natural instinct for imitation, that is, for singing, and thus managed to determine the essence of poetry apart from its effects (such as pleasure, instruction, marvelling) as well as apart from its content. He thought that the essence of poetry lies exclusively in its function to grasp the universal *forms*.[20] The universality of Platonic forms represents, to Fracastoro's mind, freedom.[21]

[20] *Naugerius* (H. *Fracastori Opera Omnia*, Venetiis, 1584), c. 115–116.
[21] 'Vult quidem, et ipse, et docere et persuadere et de aliis loqui, sed non quantum expedit, et satis est ad explicandam rem, *tamquam adstrictus eo fine, verum ideam sibi aliam faciens liberam* et in universum pulchrum, dicendi omnes ornatus, omnes pulchritudines quaeret, quae illi rei attribui possunt'. 'Non . . . rem nudam, uti est, . . . sed simplicem ideam, pulchritudinibus suis vestitam, quod universale Aristoteles vocat. . .' In a letter to Ramusio there is an interesting and very disparaging reference to the commentators of the *Poetics* (*Lettere di XIII huomini illustri*, pp. 738–39).

CHAPTER VII

MORALITY

1. RULES OF BEHAVIOUR

ONE of the truly classical works among the treatises of the
16th century was the *Galateo* by Giovanni Della Casa. This
treatise, in which a young man is instructed as to the right life in
society, begins with a series of highly interesting observations.
It is not the business of man to prove himself in tragic conflicts
in every moment of his life; nor is it necessary for him to test
all the time his highest virtues. In daily life there are no opportunities for fighting Circassian tigers and African lions. On the
contrary, most of the fighting that takes place is against the
nuisance of flies and sandflies which abound in our climes. 'It is
only very rarely that an occasion for the assertion of one's sense
of justice, of one's valour and of one's other sublime virtues
occurs. People who are generous and magnanimous are not
expected to act generously and magnanimously all the time. On
the contrary, nobody is capable of always acting thus; and courage-
ous men are very rarely compelled to prove their courage by
actions'. But if virtue in its heroic aspects is something that is
relegated to holy days, the active cooperation with one's fellow-
men belongs to everyday-life: 'the decorousness of gestures,
words and behaviour is no less useful . . . than magnanimity.'
The 'rules of comportment' are those that link us to our fellow-
men. And even if it is not a mortal sin to fail in those rules, we
are, if we fail to observe them instantaneously, punished by
nature with the utmost severity, 'for (nature) then deprives us of
the company and the benevolence of men.'

A large part of Della Casa's treatise is based upon the distinction between the value of good behaviour and the value of
moral virtue, i.e., between sociability and morality. For that
matter, he argues that all morality comes genuinely from living in
obedience to human custom. And this custom becomes, 'to
every man determined to live not in solitude as a hermit but in a

city among men', a fundamental basis for all seriously valid
action. Moreover, this custom gives both shape and substance to
virtue which is thus transformed from a solitary exercise into a
concrete life.[1] A similar conclusion is contained in a letter which
Della Casa wrote in 1549 to Annibale Rucellai. In that letter he
argued that eloquence changes the dead letter into a living spirit
and thus helps to transform science and even the gospels into
persuasive convictions. 'The gospels teach us to love our neighbour; but the preacher, provided he is a good one, will compel us
to go to our enemy and to embrace him.' Works do not mature
through cold knowledge but through the warmth of human
contact. 'The things that I do not do . . . when I read the Scriptures, but do after I have heard a sermon, these things are the
fruits of eloquence.' Eloquence, therefore, is the art of giving
consent, of communicating and of living together. It 'differs from
mere knowledge and from erudition'.

Hence Della Casa arrived at a conception of the rules of
behaviour which based, above, all upon sincerity in the relations
between man and man and also upon a complete education. It is
the same thing as the *training*, defined by Castiglione in *The
Courtier*. According to Castiglione there is no doubt that there is
in every man 'enclosed and buried in the soul' a seed of moral
virtue. But the seed requires a 'good tiller' to cultivate it and to
open the way for its growth. There is need for 'artful custom' to
transform man and make him truly human. This transformation
does not result, as the Stoics were wont to believe, from the
eradication of sentiments and passions, but from the *measure* of
virtue in which those passions and sentiments, are harmoniously
combined.[2]

The whole of *The Courtier*'s unmistakable spirit, is to be
found in this assessment of human passions. They are supposed
to be subdued and tempered, but not eliminated. Similarly,
Agostino Nifo observed in his small work *De Principe* (published
in Florence in 1521) that the man who is to be considered
temperate is not the man who has no desires but the man whose
desires are temperate.

---

[1] Della Casa, *Galateo*, p. 4–6; *Lettere*, p. 75. On Della Casa cp. L. Caretti, *Giovanni
Della Casa, uomo politico o scrittore, Filologia e critica*, Milano-Napoli, 1955, pp. 63–80.
[2] Castiglione, *Il Cortegiano*, I, 14.

It is therefore understandable that the problem of education remained a fundamental one. And by education people meant the attempt to make the hidden seeds of virtue blossom, to remove the 'thorns and tares' so that desirable fruit may ripen. It is no accident that the two works mentioned are the ones that occupy an eminent place in the literature of the century for they are concerned with the education of man as a 'civic' and social being.[3] In this connection one ought to mention also Felice Figliucci, one of the most cumbersome commentators on the *Nicomachean Ethics* who published his vast and successful book, *Della filosofia morale* in the middle of the 16th century. The book contained much of Plato; but Figliucci insisted that it was necessary to get to know our sentiments and passions well in order that we may temper and master them before we 'begin to devote ourselves to speculation and contemplation'. Only when our emotional life has reached some kind of harmonious balance 'is our mind ready to receive the seed planted by contemplation'.

But we ought not to be misled by Figliucci's praise of contemplation. It is true that he conceded primacy to contemplation as the highest form of activity of which reason is capable. For this very reason, however, it is reserved for angels and other pure spirits 'while moral and virtuous action and works are appropriate for man'.[4]

2. ALESSANDRO PICCOLOMINI's *Institution*

According to Alessandro Piccolomini, a man is 'a social and communicative being'. He thought that man is both the object of our inquiries and of education. Even though it may be possible for man to live, in a purely material sense, by himself and to satisfy all his material requirements in solitude, such a man would not be truly human but a being of 'iron and marble'; for he would have no relationship with his neighbours. Man can raise himself to the level of God and reach beatitude only by communicating with other men.

[3] Here belongs *L'Anassarcho del Lapino* (Frosino Lapin), *o vero Trattato de' Costumi, o modi che si debbono tenere, o schifare nel dare opera agli studii. Discorso utilissimo ad ogni virtuoso e nobile scolare,* Firenze, 1571, p. 74; for Lapini, the biographer of Diacceto, see *Stanze sopra la dignità dell'huomo,* Firenze, 1566, and *Lezione del fine della poesia,* Firenze, 1567.

[4] Felice Figliucci, *Della filosofia morale libri dieci sopra i dieci libri dell'Etica d'Aristotele,* Venezia, 1552, cc. 3–5.

Piccolomini was an Aristotelian and therefore not content with a deification of everyday activity. On the contrary: he tied both science and contemplation to man's 'social, friendly, benevolent and communicative' situation. For man differs from all other animals through his mastery of language. He emits not only sounds and cries, but words and discourse. Through the latter 'he can not only formulate his thoughts and inventions for the benefit of others, but he can also, by collaborating with other men, perfect them in a way in which no man living in solitude could'. By rigorous argumentation, Piccolomini insisted upon the continuity between the education of mankind and the formation of a body of knowledge which can have originated only through the tradition of collective efforts. 'It is appropriate for man . . . to consider more than the painful and pleasurable excitations of his senses. And since his voice by itself is not sufficient to communicate the things he wants to express, nature has given him speech. The latter enables him to communicate the various inventions which he has made in regard to science and to useful and virtuous behaviour. Mutual help and the exchange of opinions has enabled man to perfect the inventions in science and virtue which he had begun on his own. For these two things (science and virtue) constitute his highest good and on them depends his greatest happiness.' The man who places himself outside human relationships and flees into the forests and mountains, 'driven by a foolish mood or by misfortune' will have to stoop, as long as he retains the appearance of a man, to 'conversing with thorny shrubs and stones'. But even so something will have been subtracted from his human nature; for 'the solitary man will be taken for a wild beast rather than for a man. For man needs 'to decorate his existence and to make it comfortable', things 'which he cannot do without the help of others'. For this reason, Piccolomini came back, time and again, to the two subjects of continuous education and of civic life. In his view, the state 'comprises in itself all other relationships such as friendships and the bonds of kinship. Therefore, man must sacrifice his property, his friends, his relatives, and if necessary, even his blood, for the well-being of the state'. Thus there originated about 1540 his *Instituzione dell'uomo nobile nato in città libera*. This work came to be revised frequently and enjoyed an immense success and popularity during the rest of the 16th century. This work, as its author was pleased to remark, dealt with moral questions as well as with economic and political matters. It began with a consideration of the 'free' city and subordinated all sciences and arts to the exigencies of civic life. Eventually it got around to considering the arts and sciences themselves, but solely as functions of society. For society alone is capable, provided it possesses a proper unity, of affording man genuine happiness. 'We are men,' Piccolomini wrote, 'and not angels; and pure speculation is a divine matter' and not becoming to men 'as long as they are men'. 'For this reason we may well be surprised to find that so many scientists devote so much industry to teaching the physical, mathematical and metaphysical sciences to men desirous of learning them,' whereas they neglect 'the most honourable of the sciences which teach the art of living, that is, the ways of virtue and morals which lead us to happiness.'

Piccolomini dared to turn the theory of the Aristotelians upside down: we become citizens of the heavenly city not through metaphysical speculation but through concrete acts of morality performed in this world. The natural sciences over-estimate the importance of the body at the expense of inwardness and therefore, instead of bringing us closer to the supreme intuition blessed spirits are capable of, they move us further away from it. 'We consist of two parts. One part has minor value and is soon lost; another has greater dignity and is everlasting. In spite of this fact people spare no labour and expense in filling whole volumes with medical treatises on the former; and the schools resound of such matters. But nobody bothers to waste a single word on the well-being and care of the other part—unless, of course, one wishes to suppose that those people who expound the law according to the criterion of justice and explain the intentions of legislators in our Italian academies, have charged themselves with the care of our minds.'

On the other hand, Piccolomini was by no means a fanatical supporter of the idea that education ought to be concerned with grammar. On the contrary, he remarked very sensibly that the Greeks themselves whom we hold to be the very model of *humanitas*, did not educate themselves through the study of languages. Grammatical and linguistic studies are totally different from *studia humanitatis*, such as, for example, the historical and poetical studies by which alone a young man can grasp the sciences that are important for civic life. Indeed, history is something 'like a mirror of life and allows us to learn from the labours and dangers of those who have lived before us'. And the poets, 'if they are explained prudently, will be most useful to all boys in matters of morals and will do for them what Homer used to do for the Greeks'. For the object of the literary studies that represent the true school of *humanitas* is Homer, not the Greek language; and Virgil and Horace, not Latin grammar.[5]

In one of the many editions of his work, Piccolomini promised to treat the subject *peripateticamente et platonicamente*. In practice, however, he not only remained faithful to Aristotle but also detached himself even from those remnants of asceticism that can be found in the *Nicomachean Ethics*. He did this in the same manner in which Mureto had concentrated his attention upon the fifth book, *On Justice*, which he had singled out for commentary. Even Francesco Piccolomini, author of a cumbersome moral treatise entitled *Universa Philosophia de Moribus* which stood under the influence of Platonism, isolated in his *Compendio della scienza civile* a 'civic virtue' and recommended it. He considered that virtue capable of realising man's goal on earth, while heroic virtue could do no such thing and was reserved, as its name indicated, for heroes. He called the science which was the subject of his book the 'rule of human life, the law of action, the faithful leader on the dangerous path of earthly existence; in short, the secure path which led back into the heavenly fatherland.'[6]

[5] Alessandro Piccolomini, *Della Institution morale libri XII. Ne' quali egli levando le cose soverchie, e aggiungendo molte importanti, ha emendato, e a miglior forma, e ordine ridotto tutto quello, che già scrisse in sua giovanezza della Institution dell' uomo nobile*, Venetia, 1582. The first edition Venetiis, 1543, had the curious title: *De la institution di tutta la vita de l'huomo, nato nobile e in città libera. Libri X. In lingua toscana, dove e Peripateticamente e Platonicamente, intorno a le cose de l'Ethica, Iconomica, e parte de la Politica, è raccolta la somma di quanto principalmente può concorrere a la perfetta e felice vita di quello. Composti dal S. Alessandro Piccolomini, a benefitio del Nobilissimo Fanciullino Allessandro Colombini, pochi giorni innanzi nato, figlio dela Immortale Mad. Laudomia Forteguerri. Al quale (havendolo egli sostenuto a battesimo) secondo l'usanza dei compari: dei detti libri fa dono.*

[6] Francesco Piccolomini, *Breve discorso della istituzione di un principe e compendio della scienza civile*, ed. by Sante Pieralisi, Roma, 1858; *Universa Philosophia de Moribus*, Venetiis, 1594 (this is the 2nd edition, the first was in 1583). The commentary by Mureto is in his *Orationes*, Lugduni, 1590, pp. 103–117; his version of 1565, pp. 371–410.

3. ARISTOTELIAN INFLUENCES AND COMMENTARIES ON THE *Nicomachean Ethics*

On December 16th, 1563, Marco Antonio Mureto delivered a lecture in Rome under the title *De Moralis Philosophiae Laudibus*. In this lecture he mentioned the famous passage from the *Republic* —*nobilissimam vocem, tamquam ex oraculo*—in which Plato asserted that there could be no happiness for states until either their heads had become philosophers or philosophers had become their heads. In explaining the passage, Mureto added that true philosophy consisted neither of Logic nor of Physics, but of morals and political theory, that is, in the endeavour to achieve happiness for men. In view of this fact, moral and political thought preferred to derive their inspiration from Aristotle rather than from Plato. Indeed, the former's ethical writings were coming to be commented upon and imitated more and more frequently. When, in the middle of the century, Bernardo Segni dedicated his Italian translation of the *Nicomachean Ethics* together with a voluminous commentary culled mostly from the Latin of Accialiuoli, to Grand-Duke Cosimo de'Medici, he described this classical treatise as the best possible instrument for the political education of man. He even added that 'pure speculation is not becoming to man as such but has its rightful place only in a super-human form of existence'. For this reason he considered it more suitable to treat of 'the active life in which men engage to a much greater extent'.

But when one is leafing through the commentaries by Nifo, Javelli, Figliucci, Scaino and others or when one consults the diffuse and heavy-handed compilations of Brucioli, one will very rarely discover anything new. The most one can hope to find are some interesting echoes of more famous men, like Pomponazzi and Porzio, echoes which turn up everywhere in the literature of the 16th century.[7]

Galeazzo Florimonte's *Ragionamenti* on Aristotle's Ethics owe much to the doctrines of the cantankerous philosopher Nifo. Similarly, Della Casa's work *Galateo* owes much to the

---

[7]Segni's Italian translation appeared in Venice, 1550. In 1547 Pier Vettori's Latin translation had appeared in Florence. Cp. A. Scaino, *L'etica d'Aristotele ridotta in modo di parafrasi con varie annotazioni e diversi dubbi*, Roma, 1574 (*The Politics*, in 1578). *Dialoghi della naturale e morale filosofia* by Brucioli, Venice, 1544. *Gli otto libri della repubblica che chiamono politica d'A.*, dedicated to Pietro Strozzi, Venice, 1547.

example of Florimonte.[8] Both are dialogues in the vernacular, written in a smooth and pleasing manner, anything but original, except that they may contain the odd addition of a theological or an Augustinian theme. Nifo himself, and this is no accident, appears as one of the speakers in two of Torquato Tasso's dialogues (*Il Gonzaga, ovvero del piacer onesto* and *Il Nifo, ovvero del piacere*, the latter being a revised version of the first). In these dialogues the philosopher Nifo, who was full of spirit and anything but ascetic, is portrayed in a very lively fashion.

The same Tasso entitled his dialogue *Delle virtù* after Porzio, 'the best and most famous philosopher not only of Naples but of the whole of Italy'. Simone Porzio, a pupil of Pomponazzi, had often treated of moral questions. In his *De Dolore* of the year 1551 he had described the essence of pain as mental rather than physical. Of his treatises on liberty only the booklet on whether man is willingly good or evil has come down to us. It too appeared in 1551 simultaneously in the Latin original and in a translation by the above mentioned Florentine shoe-maker Giovan Battista Gelli, a Dante scholar, a philosopher and a witty author. Porzio was a close friend of Alexander of Aphrodisias and had much in common with him. But Gelli, gracefully, took up some of the positions of 15th century humanism and asserted in the dedication of his *Circe* that man and man alone is capable 'of choosing for himself both a status and a goal; of travelling along the path that pleases him most; of conducting his life as he wills, guided by his will rather than by his natural inclination'. Man, he maintains, is both a Prometheus and a Chameleon. The fable of Circe is clear and the conclusion reached by the mole and the oyster is instructive: their condition is happier than that of man for it knows no unquietness and enjoys its own perfection. For the whole of man's dignity and perfection consists in an incessant discontent,

---

[8] Mons. Galeazzo Florimonte, bishop of Sessa, *Ragionamento sopra l'Ethica d'Aristotile*, Venice, 1567. The author rejected the first edition of 1554 because he alleged that it had been published without his consent: 'which fact gave me no little pain'. He spoke of his treatises in the vernacular thus: 'I do not expect great praise for a work which has no distinction . . . I would not have undertaken it at all had I known that Signor Alessandro Piccolomini or Figliucci or any other distinguished mind had treated of this matter in our language'. In truth, and this is worth emphasising, the first edition was put forward as a faithful reproduction of the moral thought of Nifo: *Ragionamenti di M. Agostino da Sessa, con l'illustriss. S. Principe di Salerno sopra l'Ethica d'Aritotile raccolti dal Rev. Mons. Galeazzo Florimontio . . .*, Parma, 1562.

in a lack of equilibrium, in an imperfection that is known and that causes suffering; in an eternal need and a continuous decay due to the passage of time, in the discovery of genuine as well as of imaginary impediments: 'there is little security in respect of present things, fear . . . and worry about those of the future, suspicion . . . of all members of his own species with whom he is compelled to have uninterrupted relations; fear . . . and respect for the laws.'

Only the elephant can understand that man's greatness lies in his ability to suffer and that that ability is his freedom. 'For all other creatures are subject to a certain law and for that reason cannot reach a goal other than the one set by nature. They cannot transgress the limits that have been laid down for them by nature. But man, since he has a free will, may set himself goals that are more worthy and goals that are less worthy. This is left to his discretion. He may lower himself towards base things or keep higher ones in his mind.' The elephant, because he was able to understand Ulysses' speech, became a man.

The *Capricci del bottaio*, too, are full of reflections on the condition of man. That condition is depicted as ambiguous and full of sufferings, but also, through man's links with the earth, as noble. The spirit of Platonic asceticism crept again and again into this work: 'for these earthly goods are . . . not goods.'[9] In *Circe*, however, we can discover an interesting reference to the problem of money. Money is described as a useful tool which has been turned into a source of suffering and slavery by the greed of man.[10] In a similar vein, Doni, a contemporary and fellow-citizen of Gelli, insisted in his *Marmi* that all property amounts to infinite misery and considered that man's unquietness is a kind of damnation rather than a cause for pride. Originally, he wrote, man had been destined, like Adam, for paradise. But through sin man became subject to time and death and to vain imaginings. 'Time and death are omnipotent rulers. In the end, one sees in the whole world nothing but opinions: every man keeps some damned bee in his bonnet and clings to it until the end of his

[9] *Simonis Portii De Dolore*, Flor. 1551; G. B. Gelli, *La Circe, I Capricci del Bottaio, ecc.*, Milano, 1878. 'Urbane' moral reflections drawn from the medieval tradition of the *Panchatantra*, can be found in Firenzuola's *Prima veste dei discorsi degli animali* and in G. B. Doni, *La filosofia morale*, new ed., Ferrara, 1610.

[10] *Circe*, ed. cit., p. 67; for Bernardo Davanzati cp. the two works of 1588, *Sulle monete* and *Sui cambi*.

days. Today he is troubled by worries about his wealth, tomorrow he will be incensed on account of his dignity. The next day he moans on account of his children. Sometimes he is dying of misery, sometimes he is bursting with joy. Thus he is changing his mood, his occupation and his condition every day, nay, every hour.'[11]

4. THE ACTIVE AND THE CONTEMPLATIVE LIFE

Tasso's dialogues are less lively. They contain all the obligatory themes without the slightest trace of any original twist. It is probably more profitable to collect the observations made by Varchi in his lectures on envy and jealousy or to go through the collections of letters where the old epistle achieves the format of a real treatise, as for instance Claudio Tolomei's letter to Dionigi Atanagi on wealth and poverty.[12]

The dialogues and treatises which are expressly concerned with morals always take up the usual subjects and offer nothing but tiresome and banal variations on them. There are endless discussions on honour, on duelling, on the virtues of a nobleman, on aristocracy, and so forth. We find them everywhere, from the massive work by Antonio Bernardi Della Mirandola, plagiarised by Possevino, to the writings of Farra, Sardo, Romei, Nobili; we find them in the conventional works of Muzio as well as in the above mentioned dialogues of Tasso. Verino the Second wrote a *Trattato della lode dell'honore e della gloria*; Bernardino Baldi, a dialogue *Della dignità*. There are comparisons between arms and literary studies and Romei dedicated the whole of the seven days into which his *Discorsi* are divided to this subject.[13]

[11] A. F. Doni, *I Marmi*, ed. by E. Chiorboli, Bari, 1928, vol. I, p. 268 sqq.
[12] B. Varchi, *Opere*, II, p. 568 sqq.; C. Tolomei, *Delle lettere*, Venezia, 1585, p. 162 sqq.
There is a rich harvest to be gathered from letters. Cp. e.g. Caro's letter to Bernardo Spina in which the usual subjects are discussed, i.e. monastic life, solitude, withdrawal from the world, etc. Annibal Caro, *Del le lettere familiari*, Venetia, 1587; *Lettere familiari* (1531–1544), Firenze, 1920.
[13] Cp. e.g. A. Bernardi della Mirandola, *Eversiones singularis Certaminis*; G. B. Possevino, *Dialogo dell'onore nel quale si tratta del duello*, Venezia, 1553; Pompeo Della Barba, *Due . . . dialoghi. . . . de' segreti della natura . . . sull'armi e le lettere*. Venezia, 1558; G. Muzio, *Il duello*, Venezia, 1553; *Il Cavaliere*, Roma, 1569; *Il gentiluomo, trattato della nobiltà*, Venezia, 1571; *Avvertimenti morali*, Venezia, 1572; F. Nobili,

Speroni's *Dialoghi*, however, which we have already mentioned deserve a special place. Alessandro Piccolomini, in writing his own *Instituzione*, followed the first version of Speroni's work all too closely. Speroni, as we have seen, had a very lively sensitivity for human 'communication' and devoted some of his most important pages to language and to rhetoric. In the second part of the work he also touched at length upon other serious and fundamental problems, especially upon the problem of the relations between the active and the contemplative life and upon the problem of history. As far as the first problem is concerned, he made Antonio Brocardo, one of the participants in the dialogue, condemn the contemplative life very sharply: the contemplative life is neither human nor Christian. When the first cities were founded, he is made to say, there was among the weak, useless, miserable 'and not truly lively people' a certain man. He was 'no better, but perhaps less naive than his fellows. In order to disguise his cowardice, he invented a new form of life. In this way he made himself appear as if he despised those goods which he was not capable of achieving anyway. To this sterile life, spent in the fruitless contemplation of the grounds of the works of God and Nature . . . he gave a beautiful and high-sounding name which nobody can understand: he called it the speculative life.' Thus 'originated, grew and flourished . . . happy among the foolishness of ordinary men, the vain, contemplative mode of life'. It is indeed vain because, since it is completely absorbed by the investigation of the world of God, it faces our world, the world of men, as a stranger would. Our 'speculative philosophers . . . who are devoted to this idle speculation, know as little of our human existence as a man . . . who is born among the mute and who lives outside the world'. Man is like a sword fashioned by God for battle, not for meditation. Man is not supposed to waste his time by indulging his curiosity and investigating how God created our souls. His task is, on the contrary, to avail himself of that soul, no matter how it was made, 'so that all his

De Hominis Felicitate; De Vera et Falsa Voluptate; De Honore, Lucae, 1563; A. Farra, *Settenario . . . sull' innalzarsi dell'anima alla contemplazione di Dio*, Venezia, 1594; Francesco de' Vieri, *Trattato dell'honore, della fama, et della gloria*, Firenze, 1580; B. Baldo, *Della dignità*; *L'arciero, in versi e prose*, Firenze, 1859, pp. 293–402. The commentary on the *Nicomachean Ethics* by Bernardi della Mirandola, in Urb. lat. 1414.

actions, provided he has a good disposition, aim at goodness and at having a good reputation'.[14]

Through the words of Brocardo, Speroni reached an extreme and significant position, a position openly opposed to the prevailing academic culture, which, no matter whether it had espoused Plato or Aristotle, always insisted upon the greater dignity of contemplation. It was no accident that Tasso made Porzio say: 'Our human cleverness . . . ought not to become too proud. It ought not to over-estimate itself because it is not comparable to wisdom; for the things it concerns itself with are human. But there are many things that are more divine and stand above those that are human . . .' And earlier, when the discussion had turned upon the virtue of those wise men who escape from the world, he had remarked that if he ever escaped, 'it would not be to inferior things, but to higher things; not to earthly matter, but to heavenly things; and that such an escape made him similar to God.'[15]

If we take hold of the third volume of the Aristotelian-Averroistic *Corpus*, published in Venice by Giunta, we will come across a preface to the moral books by Giovan Bernardo Feliciano. This preface is entitled *De Duplici Hominis Felicitate, Duplicique eius Vita, Activa et Contemplativa*, and exalts the happiness of the contemplative life, even though it is led in total solitude.[16]

In this connection, the broad and complicated treatment by Paolo Paruta in the dialogues entitled *Perfezione della vita politica*[17] assumes a special significance. In these dialogues, published in 1579, there appeared one of the characters from Speroni's dialogue, Gaspare Contarini. The course of the discussion reminds one strongly of the discussions on the civic life of the 15th century and touches upon all the traditional topics, such as, for example, that of *fortuna*.[18] But it also touches emphatically upon the problem of the active life. Paruta remarked that nobody

---

[14] *Dialoghi del Sig. Speroni, nobile Padovano di nuovo ricorretti a'quali sono aggiunti molti altri non più stampati*, Venezia, 1596, pp. 180–215.

[15] T. Tasso, *Prose filosofiche*, Firenze, 1847, I, pp. 22, 33.

[16] *Aristotelis Stagiritae Libri*, vol. III, Venetiis, 1574 (*Feliciani praefatio*).

[17] Paolo Paruta, *Opere politiche*, ed. by C. Monzani, Firenze, 1852, vol. I, p. 118 sqq.

[18] Speroni composed a bizarre dialogue on *fortuna* in which he argued that 'even as our understanding is no accident but a human artifice; an accident is not understood by anybody and is for this reason, an accident. For if it were intended, it would be known, and then it would not be an accident'. (*Dialogo sopra la fortuna, ed. cit.*, pp. 509–15).

O

wants to deny that pure contemplation in its ultimate perfection as realised by angelic intellects, is something sublime. But since men are tied to their senses, they cannot reach these peaks. 'The man who practises an art to perfection, even though that art may not be the noblest one there is, will be considered a better artist than the man who has merely learnt the elementary steps of an art no matter how noble. Even so it is necessary to consider the man who always shows himself prudent in his behaviour as more genuine and happier . . .' This argument does not amount to a renunciation. For it is perfectly true that man, in his relations with other human beings, can reach God. 'All that is necessary is to make allowance for the good deeds done by one man to another in the course of civic life. Is there a more noble study and a truer philosophy than the ones that improve our human behaviour and instruct us as to how we ought to conduct ourselves in regard to our family and our fatherland? Pindar was right in saying that philosophy is anything but a mere art of sculpture which creates insensitive and mute beings. On the contrary, it is the function of philosophy to awaken the mind and to prepare it for civic action . . .'

A few years earlier, in 1574, Stefano Guazzo had used the same idea as the basis of his dialogues on *La civile conversazione*. These dialogues had been meant to be both a handbook of good manners and a popular outline of morality. He said that men are like bees 'which cannot live by themselves' and in the course of his six hundred pages there is a tediously repetitive insistence upon the importance of language and on morality as essential to society. The whole work was a modest but significant conclusion to a train of thought which had hoped, in spite of the political collapse of Italy, for a dawn of moral regeneration.

5. HISTORY AND POLITICAL LIFE

It is not difficult to see that these thoughts had a close bearing upon ideas of history and of historical research. When Sigonio, in an oration, praised the study of history, he remarked that it is nothing but 'an industrious and clear demonstration of the truths of moral science'.[19] Historians prove the reality of the things

---

[19] *G. Sigonii Orationes*, Lugduni, 1590, p. 87.

taught by moralists and demonstrate the correspondence between the *is* and the *ought* in real life. Moral precepts are without foundation if they are not confirmed by historians. They would be vain and idle appeals if it were not for the examples provided by historians which turn them into solemn instructions and into directives with a genuine bearing on life.

Speron Speroni wrote an immense dialogue, almost a real treatise, in order to determine the nature of history. In the course of his discussion he appealed several times to Pompanazzi and never strayed far from the Aristotelian parallelism between poetry and history. He reduced history to a description of the particular and described the particular as *truth*, reported by the historian with the help of rhetorical artistry.[20]

Patrizi, a Platonist, whose dialogue *Della historia* was published in Venice in 1560, did not go much beyond this position.[21] It is true that he sought to discover the presence of a divine providential plan in the course of events. But his main concern was with the instructions for political prudence and the motives for a virtuous life which this plan was supposed to furnish. In this he was followed by Aconcio, who, four years later, wrote notes on these dialogues.

The positive value of these ideas on history, however, lies not so much in the theoretical expositions as in their relevance to political reflections. The latter are to be nourished by history and are to be regarded both as admonitions to the citizen and as philosophical meditations on the changing fortunes of human life. In this sense, politics represents an effective fusion of history and moral reflection; for the politics of the present stand between the explanation of the past and all thoughts about the planning of the future, i.e. on the edge between history and ethics. In this sense, moreover, politics stands between the Platonic dreams of utopia and the knowledge of the brute reality of the actual course of events which cannot be judged but have to be accepted in their entirety. Thus we find a large number of

[20] Speroni, *Dialoghi*, pp. 361–502 (between Silvio Antoniano, Paolo Manuzio e Girolamo Zabarella).

[21] *Della Historia dieci dialoghi di M. Francesco Patritio, ne' quali si ragiona di tutte le cose appartenenti all' Historia et allo scriverla et all'osservarla*, Venezia, 1560; J. Aconcio, *Delle osservationi et avvertimenti che aver si debbono nel leggere delle historie*, in *Opere*, Radetti ed., p. 303 sqq. (Cp. Fr. Robortellus, *De Historica Facultate*, Florentiae, 1548).

political treatises in the form of commentaries on historical works.
For the latter were supposed, in the words of Giannotti,[22] 'to
furnish the living examples of the things one ought to imitate and
the things one ought to avoid.' Such instruction, he continues, is
not derived from the fact that the ancients have some kind of
paradigmatic value, but from the fact that they were subtle and
exact interpreters of events. 'For this reason I am of the opinion
that one ought to praise all those who . . . when they investigate
the customs of our age, do not despise them but derive from them
such fruits and use as can be derived from things that are imperfect.' History unfolds in front of our eyes the dynamics of society
and permits us to understand those elements of human nature
that are unchangeable, and which have remained the same
through the course of centuries. It is true, as Machiavelli
remarked, that human affairs are in constant flux. But, as both
Cardano and Bruno stressed, there is no question of a continuous
development: the flux is much more like the up and down of the
movement of waves. Our admiration for antiquity is entirely
due to the great distance which separates us from it. Owing to that
distance, the passions have become extinguished and the eye has
become able to understand the essence of mankind in its political
behaviour. So much so, that even every reason for praise or
criticism seems to have disappeared. 'When I come to reflect
upon the course of events, I reach the conclusion that the world
has always been the same. There has always been good and bad;
but the good and the bad have differed from country to country'.[23]
Historical reflection had convinced Machiavelli that, essentially,
human nature was always the same and that the margin allowed to
virtue by objective necessity is pretty small. One can therefore
never know whether, when there appears to be such a margin,
it is not the result of subjective opinion or perhaps, of ignorance.
Such a view gives rise to an equivalence of criminality and
virtue. This equivalence cannot be justified in terms of our moral
conscience; but it can always defend itself by an appeal to a sober,
rational contemplation of the unchanging course of events. Such

[22] D. Giannotti, *Opere* (*Della republica veneta*, pref.), in *Scritti politici*, Milano,
1830, p. 32.
[23] Machiavelli, *Discorsi sopra la prima deca di Tito Livio*, II.

a contemplation includes even religion: for religion is conceived as a purely human phenomenon.

As far as Machiavelli was concerned, these views amounted to a transition to a metaphysical plane. This transition resulted from the fact that he imported a rigidly naturalistic and causal conception into his vision of purely concrete, mundane and human affairs. Guicciardini, in his subtle way, was well aware of this transition, for he himself had a great predilection for a faithful adherence to particular and ever changing human experiences. 'I, for my part, know no greater pleasure than listening to an old man of uncommon prudence speaking of public and political matters which he has not learnt from the books of philosophers but from experience and action; for the latter are the only genuine methods of learning anything.'[24]

Guicciardini always stopped at the limits of the undefined. But Machiavelli, interested in determining the *essences* of things, crossed them. Guicciardini never spoke of the things that are essential, natural and necessary and never mentioned those that *never* change. He always stressed the 'variety of circumstances', 'diversity', the flux of 'experiences', the accidental, coincidences and man's 'different natures'. He taught that it is necessary to judge affairs 'from day to day'. His decisive rejection of all philosophical abstraction in regard to politics was the highest mark of his political insight. It was also a conscious beginning of a philosophy of humanity, which was to do justice to the way in which human relationships cause their effects. In this way Guicciardini went beyond the thought of the end of the 16th century. This thought, although it had freed itself from Livy and had found a basis in Tacitus instead, had never managed to steer clear of Machiavelli and had therefore continued to regard history, politics and morals as an attempt to determine the 'unchanging truth' about the nature of man and of things.[25]

[24] F. Guicciardini, *Del reggimento di Firenze, I, Opere inedite*, Firenze, 1858, vol. II, p. 13. (Cp. V. de Caprariis, *Francesco Guicciardini. Dalla politica alla storia*, Bari, 1950, p. 14 sqq.).

[25] *Discorsi del Signor Filippo Cavriana, cav. di S. Stefano, sopra i primi cinque libri di Cornelio Tacito*, Firenze, 1597 (*Al Lettore*).

CHAPTER VIII

THE INVESTIGATION OF NATURE

1. LEONARDO DA VINCI

THE assumption, clearly expressed by Ficino, that there is a perfect correspondence between the human mind and reality by virtue of mathematics, is the hidden root of a large part of the natural science of the Renaissance. It was held, for example, that mathematics mirrored the exact rhythm according to which God had created the universe. This Pythagorean-Platonic assumption amounted to a kind of pre-established harmony between the world and man. It was based upon the idea of a Platonically geometrical God and was common to Leonardo who called himself *omo sanza lettere* and to Galilei who, though he loathed people who reiterated 'trumpet-like' everything that was old, adhered nevertheless dogmatically to the notion that God had written the universe in mathematical symbols.

This theory was an implicit reference to the true God and the unchanging fundamentals of divine reason—a reference which was to become explicit with Descartes. At the beginning of the 16th century, Luca Pacioli had remarked that 'God can never change' and that 'everything unfolded either in the higher or the lower world is necessarily subject to number, weight and measure.'[1] Similarly, the cabbalism of Pico and his followers, right down to its last echoes in the 17th century, was based upon this Pythagorean confidence in the power of numbers. And Leonardo, in spite of the fact that he despised the grammarians who had become so rigid with their idea of a contrast between the natural and the humanistic sciences, did not depart from this view. He considered nature, in the manner of Ficino, to be pregnant with divine thought and reason, so that the latter 'lives as if it had been infused into nature'. His attitude did not differ from the humble respect which the humanists preached one ought to show to the texts they read and interpreted. The only

[1] L. Pacioli, *Divina Proportione*, Vienna, 1889 (I ed., 1508).

difference was that Leonardo wanted to read the book of the world, i.e. the work of God, instead of the works of the poets. 'They do not know', he exclaimed, 'that the things (I investigate) ought to be learnt from experience rather than from the words of other people. For experience was the teacher of all those who write good things; and thus I too take her for my teacher.'

In his way, even Leonardo was the son of the humanists. Their method was to break through any screen and to return to a genuine reality. And this was also Leonardo's method. The only difference was that, in order to return to physical reality, it was necessary to dispense with all authority and to liberate things of their 'accidental disguises'. 'Wisdom is the daughter of experience. People who appeal in discussion to authority, do not avail themselves of their ingenuity but of their memory. One ought to escape the precepts of those thinkers who give reasons not confirmed by experience! Experience is an open door through which one can see the grounds of things. It is not a denial of reason but a respect for the reason of things, even though it may lead us beyond our own reason. 'There is no effect of nature without a reason. If you can understand that reason, no further experience is required.' There is *one* thing of which Leonardo was most firmly convinced: nature, in its profoundest aspect, is dominated by a rational rule and that rule expresses itself in mathematical terms. This rational world-soul enters into everything. It is something like a multiple seal of the unique sun of the universe: 'Its light illuminates all heavenly bodies which are distributed in the universe. All souls derive from it because the warmth, which resides in animals, comes from the soul and there is no other warmth and no other light in the whole of the universe. There is no denying that this conception of the sun owes much to Ficino.

Experience plays only a mediating and confirming role. It reveals that the human mind is capable of more than purely rational discourse. 'If you want to argue that the sciences which begin and end in the mind, contain truth . . . one must object; for such mental exercises are devoid of experience and without experience there is no certainty.' Human thought stands in need of such confirmation because the human mind is not creative like the divine mind. The latter is more like that of the artist whose mind is geared for creation rather than for verification. 'The deity which resides in the science of the painter transforms itself into something similar to the divine mind because its free power is a procreative power.'

2. GIROLAMO CARDANO

In Girolamo Cardano, whom Giordano Bruno in his *De Immenso* condemned out of hand as *rudis et amens fabulator*, there was much that was reminiscent of Plato. At the same time, he had a lively interest in the study of nature. In the *Epistola Nuncupatoria* which prefaces his curious and voluminous encyclopaedia entitled *De Rerum Varietate*, Cardano gave a very effective description of the unquenchable thirst for knowledge that had prompted his researches: 'Man's greatest joy and happiness consists in the knowledge of the deepest mysteries of the heavens, of the hidden corners of nature, of the divine intelligences and of the order of the universe.' This knowledge liberates man from the burden of his mortality. Cardano fancied that he had grasped this knowledge in its totality and unified it by reaching its original, divine source: 'In my seven books *De Aeternitatis Arcanis*, I have scaled those sublime heights which, since Plotinus, have not been scaled by anybody. I have grasped the origin and the goal of all things. And in the four books *De Fato* I have seized the order of the universe as well as of all single things.' Cardano admired experience and was a determined advocate of natural science. But at the same time he was aware of the insufficiency of empiricism and insisted upon the justice of the claims of mathematical reason. He even went so far as to stress that our knowledge can be protected against uncertainty only by the employment of a method of reasoning that led from the one to the many. He held, however, that owing to the way in which the mind is tied to the body, the synthesis between reason and sensuous knowledge was most precarious and prevented a perfect understanding of those ideal and incorporeal essences which constitute the principles of bodies. It also makes it impossible for us to visualise adequately the original connections through which the separate things arise out of their principles. Our physical knowledge is a *superficial* knowledge. It makes us glide over things without probing their souls and is based upon analogies and parables.

Mathematics is valid in its abstract formality and its certainty resides in the mind which produces it. And since this mind is at the same time its product, the mind possesses the fullness of mathematics. But this possession is confined to the circle in which the mind has been produced and does not enable one to assess the validity of mathematics in respect to the knowledge of the whole of physical reality.

In short, Cardano was fully aware of the difficulty of the passage from the mental to the real, from ideas to things. He was convinced that there is an order of the universe and that there is a link that holds everything together. But he cannot find the nodal point, the point at which the link occurs, and therefore remains puzzled in front of the unity postulated by reason and the disunity taught by experience. As a consequence, he was inclined to deny dogmatically that the universe has life and movement, for, through his doctrine of an eternal recurrence which reduced all becoming to a mere appearance, he made it appear all rigid. 'Not only natural things but also our opinions recur. . . . The same souls remain, equal in number . . . and the same opinions are repeated infinitely, the true ones as well as the absurd ones.' Like Bruno, who was to insist eloquently on the same conception, Cardano believed that the many and the one are fixed without development and that the processes of the intellect that extend, as it were, to the universe, evaporate in a rhythm which becomes mechanical and loses its significance. As a result, the transition to the divine, which Cardano does not deny and which opens to man the possibility of a miracle, remains both mysterious and miraculous. Nevertheless, the secret of the multiplicity of things and of their order, lies in the connection of the one with the many; but man cannot grasp it: *si scirem, Deus essem*.

It can, therefore, be no surprise that, to Cardano, experience remained split into a thousand separate observations and that metaphysics exhausted itself in the abstract postulates of Plotinus' conception of the One. It was perhaps for this reason that Cardano, like Della Porta after him, did not look so much for the normal course of events as for the extraordinary and the mysterious and kept on dreaming of the illuminating ray of a divine revelation.[2]

---

[2] Cp. the ten volume edition of his works, Lyons, 1663.

3. GIROLAMO FRACASTORO AND G. B. DELLA PORTA

Girolamo Fracastoro was determined to pursue his researches on a very much more rigorously empirical plane. His concern was always to find the particular and proper causes rather than the universal and first cause. This is the subject of which he treats in his *De Sympathia et Antipathia Rerum*. In his investigation of the causes of 'miraculous consensus' which governs the links between the most minute elements of things, he considered sympathy and antipathy in the sense of purely physical forces, and excluded all traces of mysterious or 'spiritual' factors. In the same sense he fought against the application of astrology to medicine and gave in his *Turrius* a phenomenological description of the processes of knowledge.

The scientist as scientist, he held, describes and determines particular causes. Better, he describes the permanent connections between appearances. The *cause* which generates things is to be sought on another plane, that is, on a plane that lies beyond human knowledge. In his capacity as a poet—and Fracastoro was a gifted poet—he sang of these causes and praised the freedom of divine and creative nature which, if it wants to, is capable of altering even the order of things.

In a letter to Giovan Battista Ramusio, Fracastoro prided himself of having *saved* in the course of his 'bizarre' studies of astrological medicine *everything* through the determination of natural causes. 'I save everything through (an understanding of) the movements of our humours.'[3] In his numerous writings on magic, astrology and similar subjects, G. B. Della Porta too, started from the same premises. He wanted to discover through scientific research the manifold correspondences between body and soul which *seem* to belong to the realm of the miraculous and the extraordinary. 'One must watch the phenomena with the eyes of a lynx so that, when the observation is complete, one can begin to manipulate them.' *Natural magic* has thus become a science that permits a quick passage to technology.[4] Physiognomy is the determination of the mutual correspondences between body

---

[3] *Lettere di XIII uomini illustri*, p. 713; H. Fracastoro, *Opera*, Venetiis, 1584.
[4] *Jo. Baptista Portae* . . . *Magiae Naturalis Libri Viginti*, Hanoviae, 1644, I, 2.

and soul, matter and spirit, the stars and human life. 'Experience teaches that the soul is not insensitive to the motions of the body, even as the body is moved by the passions in the soul.'

But Della Porta was soon seduced by the presence of the miraculous, the marvellous and the extraordinary and did not hesitate to proclaim that 'he who seeks a cause for everything, destroys both science and reason. And he who has no faith in the miracles of nature, somehow destroys philosophy.' Unlike Fracastoro, he did not recognise the humble obligation to observe the behaviour of phenomena, but was dominated by the desire to discover the key of the efficacy of things. He was for ever on the search for the 'secret and cause of efficacy ... which is high and most worthy,' for the stone of philosophers, for the art of the miraculous. It is indeed curious to observe how the wheel had come full circle. One had started with the intention of building scientific knowledge upon the observation of regularities. And now one was determined to recognise the exceptions as the signs of the creative forces of divine nature. In the last analysis, it was merely a different way of formulating the problem that had interested Cardano. It was a search for the transition from the divine One to the manifoldness of reality. Man is capable of describing the transition, but he cannot explain it.[5]

4. ANDREA CESALPINO

In contrast to the above thinkers, Andrea Cesalpino's *Quaestiones Peripateticae* offer a more faithful Peripateticism. This work was published in Venice in 1571. It was completely opposed to any indulgence in dreams of magic and understood Aristotelianism to amount to a concrete empiricism. Cesalpino did not deny that Aristotle had raised philosophy to the greatest heights of human achievement 'so that even after almost two thousand years the greatest efforts are devoted to attempts at understanding Aristotle correctly.' But he added that it was equally undeniable that to follow Aristotle meant nothing else but to observe nature. 'If the observation of natural bodies can give us true knowledge, why should we have greater confidence in

[5] *De Furtivis Literarum Notis, Vulgo de Ciferis, Libri Quatuor*, Neapoli, 1563, introd.

pure reason? It is a weakness of the intelligence to abandon observation in favour of reason.' The things which are immediately given can never deceive us: 'Is it possible to imagine that nature lies to us when she indicated the pole with the magnetic needle? . . . or ought we not rather to attribute the lies to reason when reason departs from nature?'[6]

Always following Aristotle, he took it that nature is striving for a certain goal and that it is ordered by grades in such a way that every grade possesses its own perfection. The teleology implied in this conception does therefore not imply that things on the lower grades are inferior, by comparison, to the things on the higher grades. On the contrary, it means that one recognises the full value of every individual moment considered by itself. 'There is nothing shameful in nature; for even the lowliest things partake of the divine.'

The positive evaluation of every moment of reality and of every grade, as if it were in itself perfect, was to lead him to the view that the soul is fully immanent and that reason is linked to the senses in the closest possible way. It also led him to the question 'whether it was possible to distinguish the souls of men from those of other mortal beings'. Naturally, he did not content himself with this question and tried, albeit in a very ambiguous manner, to save the doctrine that the individual soul is immortal. His whole position is of the greatest interest not so much because of his subtle comments on individual points as because of its Aristotelianism which amounted to an open and determined defence of the claims of experience and the immediate observation of nature. It was no accident that soon afterwards, Telesio's work *De Rerum Natura iuxta Propria Principia* was to appear in the guise of a commentary on Aristotle's *Physics*.

5. BERNARDINO TELESIO

Bernardino Telesio was born in Cosenza and had begun as a pupil of an uncle of his, Antonio Telesio. The latter was an obscure poet and the author of a eulogy, in Lucretian verse, of *omniparens natura*. It would be far-fetched to regard this as an original inspiration, for in those days it was fashionable to write

[6] A. Cesalpino, *Questiones Peripateticae*, Venetiis, 1571.

poetry after famous examples. Bernardino Telesio himself was no stranger to the philosophical culture of his age. He had pursued his studies in Padua and had a great respect, amounting almost to worship, for Vincenzo Maggi, a famous Aristotelian. In fact, he submitted the first two books of his *magnum opus* to him, discussed them at length with him and obtained Maggi's approval of them. This shows (and one ought not to overlook the importance of this fact) that he had the closest of connections with the leaders of the most intelligent and official Aristotelianism of his age.

Telesio's main charge against both his contemporaries and all his predecessors was that they had erected arbitrary systems, consisting of a curious mixture of reason and experience. They had done this without consulting nature and had, indeed, ravished her in a barbarous manner. 'They had had far too much self-confidence and have not, as they ought to have had, observed things in themselves and their forces. They have not recognised the greatness, the intelligence and the capacity that reside in all things. Instead, they have competed with God in investigating the principles and origins of the world with the help of their reason. In their attempt to discover what they could not discover, they have obtained an arbitrary idea of the world.' They have managed to recreate the world, albeit in a completely fictitious manner. They have recreated it in their own image and have thus 'imitated not only God's wisdom but also His power'.[7]

Telesio rejected these methods and was determined to follow not God's, but man's wisdom, humble and devout. He stressed that there was nothing very wonderful in his work and thus betrayed a tacit polemical edge against the concept of man as the measure of all things. He considered that nature herself is the measure of our knowledge and of our works—that is nature as she reveals herself to our senses which are, themselves, part of nature. 'We have followed the senses and nature. Nature is at one with herself and therefore always does and effects the same things in the same manner.' The most important feature of this attitude is the belief, both naive and dogmatic, in the regularity and uniformity

[7] *Bernardini Telesii de Rerum Natura*, ed. by V. Spampanato, Modena, 1910, Roma, 1923; *Delle cose naturali*, transl. by Francesco Martelli (1573), from the edition in two books (*I manoscritti palatini di Firenze*), ed. by F. Palermo, III, Firenze, 1868, pp. 1–232

of nature, unchanging, rigid and dominated by unchanging laws. The nature that reveals herself fully to the senses is uniform and is herself capable of being experienced sensuously because sensuousness is universal.

When he came, however, to an examination of the structure of reality, Telesio departed less from Aristotelianism than one might have expected. He emphasises that the substance of every real being is complex and consists of a receptive substratum called matter and of two effective forces, coldness and warmth. Even though, at times, he described each of these elements as a substance, in reality he considered every little particle to be a complex unit that had resulted from an intimate relation between passivity and activity, i.e. from an effective force and a resistance. In short, he considered every particle to consist of several elements which can be isolated and considered by themselves only in abstract thought.[8]

But other things also have to be taken into account. The whole of reality is, at every moment, possessed of sensibility. It follows that reality, since all knowledge is derived from the senses, is filled with a certain form of dawning knowledge. The ability to feel is intrinsic to nature which, in order to preserve herself, must have, no matter how opaque, an intuition of what is good and what is bad for her. In his first version of his two volume work, Telesio wrote as follows: 'If natures are to preserve themselves, it is not only necessary that they should possess a strong desire for self-preservation and a powerful hatred of self-destruction but also the ability to recognise the things that are similar and adequate and the things that are dissimilar and inadequate. For they would be striving in vain to preserve themselves and they would be striving in vain to resist destruction, if they could not recognise those things that preserve them and those things that ruin them.'[9] Telesio had a reason for insisting upon this primeval gift to the world, a reason which had an almost Platonic and teleological flavour: God is good and has no envy and has created a perfect world. And for this reason He cannot have deprived His creatures of the means for their self-preservation: 'We find that these properties are given to all

[8] *De Rerum Natura*, I, 2.
[9] *Delle cose naturali*, I, 34, p. 57 sqq.

active natures so that it should not appear as if their Creator had
forgotten to preserve them and as if He had been a lazy artist
Who had not given to all things the properties they require for
their preservation, i.e. the power and the senses . . .'

No matter how small the particle of reality, activity and
passivity are always inherent in it. In every such particle there
is both an effective force and a material resistance. And similarly,
in every particle there is, inseparable, a capacity to feel and hence
to know. Knowledge and being are therefore mutually suffused
with one another in the same way in which the Ionian philosophers
considered that life and being were suffused with one another.

To the objection, which was to be raised also against Campanella, that the beings that do not belong to the animal kingdom
have no organs of sense, Telesio replied very clearly that these
organs are merely means of sensuous experience. 'The fact that
the other beings do not possess the organs or instruments by
which animals show themselves capable of feeling, does not
entitle us to claim that only animals can feel and the other beings
are incapable of feeling. For it does not appear to be true . . .
that the organs of sense are the cause of the ability to act and to
feel or to assist the soul in feeling. On the contrary, they do no
more than to initiate the actions of sensible things . . .' Indeed,
where no differentiation has ever taken place, the whole of the
being in question is an organ of sense: 'They need neither apertures nor canals . . . Since they are homogeneous and truly
uniform, it is necessary that they absorb experiences uniformly
and have feelings in their external parts as well as in their interior
ones.' Bruno was to express this idea more succinctly: they have
their eyes wide open to the whole of the horizon.[10]

Telesio, in order to make himself clearer, added that the senses
are neither a 'passion' of the *spiritus* or of the subtle matter which is
alive in the interior of the sentient being, nor an external effect
or stimulus of things. They are no more and no less than the
experience or intuition of such changes. This view amounts to
an acceptance of the theory of the universal animation of things.[11]

One can see that Telesio's initial assumption that nature has
to be studied *iuxta propria principia*, i.e., that the study of nature

[10] *Delle cose naturali*, I, 35; p. 60.
[11] *De Rerum Natura*, VII, 2; III, p. 3–4.

has to be based solely upon sense experience, was severely impaired by a whole series of dogmatically accepted metaphysical presuppositions. In this respect, Patrizi remarked that in Telesio *magis metaphysica videtur, quam physica* and wanted to know what possible meaning the inner structure of the world, matter and universal sensibility could ever reveal to him.[12] Telesio's plan to oppose to Aristotle's physics, dominated entirely as it was by metaphysical conceptions, a *pure* physics grounded upon empiricism, was condemned to failure. Modern criticism has maintained that Telesio's failure was due to his almost Cartesian attempt to postulate that the world was created by a God or to the fact that he was determined to make natural science independent of morals or by his insistence that man, though nothing but a sensuous mechanism, possessed a separate and created soul. But the truth about Telesio's failure is that he contradicted his own premises when he postulated the uniformity of nature and made certain *arbitrary assumptions* as to the structure of substances and that he conceived the idea that there was a universal sensibility without being able to demonstrate it. In spite of all this, it is true, as Patrizi sensitively wrote to Telesio, that though his physics was untenable as science, it could stand up to criticism as metaphysics. Telesio's idea that nature and sense, passivity and activity and consciousness suffuse each other incessantly and his idea that the world is uniform, be it a real world or a feeling one—was to open fertile vistas to Campanella's reflections on the structure of Being. But it is true that this line of thought led to Campanella's metaphysics, not to Galilei's physics.

6. THE METAPHYSICS OF LIGHT

Telesio had many disciples. There was first, his faithful commentator Sertorio Quattromani who combined a deep love of Petrarch with an admiration for the new philosophy. Then there was Antonio Persio who defended him against Patrizi. And finally, the greatest of them all, Campanella, who defended him against Marta.[13]

---

[12] Patrizi's objections and Telesio's answers (*Solutiones Thylesii*) in F. Fiorentino, B. Telesio, Firenze, 1872, II, pp. 375–396.

[13] *La philosophia di Bernardino Telesio ristretta in brevità, et scritta in lingua toscana dal Montano Accademico Cosentino* (Sertorio Quattromani), Napoli, 1589, E. Troilo ed., Bari, 1914; *Antonii Persii Apologia pro B. Telesio adversus Franciscum Patritium.*

But not even Francesco Patrizi from Cherso, professor of Platonic philosophy in Ferrara, was able to escape his influence. In Padua he had been a pupil of Tomitano, Passero, Lazzaro Buonamici and Francesco Robortello. The point, however, is that he derived from all these Aristotelians nothing but a deep hatred of Aristotle. The outcome of this hatred was his *Discussiones Peripateticae*, a monumental critique in which he opposed the pre-Socratics and their naturalism to Aristotle and in which he charged the Stagirite with the same inconsistency which, as we have seen, he had found in Telesio. If one insists upon the fundamental importance of the senses, he argued, how can one maintain that physics is based upon propositions the truth of which can never be ascertained by sense experience?

But in his metaphysics, derived as it was from a large variety of Stoic-Platonic sources and entangled with the most confused elements of the Hermetic-Chaldean tradition, he went back to the school of Ficino which by now had become classical. Even so it is true that he wanted to base his edifice on the senses. Among these the foremost position is occupied by the sense of vision, the object of which is light; and light is an incorporeal body, both form and matter, and hence the first foundation of the whole world. *Ille primaevus fluor* derived directly from God, *pater luminum*, and is almost identical with space which is suffused by it. It is infinite like space; in fact, infinite like the world.[14]

On one hand, his panpsychism and the importance he attributed to the senses and his conception of space, all linked him to Telesio. On the other hand, his idea that space is infinite, reconciled him with Bruno who had attacked him as a 'dirty pedant'. And finally, the inspired glorification of light makes one think of the *Zodiacus Vitae* by Marcello Palingenio Stellato, a Platonist of

Responsiones ad obiecta F. Patritii contra Telesium (Cod. Magliab., Cl. XII, 39); cp. also *Apologia* of Antonio Solino (Cl. XII, I). *J. A. Martae . . . Propugnaculum Aristotelis adversus principia B. Telesii . . .*, Romae, 1587; Th. Campanella, *Philosophia Sensibus Demonstrata . . .*, Neapoli, 1591; *Prodromus Philosophiae Instaurandae, id est Dissertationis de Natura Rerum Compendium*, Francofurti, 1617.

[14] *Fr. Patritii Discussiones Peripateticae*, Basileae, 1581 (the first part appeared in Venice, 1571); *Nova de Universis Philosophia, Libris Quinquaginta Comprehensa: in qua Aristotelico Methodo, non per Motum, sed per Lucem et Lumina ad Primam Causam Ascenditur. Deinde Nova quadem et peculiari Methodo tota in Contemplationem senit Divinitas. Postremo Methodo Platonico Rerum Universitas a Conditore Deo Deducitur . . .* Venetiis, 1593 (Ferrariae, 1591). In 1553 he had published the Platonic *Città felice*.

the deepest dye.[15] According to the latter, light is an image of the
infinite power of God, extended throughout the super-celestial
world. The infinite God has thus revealed Himself in the infinite.
This thought was also dear to Bruno and in him it assumed, at
times, a flavour of Spinoza.

Light penetrates into the celestial and earthly worlds and thus
becomes visible light. Down here, among the ever changing
accidents of earthly life, caught in the vain flux of things, man is
filled with a longing for the celestial country of his origin:

> *Patrias optate revisere sedes*
> *Hanc igitur fragilem vitam contemnite, cuius*
> *Principium est fletus, medium labor et dolor, at mors*
> *Finis.*

[15] Cp. *Marcelli Palingenii Stellati . . . Zodiacus vitae . . . libri XII*, Lugduni, 1608;
See also *De Immortalitate Animarum* by Antonio Paleario (*Opera*, Amstelaedami,
1696, pp. 573–632) and *De Principiis Rerum* by Scipione Capece.

CHAPTER IX

FROM GIORDANO BRUNO TO TOMMASO CAMPANELLA

1. RENAISSANCE AND REFORMATION

IT was inevitable that the powerful urges for a radical renovation that were alive in many spheres of humanism, should also have their effects upon religion. The Protestant Reformation did not find much of a response in Italy and its flame was fanned only among isolated intellectuals who were regarded with suspicion and whom most educated people criticised sharply. But in the sphere of philosophy there was no lack of endeavours to renovate radically the communal life of mankind. These endeavours assumed political as well as religious guises. The Reformation degenerated, at times, into a new confessional narrow-mindedness and into a rigid intolerance, both of which amounted to a lowering of the respect for man in particular and a condemnation of the world in general. As against this, Humanism had stood for freedom, a revaluation of humanity, a respect for every belief, free criticism and universal toleration. Valla had taught how one ought to read the Holy Scriptures with alert eyes, free from dogmatic encumbrances and for this reason he had received Erasmus' unreserved praise as the founder of a new Biblical philology. Ficino had demonstrated the hidden correspondence of all confessions of faith and the profound agreement between all religions and philosophies in the *Logos*, by which they were justified and upon which they were founded. All this added up to free criticism and tolerance out of which there was to emerge a plan for a new, morally regenerated, human community capable of securing for men earthly happiness as well as the true salvation of their souls.

During the second half of the 16th century, Francesco Sansovino, in his ideal *Republica d'Utopia*, defended a religion based upon a 'hidden and eternal deity, beyond all human conceptions, which extended throughout the world because of its virtue and

not because of its majestic grandeur.'[1] The supporters of his
Utopia were prepared to recognise God the Father of the Christian religion as that deity and thus Christianity was made to
appear as the perfectly rational religion. Sansovino's conception
of community life was a religious one and he made religion the
basis of civic life.[2]

There is no denying that there was a close relationship between
such a Utopian Republic and the *Kingdoms of Christ* or the *Catholic
Republics* and other forms of universal assemblies, the ideas of
which sprang up like wild-fire in religious, albeit heretical,
minds.[3] There is no doubt that the high-minded speculations of
the major thinkers of the late Renaissance were inspired by such
and similar hopes for the spiritual reconstruction of human life.
Bruno and Campanella had one thing in common. They both hoped
for the renovation of the world, even though, on other matters,
these two men stood at opposite ends of the pole. They certainly
represent a strange mixture of astrological superstition, magical
practices and messianic dreams. But both men were inspired by
the same passion for the liberation of man. And this passion
ennobles both of them and makes up for their errors and their
ingenuousness. 'This philosophy,' Bruno once exclaimed,
'enlarges my soul and elevates my spirit. Therefore, if the transformation should occur, no matter where the end of the night
which I expect may be, I am confident, now that I am in the darkness, of the light of day.' Bruno was willing to wait until 'in this
our country' the light should illuminate with the brilliant radiance
of the sun 'the shadows of those ideas' which so far are alive only
in the minds of the wise and which 'frighten all beasts and leave,
as if they were Dante's devils, all asses far behind.'

2. RELIGION AND PHILOSOPHY IN BRUNO

It is obvious at first sight that the whole of Bruno's work is
suffused by a deep longing for spiritual regeneration. One may

[1] Francesco Sansovino, *Del governo et amministrazione di diversi regni et republiche,
così antiche come moderne*, Venezia, 1578, p. 197.

[2] Sansovino, *op. cit.*, p. 189.

[3] Cp. the anonymous *Forma d'una Republica Catholica*, 1581, Cantimori ed., in
Per la storia degli eretici italiani nel XVI sec. in Europa, Roma, 1937, 'Studi e documenti
della R. Accademia d'Italia'. *Forma* is really by Pucci; see the edition by Firpo, *Gli
scritti di Francesco Pucci*, 'Memorie dell'Acc. delle Scienze di Torino', s. III, t. 4,
parte II, 1957, pp. 69–104.

doubt the precise nature of one or the other of his reforming intentions. But all his writings are inspired by a religious sentiment even though this same sentiment led him eventually to curse *his own* religion. He was highly critical of popular superstitious beliefs and, at times, extended this criticism to every form of positive religion. This critical attitude led him eventually, in his *Spaccio*, to the well known attacks on the divinity of Christ in particular and on the worship of saints in general. But in spite of all this, he was quite sincere when he insisted in front of his judges on his own conviction that all positive and rational religion was based upon the necessary assumption that there is 'a supreme first sustainer'.[4]

It would be very difficult, however, to attempt a description of this very sincere religiosity in terms of any known religious confession, catholic or protestant. During his interrogation in Venice he prided himself on having repeatedly criticised the protestants for their doctrine of justification by faith alone. Bruno was an ardent believer in the efficacy of human action and as such he could not but attack the modern 'corrupters of law, faith and religion' who taught people the possibility of salvation without works—'when works are in truth the goal of all religions'. Again and again he came back to the same topic and in the *Spaccio* he charged Calvinism with the denial of human freedom and thus of the possiblity of men espousing the true religion. But even if one cannot give much credence to the blasphemous statements attributed to him and reported by his fellow-prisoners, it is nevertheless not possible to imagine that he was in any sense a catholic or even, vaguely, a Christian. In the *Spaccio* there is an obvious allegory of Christ in the character of the centaur Chiron. But it ends in an utterly irreligious ridicule of Christ, hardly mitigated by an all too transparent veil of imagery.[5]

It is certain that Bruno was drunk with God. He longed to be an Actaeon, to see Diana in the nude and to be devoured by her dogs. He was dead to the world and completely open to the grandeur of God. 'The dogs, being the thoughts of divine things, devoured Actaeon and killed him as far as the vulgar crowds were

---

[4] *Spaccio della bestia trionfante,* in *Opere italiane,* Gentile ed., Bari, 1925–27, II, p. 201: Cp. A. Mercati, *Sommario del processo di Giordano Bruno,* Città del Vaticano, 1942, p. 90.

[5] G. Bruno, *Opere italiane,* I, p. 301; II, pp. 65, 223–24.

concerned. Thus they liberated him from the carnal prison of matter so that it was no longer necessary for him to see Diana through mere apertures and windows. The walls razed, the whole of the horizon was revealed to his eyes.' The 'heroic' man realises this infinite horizon in himself and he reaches God not as a reality outside himself. But man is no God. However, he is vanquished by the *thoughts of divine things* which make a breach into his limitations. And thus the infinite horizon is opened up: 'He himself became the longed prey of his own dogs, of his thoughts. Since he had grasped them in himself, there was no need to go on seeking the deity outside his own self.'[6] This deity is nothing but the unity of Being, the original simplicity which is infinity itself. This unity overcomes the sensuously perceived multiplicity and, at the same time, verifies and illuminates it by reducing it to itself.[7] 'This is done in such a way that man sees everything as One and can no longer regard things in terms of differences and numbers, which, as is proper for the senses . . . make him see and perceive things in confusion. He then sees Amphitrite, the source of all numbers, of all species, of all reasons. For Amphitrite is the Monad, the true essence of every thing.'

This radical *conversion* of multiplicity into the One, of appearances into the root, is conditioned by religion: 'They did not worship Jupiter as if he were a deity, but they worshipped the deity as if it were Jupiter.' He saw religion not as a worship of things but as the worship of God in things, 'provided one regards the deity as something close and familiar and not as something on high, absolute in itself and without relation to creatures'. This idea of a contact with the deity which reveals itself and communicates itself had a religious basis. 'God, as an absolute, has nothing to do with us. But in so far as He communicates Himself to the effects of nature and is intimately connected with them (he is related to us). And even if God is not the soul itself, He is the soul of the soul of the world.' For this reason, people have wisely worshipped God in worshipping things: 'He is hidden in nature. He works and shines in different ways in different things and through different physical forms'. The faith that grasps the divine beyond the veils in which it is clothed, will verify itself in propor-

[6] Bruno, *Opere italiane*, II, pp. 472–74.
[7] *Opera Latine Conscripta*, 1879–91, I, 3, pp. 136, 146.

tion to the degree to which the divine is grasped in mortal beings.

'Thus one can explain that in reality people never worshipped crocodiles, cocks, carrots and onions, but always the gods and the deities that were latent in crocodiles, cocks and other creatures.' Times and forms of worship keep changing and altars are over-thrown. The deity alone 'which was, is and will be in certain times and places, successively and simultaneously, in different mortal beings', remains. The deity changes form and name as it reveals itself on earth and therefore will be invoked in different manners 'and sought in countless ways for good reasons and bad ones and worshipped and honoured with countless rites'. Names and prayers change with time and place, only God, as the unique light reflected by an infinite number of mirrors, remains always the same. 'One finds in the end that the whole of the deity is reduced to *one* source, even as all light is reduced to the first light in itself; and as all pictures which appear in so many different mirrors as if they were so many separate beings, are reduced to one formal and ideal principle which is their source.'[8]

It is an asinine idolatry to reduce God to things and to direct our worship to inferior objects or to 'mortals'. Religion means an ascent from 'natural forms' to the deity which is 'uniquely and simply absolute in itself, but multiform and omniform in all things . . . A religious man who is not yet one with God is not the hero who left his flesh to be devoured by the dogs once he had seen the naked Diana. At best, he is a pious man who has been *converted* to begin the ascent in order to reach towards the deity. This ascent is the hunt, in the course of which the hunter will be transformed into the prey'.[9]

Bruno's idea that God is internal to things and his conception of the encounter between the wise man and God, explain why he stressed the magic elements in religion. According to him, the founders of religion availed themselves of their knowledge of the secrets of things in order to persuade and to educate. 'Moses, who had acquainted himself at the court of Pharaoh with the know-ledge of the Egyptians', performed miracles by availing himself of the laws of nature. 'Magic, be it that of Moses or be it magic in

[8] *Opere italiane*, II, pp. 188–200; cp. *De Visione Dei* by Cusanus.
[9] *Sommario*, p. 87 (and p. 101); *Spaccio, Opere*, II, p. 198; and *De Magia, Opera Lat. Conscripta*, III, p. 403.

general, is nothing but a knowledge of the secrets of nature joined to the ability to imitate the workings of nature and to perform things that appear miraculous in the eyes of the people. As far as mathematical and superstitious magic is concerned, I am of the opinion that Moses as well as all other honourable minds were strangers to it.'

3. BRUNO'S CONCEPTION OF THE UNIVERSE

Bruno's attitude to religion was only a preparation for his philosophical standpoint. We ought not to be misled by certain declarations of his faith in St. Thomas Aquinas which were made sincerely enough at the most tragic moments of his life.[10] He worshipped in Aquinas the triumph of reason and a compact Aristotelianism, but not the triumph of faith. For Bruno's world was not a Christian world. Bruno's world was a living nature which turned, without development, in upon itself and, subject to an inexorable cycle, was resting immobile. We have already had occasion to note the lapidary pronouncement of the *Candelaio*, the certain expectation of the man who knows that the tide which is rising today is bound to subside again tomorrow. Hence he took it that all life remains immobile in itself and is, therefore, nothing but an appearance of life.

On several occasions Bruno espoused as his motto the saying of *Ecclesiastes* which he inscribed with his own hand into the register of the University of Wittenberg in 1587: 'Salomon and Pythagoras. The thing that has been, it is that which shall be; and that which is done, is that which shall be done: and there is no new thing under the sun.' In the dialogues *De la causa*, in his *Sigillus Sigillorum* and in the famous answer to his judges[11] he returned again and again to this basic conception. As far as the divine spirit, understood as the soul of the universe, was concerned, he added: 'According to my philosophy, that spirit, which is called the life of the universe, flows into the life and soul (both of which I consider to be immortal) and also into the bodies of all beings that have life and soul. As far as their substances are concerned, they are all immortal, for death is nothing but a

[10] *Documenti della vita di G.B.*, ed. by V. Spampanato and G. Gentile, Firenze, 1933, pp. 40, 107, 154; *Sommario*, p. 89.
[11] *De la causa, Opere*, I, p. 191; *Opera Lat. conscripta*, II, p. 213; *Documenti*, p. 96; *Sommario*, p. 115.

division and a congregation, which doctrine seems to be expressed in *Ecclesiastes.*' Some of his answers, written down during his trial in order to defend and explain his theory, are even more precise. In respect of souls, he remarked: 'The spirit that is in me, in you, in a third person, comes from God and returns to God . . . even as any particular drop of water comes from, depends on and returns to water in general'. And then, having repeated that 'things cannot be other than what they have been and what they will be and what they are', he says that 'there is only separation and conjunction or composition or division or translation'. And once again he quotes the verse from *Ecclesiastes.* Still speaking of the soul, he calls to mind an image of *Lampas Triginta Statuarum* and develops it in an illuminating manner. The universal soul is like 'a great universal mirror' which reflects an image'. Once broken into pieces, it yields 'as many whole forms as there are fragments'. But these forms are ephemeral 'like water running away'. For when the fragments are once more re-assembled as a whole mirror 'the images that are reflected singly by every fragment will be annihilated. The only thing that will remain . . . is the substance, which alone is true and will endure'.[12]

It is true that Bruno maintained that God 'through the power of His will' allows souls of men to escape their destiny, for He makes 'the spirits immortal through the grace of God'. But the logic of his own conception was to drive him into a different direction: ultimately he was committed to a belief in the rigidity of cyclical development, whether of nature or spirit. And in the course of these cycles, nothing is either ever created or ever destroyed. It followed that, when he was speaking as a philosopher and not 'as a catholic', he had to deny all difference between the soul of man and the soul of animals. He had to agree with the Pythagorean view about 'an incessant metempsychosis, which is a transposition and reincarnation of all souls'. For the souls of men do not differ 'either in their specific being or in their general being from the souls of flies, oysters and plants or of any other living creature'.[13] Given the idea that there is 'no body which

---

[12] *Lampas Triginta Statuarum,* 22 (*Opera lat. conscripta,* III, p. 59 sqq.): Cp. *Opere ital.,* I, p. 196 sqq.
[13] *Opere ital.* II, p. 274 sqq. (*Cabala del cavallo pegaseo*).

does not have a more or less lively and perfect spiritual communication in itself', it follows that the only soul, 'which has an
existence separate from the organic body, no matter what
Aristotle said to the contrary', partakes without change in all
things.

Bruno's conception of the relationship between the world and
God and his conception of God, unique and infinite, all reflect his
theory that the universe as a whole was naturally rigid, without
any kind of effective creativity. As far as the soul was concerned,
Bruno stressed that *ab uno, secundum quod unum, non procedit nisi
unum*; and that, therefore, any increase is only an apparent and
temporary material dispersion. In the same way he argued that
the relation between God and the world is not one of free
creativity, but merely one of necessary revelation. Infinite nature
is nothing but the appearance of a God, Who, because He is
infinite, is compelled to manifest Himself in the infinite. 'I presuppose that there is an infinite universe which is the effect of the
infinite divine power. For I do not consider it worthy of God's
power and goodness to have created, when He was capable of
creating besides this our world an infinite number of other
worlds, only a finite world'. Bruno never tired of reiterating this
argument which he examined even in its moral aspects. He
maintained that it was unthinkable that an infinite and perfect
power should have created something that was finite and
imperfect. If God had created something finite and imperfect,
He would have been guilty of malice and envy. Hence the
'syllogistic demonstrations' in his dialogues De l'infinito.[14]

The infinity of the universe, the eternity of the universe and
the unity of the universe are all founded upon the necessary link
between God and the world. All this was asserted categorically
in the dialogue De l'infinito and repeated again in De Immenso.[15]

It is possible to infer *necessarily* the infinity of the world from
the infinity of divine power. Similarly, one can infer the original
Oneness from the nature of the world. The infinite universe is an
image of the *inaccessible divine face* and therefore expresses God,
even as the rivers bear witness to their source.[16]

[14] Cp. *Opere ital.*, I, p. 300 sqq.; *Sommario*, p. 113.
[15] Cp. *Opere ital.*, I, pp. 295; 321.
[16] *Opera*, I, 4, p. 79.

There is a perfect correspondence between the two, even though man, as long as he is a child of this world, will not be able to see God except in His mundane diffusion. For this diffusion in the universe that is His own image, is the same as the Being of nature and amounts to a self-expression of God. It is the Oneness in its diffused wealth:

Vel nihil est natura, vel est divina potestas,
Materiam exagitans, impressusque omnibus ordo
Perpetuus.[17]

God is, and is not, in nature. For nature is God in things and the revelation of divine power. It has been held that Bruno's equation was not always formulated with clarity. But in the last analysis, one has to admit that Bruno did not vacillate: God Himself is inaccessible Oneness as such. He expresses Himself, manifests Himself, unveils Himself in the mirror of nature's multiformity. 'The Platonists said that He did it as if nature were a trace; the Peripatetics, as if it were a remote effect; the Talmudists, as if it were His shoulders or His back; and people given to apocalyptic thinking maintain that He does it as if it were a mirror, a shadow or a riddle.' God's self-expression and self-revelation is nothing but a transition from an absolute Oneness, complete in itself in a *single* act, to a diffusion; so that there are distinctions 'between time and time, place and place, part and part'. This diffused face, comprehended in its multiform totality, is nothing but the universe 'always and everywhere the same'.[18] There is no real new conquest, no genuine loss in this all comprehensive diffusion and in the cycles or 'eternal revolutions of vicissitudes'. These cycles determine everything that happens in the universe. They are like the play of waves on the 'inaccessible face' of the absolute One. And every single moment, in a different position, contains every single happening, every wave, every drop. In nature everything is cyclical. The things that are high, must fail; and the things that are low, must rise to make a total perfection. 'There is a high and magnificent change that makes the inferior waters equal with the superior ones, that turns night into day and day into night, in order that the deity be in all, in the sense in which everything is capable of everything'. One ought

[17] *Opera lat.,* I, 2, p. 193.
[18] *Opere ital.,* I, p. 247 sqq.

to note, however, that even the faint teleological hint that is contained in this thought, is ultimately suppressed:

'One and the same chaotic confusion
Assigns the same destinies to all.'

In the great ocean of Being and in the miraculous multiplicity in which the One unfolds itself, 'one always comes back, from the most diverse customs and effects, through opposite means and by contrary methods, to the same point'.[19] All change and all individuals are reduced to vain appearances, to mere variations upon the same theme. In spite of so many different appearances, everything remains the *same*: 'The Fates, not only as far as the species of bodily matter is concerned, make no distinction between the body of man and the body of a donkey. They also make no distinction between the bodies of animals and the bodies of things considered to be without soul. They also cause no differences in spiritual matter and cause the soul of man to be no different from the soul of a donkey. They make the souls of animals like those one finds in all things. For that matter, all humours are one single humour in substance; all particles of air are substantially one air and all spirits are one spirit derived from Amphitrite and returning to it'.

Nothing dies, even though individual compounds change. In reality all change is mere appearance and it is foolish to fear death. Substance persists eternally, one and indifferent to the multiplicity of appearances in which it manifests itself.[20] 'There is no room for the blind fear of death in the space surrounded by the unimpregnable wall of true philosophical contemplation, in which steadfastness rules strong and supreme, where truth is manifest, where the necessity of the eternity of every substance is clear'.[21]

4. CONTEMPLATION

In Bruno, contemplation has a liberating power. Those who contemplate will truly recognise that, intimately, all things are the same and that that is so throughout the universe which in its very root is One. One in its truth, One in its goals, One in its methods. The universe is like an incessant pulsation through which the One reveals itself, descends and returns to itself. The process of

[19] *Opere ital.*, II, p. 430.   [20] *Opere ital.*, I, pp. 191 sqq., 211 sqq.
[21] *Opere ital.*, II, p. 212.

revelation is a descent to the 'creation of things'. By contrast, comprehension is an ascent 'to the knowledge of things'. This cycle demonstrates the vital pulsation of Being in the course of which the One and its revelation, ascent and descent, diffusion and return, have the same validity. 'This is the reason why we need not fear that anything ever decreases, that a particle may be lost or escape, be dismembered or annihilated. This is the reason for the constant change in the universe. For this reason there is no evil which we might escape, and no good we might not encounter. And all along, on the infinite field, throughout eternal change, the whole of the substance remains constant and one.' Contemplation, therefore, is the recognition of the fundamental indifference of existence and the conquest of peace through an ascent to the One. It means that 'fear and suffering . . . joy and hope' are abandoned. Contemplation leads to 'the true way of true morality; it makes one 'generous' and greater than the gods worshipped by the mob: it makes one 'despise all those things that are valued by childish minds'.

Those who 'genuinely contemplate natural history' understand that there is no distance and no separation, nothing big and nothing small, nothing close and nothing far away, no good and no evil in the universe. 'There is no difference between flying from here to heaven and flying from heaven to here; no difference between ascending to that place; and no difference between descending from one end to another. As far as all these other points are concerned, we are not in a centre. And similarly, they are not centres in regard to other points . . . We walk on this earth and are surrounded by the heavens even as they are.' The insight that there is no difference between the parts of the universe amounts to a liberation 'from all vain urges and all foolish worry, to long for far away things'. For goodness is in us. This insight frees us from fears that are groundless because nothing changes and everything merely 'alters its appearance'. The infinite finds its salvation in the One; and the One reveals in the infinite its fertile and inexhaustible life. He who contemplates, rids himself of fear and hope and of all distracting preoccupations with the future or with change in general, in order to enjoy the 'true beatitude . . . of being in the present'.[22]

[22] *Opere ital.*, I, p. 281 sqq.

5. MORAL REFORM

The whole of Bruno's problem is contained in the conception of the cyclical relationship between God and the universe. From an ontological point of view this process reduces itself to an essential immobility; but on the other hand, it is transfigured into an effective becoming, even though it is taking place inside God. In the *Eroici furori*, there is an insistence on the idea that 'the body is in the soul, the soul in the mind and that the mind is either God or in God'. And in the *Spaccio* no distinction is made between the gnoseological process and ontological development, between truth and reality, between knowing and doing.[23] 'The act of divine knowledge is the substance of the Being of all things.' And again: 'there is a kind of truth which is the cause of things and which is above all things. There is another kind, which is in things and which belongs to things. And a third and last kind, which comes after things and out of things. The first is called cause: the second, thing; and the third, knowledge.' There is no difference between truth and being. Truth is 'ideal, natural and conceptual, . . . metaphysical, physical and logical'. The process by which the One always returns to itself and grasps its meaning by revealing itself in a multiplicity of forms, is a compact process, inherent in Being. This multiplicity, in turn, since it is inherent in the One, annihilates itself perennially in the bosom of the One. However, a fundamentally novel element is introduced into this cycle, in which there is nothing new and in which nothing new *can* occur, by moral reform. 'Through intellectual work and through the will that is consequent upon such work', man, who is 'by his essence in God' and who is, in fact, entirely one with God, 'relates himself to His light and to its beatifying object'. Thus he opposes to the immediacy of the original Oneness, the will to return to that Oneness. And this will is a new conquest. In this way the cycle of ascent and descent loses its cyclical and mechanical character and is transformed into a moral progress, i.e. into a cycle of love and a progressive enrichment of Being.

During the passage from the metaphysical to the moral dialogues, Bruno's point of view seems to have changed. In the

[23] *Opere ital.*, II, pp. 367, 264 (cp. *Opera lat.*, II, 3, p. 94).

fifth dialogue *Della causa*, after an exalted hymn to the unity and sameness of the universe, Bruno had asked why things keep changing and had not hesitated to answer that there was no question 'of changes that seek other Being, but simply of other *kinds* of Being'. Although there were different *kinds* of Being, there was only Oneness and substantial identity. Certainly change never led to an enrichment, a new conquest. It only led to dislocations, through unchangeable and unchanged stations inside the one infinite immobility. 'An evanescent appearance . . . of an immobile . . . and eternal Being . . . every appearance, every face, everything is vanity. It is like nothing. Indeed, it is nothing'. But in his *Spaccio* that 'nothing' suddenly comes to life; and when moral and religious reform have taken place he conceived the possibility of a change of the passive 'vessel' of the deity into 'an active artisan', in the person of which one may admire 'the excellence . . . of mankind'. Then follows the glorification of human activity as a sort of 'competition with divine acts' and of the 'new and wonderful inventions'. Hence his very significant praise of work which overcomes laziness and the sharp condemnation of the golden age and of any kind of earthly paradise. Hence also the eulogy on work for the construction of civilisation which frees itself slowly from 'animal existence'. 'In competition with divine acts and through the application of intellectual urges, battling with difficulties and newly emerging needs, the intelligence is sharpened, crafts are invented and the arts discovered. And so, from day to day, because of deprivations, new and marvellous inventions are brought forth from the depths of the human intellect.'[24]

The eulogy of work runs parallel to a eulogy of the virtue of repentance. Repentance is the crisis that interrupts man's fatal descent and afflicts the soul with sorrow on account of 'its present condition'. Thus it leads the soul back to itself, 'remembering, as it were, its high inheritance'. To repent means to introduce into one's own earthly condition 'the ardent love of sublime things'. And though repentance originates in the flesh and in sin, on earth and through pain, 'it is like the red rose that grows from dark and sharp spines'. The moral crisis occasioned by the feeling of guilt in the static condition that is proper to Being is

[24] *Opere ital.*, II, p. 152 sqq.

'like a lucid and liquid spark, caused by a dark and hard stone, rising towards the sun to which it is related'. This thought contains more than a deep moral meaning. It expresses the rhythm of Being which, in its mobile immobility, becomes a process that realises the good whenever 'the dark and hard stones' cause the lucid flame of love to spring up.[25]

Pain, work, and a bitter sense of guilt are the only methods for shaping reality in a way that is worthy of man. Where metaphysics is unable to see anything but the closed rigidity of the eternal and perfect One, morality implies a fundamental transformation. For morality transfigures into a conquest the passive acceptance of everything that is given, and chases away the wild beasts of passion. As against morality, there is the condition of asininity which consists in a blind submission to and passive perception of one's own existence. In this state there is neither sin nor redemption; nobody plucks the fruit forbidden to Adam and nobody raises the hand with Prometheus in order to grasp the divine fire 'in order to spark off the light that resides in the power of reason'. *Asininity* is a surrender without a battle and makes man into a thing. In such a condition people 'stop, cross . . . their arms, shut their eyes, cease to attend and to strive . . . and turn neither right nor left, except when the lesson tells them to . . .'[26]

The reform demanded in the *Spaccio* is in reality a reduction of the rhythm of ascent and descent to a movement of moral liberation. In this movement the knowledge which has been reached about the laws that govern the universe, becomes the norm of the human conscience. The passions cease to be the sign of submission and are replaced by love which is 'an intellectual contact with the deity as object'. Thus the sovereignty of the law, of 'an unworthy destiny' under the bonds of bestial appetites, is brought to an end and replaced by 'a rational impulse that follows the intellectual apprehension of the good and the beautiful'.

6. HEROIC PASSION

The extermination of the beast (*spaccio*) has its origin in the consciousness of one's self and of one's shortcomings as well as

---

[25] *Opere ital.*, II, p. 129. [26] *Opere ital.*, II, p. 269.

in the knowledge of what it means to be a man and of one's vocation. The extermination of the beast amounts to a conquest of passivity and of the paramount power of the flesh and represents the beginning of a human existence which is supposed to be characterised by moral deed and conscious will. Our 'inner lack of peace' forces us to the recognition that we are, though part of nature, not wholly natural. Man is capable of emerging from the blind cycle of things when he accepts the invitation of a 'certain light that resides in the mirror . . . of our soul'. This light is the voice of reason, a rupture in our existence, something that is without prejudice and ironical in the Socratic sense. It is 'an act of ratiocination of our interior counsel . . . the lantern of reason' which makes man surpass both himself and his bestial life. It makes him blush on account of his animal existence and makes him repent his sins. In this way, man begins to desire to change himself from a mere 'vessel' of the deity, from an 'ass' which merely carries the divine as all other things, whether onions or crocodiles, carry it, into a living temple; that is, into something that offers itself freely and voluntarily to God. In short, he wants to become divine himself. The passions are of two kinds. On one side there are the 'ordinary and natural appetites' and on the other side, there are the 'divine and heroic passions'. As far as the former are concerned, man is dragged along by an 'irrational impetus'. He remains blind and completely closed in himself and suffers his destiny passively because he sees, in his blindness, nothing but himself and his own pleasure. But over and above these passions, there is a love which is directed not upon itself but upon Being; not upon one's own limitations, but upon truth. This love is not a passionate forgetfulness, but a *remembering* of one's roots and a desire to break out of one's seclusion. To forget oneself is not the same as to neglect oneself. On the contrary: in such a case, one desires and loves the good and the beautiful 'in order to become more perfect by changing oneself to become similar to the good and the beautiful'. Forgetfulness, therefore, amounts to a kind of conquest and a power to remember. Doing becomes identical with suffering, and suffering, with the highest form of action. The man who is possessed by an inferior kind of love is a slave, for in his desire to subject everything to his own pleasures, he himself becomes the slave of his own desire. But the man who

Q

knows true love, that is, the man who desires with a pure will the infinite in every single thing, is able 'to become a God through the intellectual contact with the deity. For he is animated only by the thought of divine things and he is without feeling for, and incapable of being touched by, the things that the mob value most'. The one form of suffering is a passive experience of the finite; the other form of suffering is an experience of the presence of the deity, an openness towards the deity. In the second case, love is not a dumb passion which causes man 'to meander beyond the sphere of reason and prudent thought, led by accident and dragged by confusion . . .' In the second case we have a *passive experience* of Being transformed into an active co-operation with Being. And it comes about when man 'begins to grasp the divine order . . . in the pictures he can see with his senses.'[27]

The history of the conversion from passive suffering of sensible experience (i.e. from a subjection to destiny) to heroic passion (i.e. to liberation), is the history of the process which demonstrates the emergence of human morality from nature. This is the main problem with which Bruno wrestled: and it is much more important than the question as to whether the One is in the world like the pilot in the ship. The main problem was concerned with an attempt to discover how the passivity of every finite being, subject to fate, contains another kind of passivity or suffering which is in reality an activity with God in God. This was the very problem expressed by Bruno in another form in the myth of Actaeon. He said that Actaeon, chasing the naked Diana, was transformed from hunter into the prey. He represents the human intellect which, in the presence of the divine, 'is moved beyond itself by so much beauty. Thus he becomes the prey and is transformed into the very thing he sought. He noticed that he ended up by becoming the prey of his own dogs, i.e. of his own thoughts. For as he had already grasped the deity there was no further need for him to seek the deity outside himself.' The myth demonstrates that the internal and the external coincide, even as the many and the One coincide as soon as man turns away from the crowd and begins to see his Diana—no longer through windows, but 'with eyes wide open to the whole of the horizon'.[28]

[27] *Opere ital.*, II, p. 360 sqq.   [28] *Opere ital.*, II, p. 472 sqq.

7. NEW PROBLEMS IN CAMPANELLA

There is no doubt that in many respects Campanella's thought goes beyond the limits of Renaissance philosophy. It is directly related to the religious movement that stems from the Counter-Reformation, to the political controversies nourished by the reaction against Machiavelli and to the scientific interests which culminate in Galilei. It is enough to remind oneself of his Machiavellism, which he professed openly and naively in spite of persistent condemnations, in order to understand his close relation to the theoreticians of *reason of state* to whom he owed so much. 'The world has gone mad . . . and the wise, in order to cure it, have been compelled to speak, act and live as if they themselves were mad, even though in secret they have other views.' Campanella, like Descartes, wore a mask.

Campanella did not wish to hide the fact that as far as the culture of Humanism was concerned, his thought was original. Nor did he make a secret of the fact that his scientific researches were subject to his practical, moral and political aims. In a famous letter which he wrote from the 'depths of the Caucasus' of the Neapolitan prison in July 1607 to Monsignor Antonio Querengo, he compared himself to Pico. He criticised Pico, 'phoenix of the great intellects', for not having made much of a contribution to 'morals and politics', because he spent all his time in 'poring over books'. Pico was a 'philosopher who relied more on words than on nature from which he learnt nothing'; and thus Pico was the very incarnation of an intellectual attitude that was completely contrary to that of Campanella. 'The difference between my philosophising and that of Pico is this: I learn more from the anatomy of an ant or a blade of grass, not to mention the most marvellous anatomy of the world, than from all the books which have been written since the beginnings of time. This is so, since I have begun to philosophise and to read the book of God. This is the model according to which I correct the human books which have been copied badly and arbitrarily and without attention to the things that are written in the original book of the Universe.'[29] This then, is the central theme of Campanella's standpoint. It was destined to come up again in the famous comparison of the

[29] Tommaso Campanella, *Lettere*, ed. by V. Spampanato, Bari, 1927, p. 134.

Apologia for Galilei—a comparison between nature, the sacred book of God, and the Scriptures. These three, he argued, are not, and cannot be, incompatible with one another.[30]

Campanella inferred from this argument that it is necessary to recognise the direct and immediate relationship between man and thing as the sole source of human knowledge. Thus he even denied the value of the syllogism and was mindful of the fact that both Augustine and Lactantius, for instance, had used the syllogism in order to deny the existence of the antipodes. 'A sailor has proved them liars because he had *seen*.' Reasoning always leads one to the belief that all opinions are equivalent. 'In this our dark century . . . all philosophers and sophists, religion and impiety and superstition, have the same colouring and the same value.' It is not possible to decide with the help of a syllogism 'which of the three laws, the Christian, the Mahommedan or the Hebrew, is the true one. All writers are in doubt about Aristotelian impieties and in the schools people are confused and in doubt'.

In the preface to the *Metaphysics*, Campanella elaborated his appeal to the direct communication with the world and with God even more accurately. The syllogism, he argued, 'is like an arrow that hits the goal. But we remain far from the object and cannot enjoy it'. The reliance on authority implies that one touches things with other people's hands. One can have knowledge only through direct and deep contact, accompanied by a very agreeable sensation, which becomes intrinsic to the object (*per tactum intrinsecum, in magna suavitate*).[31]

Campanella insisted on the sensuous quality of this relationship because he wanted to emphasise its immediacy and the fact that it was not based on discursive reasoning. Thus he joined sensuous knowledge and intelligible intuition into a single concept, similar to Roger Bacon's *experience*. Like Bacon, Campanella started with the traditional analogy between vision and light. At the same time he insisted on the above mentioned idea that God had given man two books: nature and the Scriptures. In the preface to the *Metaphysics* he remarked that 'God speaks to us in two ways: either He creates the thing itself or He reveals it, the way men do

[30]*Apologia pro Galilaeo;* cp. *Le Opere di Galileo Galilei,* Firenze, 1846, V. pp. 507–509). Cp. *Poesie,* G. Gentile ed., Firenze, 1939, p. 30 sqq.
[31] *Metaph.* (Parisiis, 1638), pp. 2–5; *Poesie,* p. 30.

when the teacher shows something to the pupil'. At any rate, He has written a book from which we can learn by looking.

When all things are considered the famous analogy of vision no longer proved really satisfying to Campanella. It was the image he loved so much, the image of the world as 'a book and temple of God', the image of the 'original book of nature' that stimulated further research. God's word and God's Scriptures create things. For this reason the ancients used to call the world the wisdom of God; and for this same reason, since we are only men and not gods, we create words and not things. And therefore our poetry is fiction and not creation. And in the *Poetica* the poets who are not subservient to civic ends are considered *excrementa reipublicae, merito religanda*.[32] Campanella was not satisfied by the conception that knowledge is a reflection in a mirror, i.e. by a knowledge which the metaphor of vision betrays as a mere reproduction. But the idea that there is a parallelism with God opened a way to a new and more direct contact. It opened the possibility for the idea that knowledge consists in a real penetration of the object; in becoming intrinsically and effectively one with it. *Sapientia dicitur a sapore, qui sensui gustus intrinsecatur'.* Man, he argued, *sapit* in so far as he manages to appropriate the *saporem* of the object.[33]

It is impossible to overrate the particular value of this *feeling* and it is no accident that Campanella compared it, repeatedly, to the highest peaks of Platonic intuition rather than to Telesio's perception. It could have been compared to Telesio's idea of perception only if the latter is understood to be a form of intuitive wisdom. Moreover, it is no accident that Campanella's image was taken directly from the mystical tradition of the Arabs, from Sufism. It is indeed possible to find it in Gundissalinus who had approved of the Arabic transformation of Plato's and Plotinus' *seeing into tasting*.

In this sense, then, *feeling* has a meaning different from the one it has in Aristotelian empiricism. It appears to be a submergence in the object and thus a participation in its deepest essence. It

---

[32] *Poetica*, ed. by L. Firpo, Roma, 1944, p. 260.
[33] Metaph. (Parisiis, 1638), p. 65. For Gundalissinus see E. Gilson, *Les sources gréco-arabes de l'augustinisme avicennisant*, "Arch. hist. doctr. et lit. du M.A.", IV, 1929–30, pp. 90–91, and J. Teicher, *D. Gundisalino e l'agostinismo avicennizante*, "Riv. filos. neoscolastica", 1934.

is something that coincides with divine revelation and hence with the process in which God expressed Himself. It is something like Being itself, becoming assimilated to Power and Love. It is certainly not a simple form of *seeing* or mirroring, of reproducing pictures; but a way of penetrating the vital processes of the universe. In short, a *taste* of the sweetness of universal life.

The experience which removes the barriers between the inside and the outside, leads, through the innermost heart of things, into the real expression of the divine. The participation in this expression makes us somehow equivalent with God. As in Roger Bacon, empiricism was transformed into mysticism.

8. 'LEARNING AND KNOWING ... ARE FORMS OF DYING'

The mystical vein which runs through this conception of perception changes the idea that feeling is a *perceptio passionis* and brings it instead into immediate contact with the divine being. In this way, Campanella was induced to take up once again the problem of the senses. The senses, he said, are not sources of information—information in the sense of losing one's own form and of becoming one with the object. Sensual knowledge, on the contrary, is a mutation which turns the subject into the object, but not wholly. To know something is to feel it and to submerge oneself in the other, to receive it into oneself. 'The more sensitive and soft one is, the greater the capacity to feel and to become wise.'[34]

For this reason, knowing amounts to dying. 'For death is a transformation into something else and every transformation, somehow, is a death.' And since knowledge amounts to a transformation of the subject into the object, it also amounts to a form of death. This death, though, is only partial for we always remain conscious of our own selves. We always retain an intimate feeling in us; hence we do not lose ourselves in the subject but remain firmly moored to our own selves. At this point we encounter the conversion of feeling into wisdom which Campanella emphasised. *Feeling* means to become the object felt and hence is a form of suffering. It means that one reaches new boundaries and that one dies. But the contemplation of the God Who resides

[34] *Del senso delle cose e della magia*, ed. by A. Bruers, Bari, 1925, pp. 11 and 151.

in all things and Who is the highest Being which forms all things, amounts to the ability to break through the limits of negative reality and to become genuinely real. 'Learning and knowing are a . . . form of death. The transformation into God is the only form of eternal life. For being cannot be lost in the infinite ocean of Being. On the contrary, it becomes enlarged.'

In the moral field, Campanella resorted to a beautiful parable: 'Even as the incorporeal light is turned yellow, red and green by the vapours of the rainbow . . . the soul possesses itself of the passions and undoes them . . . but if she is defeated, she will suffer pain.' If man, instead of allowing himself to be defeated by things, grasps them in their true being by placing himself into true being, he will, 'because he is both penetrator of, and penetrated by', the divinity, be blessed and reach knowledge with joy. Campanella's first concern was with the possibility of pointing at the passage to the totality of Being. He discovered such a passage on the level of the senses conceived as immediate experience: 'True theology is wholly revealed to the senses of man.' The passage is possible when 'sentient cognition' touches things and frees them from their limitations and their nothingness in order to re-translate them into the divine reality of the universe. In other words, it grasps them in the very process in which God reveals and expresses Himself. Thus it affirms their positivity rather than their negativity.

Hence Campanella's persistent polemics against all types of Aristotelian abstraction which impoverishes and dilutes things and reduces them to empty forms. Such abstraction may be 'fit for children and ignorant people who know man in general but not in his particularities. It is becoming to animals to whom all men are the same, just as we do not distinguish between the eggs of a hen'. The truth of a particular man is not to be found in the abstraction of his manhood but in his concrete existence; in his peculiarities and in the knowledge of all the minute qualities of which he consists. 'To the external observer it seems as if all qualities were the same: but He who observes, learns to distinguish.' Those who penetrate the depths, eliminate the relationship between the inside and the outside because they comprehend the process of the Universe and penetrate it. 'All science is based on the senses; and by senses I do not mean the eye or the ear, but sentient cognition' (*anima in eis*). Thus we see how Campanella's new metaphysical basis, no matter how closely related to the theories of Renaissance Platonism in general, transcends the limits of that Platonism. This is not to say that in other points his metaphysics did not remain closely linked to it. His mathematically conditioned conception of physical reality and his theory of universal animation prove his debt to Renaissance Platonism. So do his practical preoccupations with the conversion of the whole of mankind to the true religion. The true religion to which he wanted to convert mankind, with the help of magic if necessary, was a faith in the Word, perfectly revealed in the world. It was a natural religion which happened to coincide with Christianity. He considered the latter the perfected expression of divine wisdom.

With this somewhat confusing web of themes, Campanella began to reach beyond the problems of the Renaissance.

EPILOGUE

IF it is true that Humanism consisted in a renewed confidence
in man and his possibilities and in an appreciation of man's
activity in every possible sense, it is only fair to give Humanism
credit for the new methods of scientific investigation, the renewed
vision of the world and the new attitude towards objects with a
view to using them and to dominating them. During the 15th
and 16th centuries, the civilisation of Italy, in spite of oscillations
and contrasts, witnessed the emergence of a fully fashioned idea
of man. This idea was made possible by the *studia humanitatis* and
by an active expansion in the world. Burckhardt's old and
vigorous conception which linked the reaffirmation of man with
the reaffirmation of the world, the reaffirmation of the spirit with
the reaffirmation of nature, ought to be connected without fear
of rhetoric to the old notion that the Renaissance succeeded in
bringing about a new harmony. This ideal of the harmony and the
measure of a complete man runs, in spite of a certain amount of
turgidity and obscurity, through those centuries. In fact, it is
the very hardness of the contrasts and the labour involved in overcoming them which gives the age an appearance of nobility. As
perhaps no other age, it was full of exemplary personalities like
Alberti or Lorenzo, Michelangelo or Bruno.

Augustin Renaudet once wrote with great truth that 'the
Italy of the Renaissance unites in herself all manner of conflicts'.
The man of the Renaissance was indeed a living synthesis, a
meeting-point, a mediator; and his world as well as the God he
worshipped, are not only the poles of this tension, but are seen
in terms of tension. The philosophical meditation of the age was
prepared to emphasise this synthesis and to educate man for the
task of realising it and was less than ever prepared to allow itself to
be reduced to systems and classifications. It informed and
animated every problem and all research. It was a constant
warning—to the artist, the scientist, the priest and the politician—
of the measure of man. For this reason it remained split up and
seemed to evaporate, now in a political oration, now in a treatise
about good manners, now in a technical manual. But all in all it

was a constant reminder of the human task in hand. It would be vain to seek this conception of universal knowledge in the scholastic systems of professors. But it was alive, as a constant reminder, in every single piece of work.

Because of this, the Renaissance was the dawn of modern thought and the whole of Europe in the 16th century was full of echoes of Italian culture. For the same reason, every future historian of the Renaissance philosophy of Italy will have to busy himself with books on politics, morals, rhetoric, logic and science, rather than with the remnants of that Scholastic philosophy which had received such a fatal blow. Ever since that blow, the country of Galilei, Vico, Giannone, Muratori and of the political economists of the 18th century and of Leopardi seemed to many observers to have been lacking in genuine philiosophy. But this was only because these men were unable to forget the lessons of Humanism even when rhetorical degeneration had dried up its sources, and could therefore never again return to abstract and systematic philosophy.

But if philosophy is understood as an unceasing exploration and taken to be a critical consciousness of the mind's activities, of its human measure and its limitations as well as its potentialities, it is impossible to exaggerate the importance of the age of Humanism.

INDEX OF NAMES